C000132355

"The President does not have power unde[r] [the Constitution to unilaterally] authorize a military attack in a situation th[at does not involve stopping an] actual or imminent threat to the nation."

Candidate B[arack Obama]

"[T}he war is illegal under the United States Constitution and our War Powers Act, because only the US Congress has the authority to declare war and the president has been unable to show that the US faced an imminent threat from Libya. The president even ignored his top legal advisers at the Pentagon and the department of justice who insisted he needed congressional approval before bombing Libya."

Congressman Dennis Kucinich

"Perhaps the greatest harm to humanity will be the long-term effects on international affairs from the use of force in a manner that is outside of the allowed exceptions of international law. In the Pact of Paris in 1928 and again in the UN Charter in 1945, States agreed not to use force against each other to accomplish their foreign policy ends. The Western world has appeared to repeatedly challenge this agreement in the last ten years, especially by its willingness to take military action against predominately Muslim States. In doing so they have sent an undeniable signal to the international community through their actions and despite some of their words, that international law does not matter to them. If this message is not answered by the proponents of international law then the advances we have made to ensure that the international community respects the rule of law may be undone for future generations."

Curtis Doebbler, *JURIST Forum*

"The legal machinations Mr. Obama has used to justify war without Congressional consent set a troubling precedent that could allow future administrations to wage war at their convenience—free of legislative checks and balances."

Bruce Ackerman, Professor of Law, Yale
"Obama's Unconstitutional War," *Foreign Policy*

"It was equally clear from the start that this Orwellian-named 'kinetic humanitarian action' was, in fact, a 'war' in every sense, including the Constitutional sense, but that's especially undeniable now. While the President, in his after-the-fact speech justifying the war, pledged that 'broadening our military mission to include regime change would be a mistake,' it is now clear that is exactly what is happening."

Glenn Greenwald
"The Illegal War in Libya," Salon.com

THE ILLEGAL WAR
ON LIBYA

EDITED BY

CYNTHIA MCKINNEY

A **DIGNITY** PROJECT

CLARITY PRESS, INC.

© 2012 Dignity

ISBN: 978-0-9852710-6-0
      0-9852710-6-X
E-book: 978-0-9853353-2-8

In-house editor: Diana G. Collier
Cover: R. Jordan P. Santos
Cover photo: Dedon Kamathi
Photo Cynthia McKinney: Wekesa Madzimoyo

ALL RIGHTS RESERVED: Except for purposes of review, this book may not
be copied, or stored in any information retrieval system, in whole or in part,
without permission in writing from the publishers.

Library of Congress Cataloging-in-Publication Data

The illegal war on Libya / edited by Cynthia McKinney.
    p. cm.
  "A DIGNITY Project."
  Includes bibliographical references and index.
  ISBN 978-0-9852710-6-0 (alk. paper) -- ISBN 0-9852710-6-X (alk. paper)
  1. Libya--History--Civil War, 2011- 2. Libya--History--Civil War, 2011---Mass
media and the war. 3. North Atlantic Treaty Organization--Armed Forces--Libya.
4. Regime change--Libya. 5. Geopolitics--Libya. I. McKinney, Cynthia, 1955- II.
DIGNITY (Organization)

  DT236.I55 2012
  961.205--dc23

                    2012023248

Clarity Press, Inc.
Ste. 469, 3277 Roswell Rd. NE
Atlanta, GA. 30305 , USA
http://www.claritypress.com

This book is dedicated to the people who want peace so badly that they will actually do something in order to obtain it. DIGNITY seeks first to find truth and work for justice, on which peace is built. The outcome of the struggle for truth, justice, and peace is Earth and human DIGNITY.

DIGNITY Members in Tripoli, Libya. (Photo courtesy of Dr. Randy Short, DIGNITY)

TABLE OF CONTENTS

EDITOR'S NOTE

Cynthia McKinney

Think of this book as your primer on war propaganda, deliberate media deception, hidden political and personal agendas, and finally, on what a set of politically powerful and well-connected people will do to a country when they have access to military power and the will to use it. We now know that they will even use military power, killing innocent people, just to hide contacts and contracts that they would rather keep secret, like, for example, the alleged payments to Nicolas Sarkozy that financed his successful 2007 Presidential campaign in France

For me, the story of Libya begins during my days in the Congressional Black Caucus when Earl Hilliard, the first Black Congressman from Alabama since Reconstruction, proposed that Members of the Caucus take a more active role in US policy toward Africa. I agreed with him. Subsequently, he traveled to Libya and began the thaw in relations between the US which, a decade earlier, had bombed Muammar Qaddafi's home in an illegal assassination attempt, killing instead his young adopted daughter. For his temerity—to actually think that he could act as a Member of Congress, serving on the House International Relations Committee, and engage Africa as a partner—Earl was targeted in the Summer of 2002 for ouster from the Congress by the pro-Israel Lobby. Then they came for me later that summer for my views and votes in favor of peace in Israel/Palestine.

Remembering Earl, I watched with sadness as, in the following Congressional term, Congressman Tom Lantos and others who represent the strength of the pro-Israel Lobby in US political circles, traipsed to Libya, purportedly to herald a new era of openness and dialogue between the two countries.

We now know of Israel's role in precipitating the 1986 crisis between Libya and the United States thanks to the writings of Victor Ostrovsky, a former Mossad agent. In *By Way of Deception*,[1] Ostrovsky writes that Israel regarded Libya as an unpalatable arms supply route to the Palestinians and recounts numerous projects of Mossad to trick US leaders into believing Israeli versions or characterizations of Libyan leaders, especially of Muammar Qaddafi.

In *The Other Side of Deception*, Ostrovsky goes even further and describes the specific "Operation Trojan" that, once again, set Libya up for US retaliation for something that Libya did not do. Ostrovsky writes:

> Ultimately, the Americans fell for the ploy head over heels, dragging the British and the Germans somewhat reluctantly in with them.
>
> Operation Trojan could be regarded a success. It brought about the air strike on Libya that President Reagan had promised. The American attack achieved a triple result for the Mossad. It derailed a deal for the release of the American hostages in Lebanon, thus keeping the Hizballah (Party of God) as the number one enemy in the eyes of the West. It also sent a message to all the Arab world, telling them exactly where the United States stood regarding the Arab-Israeli conflict. Thirdly, the office came out of it as the big hero that saved the day, having provided the US with vital information in the struggle against world terrorism.
>
> It was only the French that didn't buy into the Mossad trick and were determined not to align themselves with the aggressive American act. The French did not allow the American bombers to fly over their territory on their way to attack Libya, and in doing so placed themselves in clear opposition to the action.
>
> On April 14, 1986, one hundred and sixty American aircraft dropped over sixty tons of bombs on Libya.[2]

In the case of the 1988 bombing of the Pan Am Flight 103 aircraft over Lockerbie, Scotland, as the death of Abdelbaset al-Megrahi, the only person ever convicted of the bombing was announced, activists, politicians, religious leaders, and journalists renewed the call for an independent investigation of evidence that was concealed during the Megrahi trial.

I remember watching a Member of the UK Parliament protest at the time of the bombing and investigation that there was US intelligence involvement in the case that should be investigated. Of course, that was not investigated and ultimately Libya accepted responsibility for the bombing as a price to pay for the lifting of sanctions imposed after the earlier successful false flag operation/false accusation against Libya that saw Libya blamed as a sponsor of state-sanctioned terrorism. No further serious investigation of the incident took place after the conviction of Megrahi. Now, even *The New York Times* and other establishment sources admit that the case against Megrahi was flawed and political. One of the Lockerbie judges admitted that there was enormous political pressure applied for a conviction. In my opinion, Megrahi was as convenient a scapegoat as were Oswald, Ray, and Sirhan in the murders of President John F. Kennedy, Dr. Martin Luther King, Jr., and Presidential-candidate Robert F. Kennedy.

It was not until my 2008-2009 ordeal trying to reach Gaza with the Free Gaza Movement that Libya resurfaced on my radar. Through various friends, in late 2009 I received an invitation to come to Tripoli to tell the story of my efforts on behalf of peace and the human rights of the Palestinian people. I went and carried more than a dozen US and South African friends with me. We called ourselves the DIGNITY Delegation, named after the Free Gaza boat that was rammed by the Israelis during my first attempt to reach Gaza by sea.

In early 2011, I returned to Libya, again with more than one dozen DIGNITY Delegation members, to attend a Conference for Africans in the Diaspora and on the Continent the intent of which was to put effective structures in place to build Africa starting with Libya. Attendees were invited to relocate from the Diaspora to Africa so that they could live their lives in dignity. More specifically, attendees were invited to relocate to Libya so that they could help begin the process of building Africa. Members of DIGNITY began to discuss among themselves ways in which they could help Africa and get to know their own roots on the Continent from which they had been snatched.

We may never truly know the gamut of reasons beyond the public pretexts that the North Atlantic Treaty Organization (NATO) used to enable it to bomb Libya from March 2011 through October 2011. But what *is* clear, is that just like in 1986 and again in 1988, lies were told about Libya to a trusting and unsuspecting public in the midst of tragedy that led to horrific outcomes for everyone. Once again, the US military machine outfitted its propaganda wing with a story believable only by people who had no background on Libya or who had forgotten or preferred to overlook the lies that led the US into war against Iraq in 1993. What is also clear is that unlike the United States or its allies in NATO, Libya did not bomb another country, it did not invade another country. Libya did not directly or, through the use of proxy forces, indirectly attack another country; it did not distribute Viagra to its military to encourage the rape of its own citizens as was propagandized by the US and its NATO allies in order to justify and build public support for a grand theft of Libyan assets and resources that is one of the results and clearly one of the objectives of NATO's Operation Unified Protector.

In 1991, Paul Wolfowitz, then the Number Three in the Pentagon, told General Wesley Clark that the primary lesson of the 1991 Gulf War was that the US could act militarily near the Russian border in the countries of the Israel/Palestine region without a Russian military response. Wolfowitz declared to Clark then that "we" had another five or ten years to "clean up" the old pro-Soviet regimes (Syria, Iraq, Libya) in the region before a new superpower came along to challenge "us." In 2007, at the Commonwealth Club in California, General Wesley Clark related all of this publicly and told how he learned of a plan to attack and destroy the governments of seven countries in five years. Those countries were Iraq, Syria, Lebanon, Libya, Somalia, Sudan, and Iran. Clark further stated in this speech that the US had suffered a "policy coup" in which "some hard-nosed people" whom he identified as Wolfowitz, Cheney, and Rumsfeld and a half dozen others from the Project for a New American Century wanted the Middle East destabilized and turned upside down without a US debate on the issue. Finally, he says that Iran and Syria know about the plan, but sadly, not the people inside the US. Clark concludes that the strategy of the US in this region is the main issue that the people must engage.

Could it be that Libya is just a pawn in a larger geostrategic game of chess? Articles included in this anthology clearly point in this direction. At the time of this writing, I have been told by reliable sources that the United States maintains mercenary forces in Libya by way of an off-shore base near the Tunisia–Libya border and that these forces carry out joint operations with Al Qaeda forces in Derna, Benghazi, and Misrata. I am also told that US forces operate in Tripoli under the protection of known Al Qaeda operative Abduhakim Belhadj, where they control the shipping terminal and Mitiga airport.

Finally, an issue that I addressed while in Congress is the accountability for the private militaries being sent around the world to do battle for the US. Libyan sources indicate that many US mercenaries there have been killed, but in response to the mounting losses, the US merely imports more mercenaries into Libya from other parts of the world. These sources conclude that one can no longer recognize Libya and with the reality of bombed-out buildings and the stench of decaying corpses on the streets, Libya's better days are a distant memory, hard to even remember.

In addition, I recently learned that:

- The people of Libya see very clearly now what has befallen them.
- They are concerned about the toxic contamination of their air, soil, and water.
- There are a large number of amputees among the population.
- The Libyan economy is now in a shambles.
- NATO is still active in Libya with foreign militaries present and on the ground.
- NATO mercenaries are from US, France, UK, Qatar, and other European and Arab countries.
- NATO's Al Qaeda allies, all radicals and armed, are terrorizing the Libyan population.
- Dead bodies are on every street, "it's either kill or be killed."
- Libyans are now displaced inside and outside of their country.
- NATO has introduced instability all over the country.
- This is the most difficult time in Libyan history for Black Libyans.
- "Rebels" engage in ethnic cleansing with NATO support and backing.
- Many US mercenaries are willing to die for money.
- The Libyan peoples' primary response is this: "Libya is our country and we will never trade it for any other in the world."
- Resistance will continue until Libya is freed from the current NATO-Al Qaeda axis

The last words I heard were "We hope Gaya/Allah/God/The Creator grants us victory. Never shall we surrender, we either win or die." There is so much that needs to be said and that could be said about NATO's illegal war against Libya. The contributors to this publication are either DIGNITY Delegation members who accompanied me to Tripoli or are individuals who have personal experience in Libya and/or much-needed insight into war propaganda and the rolling tide of the NATO military machine.

Bob Fitrakis, Don DeBar, Keith Harmon Snow, Dedon Kamathi, Joshalyn Lawrence, and Dr. Randy Short accompanied me on various DIGNITY Delegations. Lizzie Phelan, Mahdi Darius Nazemroaya, and Julien Teil were among the last alternative (non-embedded) journalists to leave Tripoli and risked their lives to remain in place so the truth could be told about what was really happening in Libya. The other contributors wrote compellingly during NATO's bombing campaign of Operation Unified Protector and I befriended many of them by way of the internet. We shared a heartbreaking time together, but even our heartbreak must pale in comparison to what the Libyan people now see in their country. Libya represents another episode of what I call patricide (the wholesale destruction of an entire country) and some now call sociocide (the wholesale destruction of a society).

How many more countries need to be invaded, how many more governments will be overthrown, how many more societies totally destroyed, how many more countries completely destroyed before the people of the US and allied NATO countries actually do something to stop the killing machine financed by them and organized in their name. I am sick and tired of the killing and I will do as Mario Savio said on 2 December 1964 in front of the University of California at Berkeley's Sproul Hall so many years ago:

> There's a time when the operation of the machine becomes so odious, makes you so sick at heart, that you can't take part. You can't even passively take part. And you've got to put your bodies upon the gears and upon the wheels, upon the levers, upon all the apparatus and you've got to make it stop. And you've got to indicate to the people who run it, to the people who own it, that unless you're free the machine will be prevented from working at all!

As the US fires its drones killing innocent Somalis, Pakistanis, Yemenis, Afghanis, and others around the world, it is my hope that this book will provide a rare prism of truth through which to view NATO's illegal war in Libya, current and future events, and US foreign relations as a whole.

ENDNOTES

1   Victor Ostrovsky, *By Way of Deception: The making of a Mossad officer*, 1990, ISBN 0971759502.
2   Victor Ostrovsky, *The Other Side of Deception: A Rogue Agent Exposes the Mossad's Secret Agenda*, 1994, ISBN 9780061093524.

INTRODUCTION

Bob Fitrakis

In October 2009, I accompanied former Congresswoman Cynthia McKinney along with nine others in her United States delegation to attend the First International Conference of the *Green Book* Supporters Society. We visited Colonel Muammar Qaddafi in his really big air-conditioned tent with cushy rugs and impressive chandeliers. Forty decades earlier, Qaddafi was a 27-year-old admirer of Che Guevera and leader of the bloodless coup that overthrew the Libya government.

The controversial Libyan leader, who worked with insurgent groups throughout the developing world was also a man with his own ideology. Qaddafi wanted to compete in the marketplace of ideas. He and his supporters felt the *Green Book* offered a unique perspective to a world plagued by neoliberal global economic policies. Here's one *Green Book* idea: every citizen is entitled to one mortgage-free house, or tent. That's the way it was for 5.5 million Libyan citizens in 2009. Although it was never emphasized in the US corporate controlled media, Libya had the highest standard of living in Africa and was comparable to so-called Middle East oil-rich nations.

Our trip to Libya was in some way a response to Qaddafi's much derided trip to the United States in September 2009, when he spoke for an hour and a half at the United Nations questioning the assassinations of Kennedy and King. After a nine-hour flight to Frankfurt, Germany and a three-hour hop to the shores of Tripoli, I arrived Thursday morning, October 22, to be greeted by Society supporters at the airport. The 11-member US delegation was whisked off to the Bab-Al Bahre Hotel to mingle with hundreds of representatives from around the world.

Many *Green Book* supporters were shocked, but delighted to see a US delegation. We were the first US visitors to Tripoli of any note since President Ronald Reagan attempted to assassinate Qaddafi with F-16 fighter jets in 1986, instead killing his 5-year-old adopted daughter. United States sanctions against Libya were lifted in 2004, and in 2006 the US removed the country from the State Sponsors of Terrorism list, but the US had been slow to engage with Qaddafi. In the meantime, the countries of Africa voted him the President of the African Union and businessmen from China, Japan, South Korea, and Russia had flooded the scenic Mediterranean port city of Tripoli with development. Construction cranes were everywhere as 2000 miles of undeveloped and unpolluted Mediterranean coastline beckoned foreign investors.

Initially I planned to go to Libya as a reporter or as McKinney's attorney, but I soon became caught up as a conference participant, as other countries' delegates began asking me for my analysis of President Barack Obama and what was happening in US politics, post-Bush. There was great hope among the attendees that Obama represented change for the better in African and Middle Eastern policies. On Thursday and Friday, I worked with the US delegates, particularly Glen Ford of the Black Agenda Report, in drafting a statement of friendship to be read at the conference. It ended: "We know that a better world is possible. We are here to build it in solidarity with each and every one of you, and with our brothers and sisters around the world."

At the time, I kept thinking of the courageous writings of Tom Hayden and Staughton Lynd in their book "The Other Side" about their visit to North Vietnam during the war. In this case however, bravery was not as necessary, since Qaddafi and the United States had a common enemy in pan-Islamic fundamentalist terrorist groups like al Qaeda. After all, as the Colonel liked to point out, he was the first man to send out a warrant through Interpol to arrest Osama bin Laden. Just prior to our visit, Senators John McCain and Joseph Lieberman had met with Qaddafi. My thoughts were that if Richard Nixon could embrace Chairman Mao and his *Red Book* supporters, we can dialogue with Qaddafi.

One of my fellow US delegates, journalist Wayne Madsen, and I wandered through the old walled city of Tripoli, run-down and hard hit by the US sanctions yet currently being renovated in anticipation of a flourishing tourist trade. Libya was in the process of building the largest airport on the African continent and expected it to be a destination for people from all nations. While we were warned that we should not be in the old city without an interpreter or guide, we felt safe strolling through the incredible ancient fortress.

Four of us shopped in Tripoli's central market. Sadly, I found it virtually impossible to buy any authentic Arab wear. Most of the clothes being sold were knock-offs of US styles with names like "Calvin Place," manufactured in China or Cambodia. Also, the ubiquitous satellite dishes offered four English-speaking channels: the BBC, CNN, Fox's Action Movies, and another US action-adventure channel. I wondered about the wisdom of showering the Libyan people with movies like Mission: Impossible and Rambo Part III. The proliferation of western goods and popular culture in Tripoli ran counter to the stereotype that Libya was an authoritarian society.

On Sunday, the conference of 400 or so participants convened. A conference organizer ushered me into the first row of VIP-reserved seats, right in front of the Secretary General. Both Cynthia McKinney and I had the opportunity to address the delegates. With hope and change in the air, delegate after delegate spoke of the possibilities for a peaceful and more equitable world—one that transcended corporate capitalism.

We were surprised when they postponed the conference on Sunday and Abdurahman our interpreter, told us we were going to meet a special guest. Conference members boarded buses and headed along the seashore highway in Tripoli. The bus pulled into a military compound and we were ushered through heavy security. What else could it be— we were destined to sit in Qaddafi's big tent.

I never thought I'd be hanging out in his tent, in a compound with a shrine dedicated to his dead daughter. Once again, I found myself in the front row next to Congresswoman McKinney. Finally, the Colonel came in and we observed a moment of silence for the thousands of Libyans kidnapped and relocated by Italian occupational forces on that day in October 1911. Qaddafi spoke for more than an hour. His speech's theme was clear—corporate capitalism was failing in the West and the *Green Book*'s version of socialism offered an alternative.

He stressed over and over again that people should actually read his *Green Book* and not listen to Western propaganda about it. He emphasized that true democracy must be rooted in the religious and cultural traditions particular to each society. He specifically cited the Torah, the Bible, and the Qur'an as sources for law and democracy. His voice was strong and he spoke slowly. It was clearly legacy time for the aging leader of both pan-Arab and pan-African unity.

Why must there be People's Congresses? "The rich create the Parliament, they own the press." Denouncing the rich, he stated: "They have a right to steal, you have the right to protest." Qaddafi commented specifically on the United States: "The wealth of society is the property of all Americans and should be distributed that way."

In our current climate of economic collapse, the ideas in Qaddafi's *Green Book* may make sense to some Americans. Yet, it seemed implausible that the great vilified enemy of the US would rise from the ashes of near assassination to influence US politics. At the time, it was intriguing that a robed, revolutionary Bedouin living in a tent in Tripoli seemed to have a more realistic assessment of the US economy and democracy than most of our own elected officials. I thought, next time, let's let him set up his tent in New Jersey or New York City—particularly Wall Street—and maybe a few more people could dialogue.

President Obama and the US military industrial complex had other ideas. Dialoguing and reading the *Green Book* were not among them. Less than 18 months after my trip, the Arab Spring had presented new opportunities including an old-fashioned plundering of Libyan wealth.

During the 2011 eastern Libyan revolt against Qaddafi, the United Nations Security Council passed Resolution 1973 which called for a ceasefire and authorized military action to protect civilian lives. A coalition formed centered around NATO, with the March 17, 2011 passing of the Resolution. Its purpose—a so-called "no-fly zone" over Libya.

The great historical question is, how did the North Atlantic Treaty Organization (NATO) go from a collective defense organization ostensibly to protect Europe against the former Soviet Union to the new Barbary Pirates of imperialism in North Africa? The irony that the U.S.-dominated NATO military organization could be concerned with "protecting" Arab civilians is excessively absurd, since the United States is the nation most responsible for killing Arab civilians over the last 20 years.

Fairness and Accuracy in Reporting (FAIR) in its January-February 2008 issue pointed out that 1 million people had died in Iraq as a result of the US invasion and occupation. The for-profit corporate media liked to focus on just the casualties that resulted from US military forces. Had we not invaded Iraq and dismantled the government, police and military, how many more Iraqi civilians would be alive today?

Lancet, the highly regarded British medical journal, estimated that 100,000 Iraqis were killed during the first year of the war. In July 2006, Johns Hopkins Medical School estimated that 650,000 Iraqi civilians had been killed. President George W. Bush went so far as to accuse Johns Hopkins of having a "political agenda."

But George W. Bush was not the first to slaughter Arab civilians. His father George Herbert Walker Bush, later aided by the Clinton administration, was responsible for the deaths of more than a million Iraqis. Roughly half a million of these were children. The deliberate bombing of Iraqi water and sewage facilities, hospitals and other key infrastructure during the first Gulf War caused most of these deaths.

Back in 1996, Clinton's Secretary of State Madeleine Albright made her notorious comments to CBS' Lesley Stahl that "We think the price is worth it" in reference to the killing of 500,000 Iraqi children.

Many of these children died as a direct result of the US embargo of medical and other essential supplies.

The most interesting question I pondered as the world's foremost war criminal, George W. Bush, walks free in the United States is—how could the US public be sold such an obvious lie about NATO's concern for Iraqi civilians?

The real reasons for the attack had been dealt with most directly by America's famous reformed "economic hitman," John Perkins.

Perkins pointed out that the attack on Libya, like the attack on Iraq, had to do with power and control of resources, not only oil, but gold. Libya had the highest standard of living in Africa. "According to the IMF, Libya's Central Bank is 100% state owned. The IMF estimates that the bank has nearly 144 tons of gold in its vaults," Perkins wrote.

> It was obvious to me that NATO was attacking Tripoli like modern Barbary Pirates—to loot Libya's gold. The Russian media, in addition to Perkins, reported that the pan-Africanist Qaddafi, the former President of the African Union, had been advocating that Africa use the gold so plentiful in Libya and South Africa to create an African currency based on a gold dinar.

> It is significant that in the months running up to the UN resolution that allowed the US and its allies to send troops into Libya, Muammar Qaddafi was openly advocating the creation of a new currency that would rival the dollar and the euro. In fact, he called upon African and Muslim nations to join an alliance that would make this new currency, the gold dinar, their primary form of money and foreign exchange. They would sell oil and other resources to the US and the rest of the world only for gold dinars.

What the world witnessed in 2011 was old-fashioned 19th century imperialism—the deliberate plundering of a sovereign nation-state's resources by more powerful Western conquistadors.

Under the neo-colonialism favored after World War II during the period of the Cold War, we preferred to bribe various African leaders to help us loot their nation's resources. The US, of course, killed any pan-African aspirations as well as potential leaders like Patrice Lumumba.

The highjacking of Arab and African resources and slaughtering of Arab civilians was a longstanding plan put forth by neoconservatives in the United States. The Project for a New American Century (PNAC) has had a "hit list" of Arab nations and little regard for Arab casualties.

General Wesley Clark wrote in *Winning Modern Wars* that "As I went back through the Pentagon in November 2001, one of the senior military staff officers had time for a chat. Yes, we are still on track for going against Iraq, he said. But there was more. This was being discussed as part of a five-year campaign plan, he said, and there was a total of seven countries beginning with Iraq, then Syria, Lebanon, Libya, Iran, Somalia, and Sudan.

During the initial attacks I was pleased, but worried, that Cynthia McKinney was once again visiting Libya, condemning the bipartisan and brutal new imperialism perpetuated by the United States and the Obama administration. As NATO war planes attempted to assassinate the leader of a sovereign nation to steal its gold and hijack its oil, McKinney had the courage to speak out: "I think that it's very important that people understand what is happening here. And it's important that people all over the world see the truth. And that is why I am here ... to understand the truth," she told CNN.

McKinney's trip to Libya in 2011 was courageous and we should applaud her willingness to address the facts in a period of universal government deceit. She stated, "I want to say categorically and very clearly that these policies of war ... are not what the people of the United States stand for, and it's not what African-Americans stand for."

DIGNITY Delegation Members of journalists, activists, and attorney present during NATO bombing. (Photo courtesy of Dr. Randy Short, DIGNITY)

History has relegated a slew of over-extended militaristic empires to its dustbins—from ancient Egypt and classical Greece to the Romans, Mongols, Ottomans, Spanish conquistadors, and Brits. Perkins also wrote: "Understanding the war against Qaddafi as a war in defense of empire is another step in the direction of helping us ask ourselves whether we want to continue along this path of empire-building."

I saw the predictable "blowback" in post- Qaddafi Libya soon after the defeat of his government and his highly visible murder. The first week in February 2012, *The New York Times* ran the headline "Qaddafi's Weapons Taken by Old Allies, Reinvigorate an Insurgent Army in Mali." Mali's foreign minister told the *Times* that "The stability of the entire region could be under threat." The dormant Mali rebel movement, the Tuareg insurgents, were assaulting towns in the northern Mali desert. The Tuaregs were in possession of anti-tank weapons, anti-aircraft guns, mortars, and other weapons that were part of the former Qaddafi military arsenal. Before the end of March 2012, the Mali rebels would topple the democratic government in power.

ABC News reported as early as October 13, 2011 that former Qaddafi regime handheld missiles were popping up at Egyptian bazaars and the price for heat-seeking shoulder-fired surface-to-air missiles had dropped from $10,000 to $4,000. A follow up report by ABC News noted that out of the 20,000 portable shoulder-launch surface-to-air missiles, 15,000 remained unaccounted for, as of February 2012.

Peter Bouckaert, Emergencies Director for Human Rights Watch, supplied ABC News with videos of Libyans looting both SA-24 and SA-7 Stinger-style shoulder-fired Russian-made missiles. The Obama administration announced a program to try and re-secure the remaining 15,000 missiles that included 20 US weapons inspectors.

In late January 2012 in Cairo, Amnesty International documented widespread abuses under the US-backed interim Libyan government. Doctors Without Borders, that had been providing emergency medical care in Libya, announced on January 26 that it would suspend operations in Misurata, Libya detention centers as a result of having treated 115 detainees for torture. Many of them "... had been returned repeatedly with more wounds," according to *The New York Times*.

A 45-page report by Amnesty International issued on February 15, 2012 reported that several Libyans had been tortured to death and that scores had reported being "suspended in contorted positions; beaten for hours with whips, cables, plastic hoses, metal chains and bars, and wooden sticks; and even electric shock with live wires and taser-like electro-shock weapons."

Amnesty International reported on what appeared to be the

Weapons provided to the rebels by Qatar, along with massive propaganda assistance via their media channel, Al-Jazeera. (Photo courtesy of Don Debar, DIGNITY)

illegal detention of foreign nationals in Libya at Ain Zara Prison. They estimated that 400 of the 900 detainees were foreign nationals from sub-Sahara Africa. Reports documented that these darker-skinned Africans were being singled out for torture by the lighter-skinned Arab-speaking Libyans.

Despite western reports that the people of Libya hated Qaddafi, the Libyan leader had opened up his arsenal to his people in an attempt to defend the country from eastern-based rebels in Benghazi, backed by the United States, NATO, and forces from the United Arab Emirates and Qatar.In Mid-February, Human Rights Watch issued a report estimating 250 separate militias were then operating in the coastal city of Misurata and an equal number in Tripoli. Massive ethnic and tribal cleansing was widely reported in *The New York Times* under the title "Libya struggles to curb militias as chaos grows."

The Associated Press reported on February 13, 2012 that 100 militias from western Libya "had formed a new federation" and were posing a challenge to Libya's US-backed transitional government.

Colonel Mokhtar Fernana told the AP that the new federation was opposed to integrating fighters formerly loyal to Colonel Qaddafi.

To understand this NATO-caused chaos in Libya, one needs to understand the history of the country. Prior to 1912, the nation of Libya was under the control of the Ottoman Empire and constituted three separate provinces that were more ethnically and tribally cohesive.

Between 1912 and 1927, Italy claimed Libya as a colony acquired as a spoil of the Italo-Turkish war (1911-1912). Italy renamed the territory Italian North Africa. In 1927, they split the colony in two and later in 1934 renamed the colony Libya, and like the Ottomans before them, split it into three provinces.

During World War II and its aftermath, Britain took control of Libya from 1943-1951. In 1951 Libya became an independent nation under the rule of King Idris. He was the grandson of the founder of the Senussi Muslim Sufi order. Under Idris, Libya remained divided it to three governorates.

Prior to the US-NATO assault on Libya, the International Monetary Fund (IMF) certified that Libya was debt free and had an

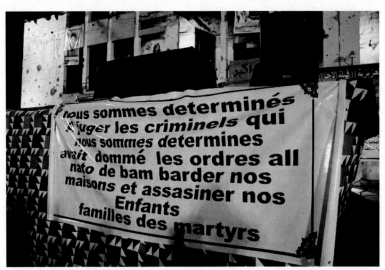

Sign at Bab al-Azizya where NATO bombed relentlessly every night despite the presence of an ever-increasing number of homeless Libyans (due to the bombing) and supporters of the Libyan Socialist Jahamiryia government. Text: "We are determined to judge the criminals whom we have determined to have given the orders to NATO to bombard our homes and murder our children. Families of the martyrs. (Photo courtesy of Dr. Randy Short, DIGNITY)

estimated 144 tons of gold under the control of its state-owned central bank. At the time of the intervention, Qaddafi was estimated to have killed 1000 civilians in the revolt.

NATO forces from France and Germany joined by elite military forces from Qatar and the United Arab Emirates, decided to escalate the mission. The newly admitted goal was to remove Qaddafi, and predictably, shatter and drive Libya into ethnic and tribal chaos. These military actions in Libya have resulted, as intended, in the permanent fracturing of an essentially non-cohesive nation-state that Qaddafi had managed to hold together for 40 years.

Perhaps "blowback" is the wrong term here. That implies unintended consequences. A better thesis is provided by former high-ranking CIA official John Stockwell, who in his book *In Search of Enemies* offers the perspective that the US military industrial complex and its cohorts in the security industrial complex intentionally keep the Third World in chaos and turmoil to justify their unprecedented budgets. Amidst this chaos, it is much easier for the former colonialists of NATO to extract 144 tons of gold and vast oil and gas reserves from the once defiant nation of Libya.

The McKinney-led delegation and this book will serve as a first-person witness to the crimes perpetrated against the people of Libya by the US and its NATO allies. But more importantly, it will be a lasting testament to the hope and possibilities briefly opened up through dialogue and discussion initiated by the *Green Book* Society and Qaddafi just a few short years ago. We must not allow the military madness and deliberate mythology to obscure the historical record and the shining moment when an alternative path was glimpsed by a handful of Americans on the shores of Tripoli.

ON THE GROUND IN LIBYA DURING "HUMANITARIAN INTERVENTION"

A supporter of the Libyan Jahamiriya Government defies NATO
bombing at Bab al-Azizya. (Photo courtesy Dedon Kamathi, DIGNITY)

NATO'S FEAST OF BLOOD

Cynthia McKinney

May 24, 2011
Dispatch From Tripoli

While serving on the House International Relations Committee from 1993 to 2003, it became clear to me that the North Atlantic Treaty Organization (NATO) was an anachronism. Founded in 1945 at the end of World War II, NATO was founded by the United States in response to the Soviet Union's survival as a Communist state. NATO was the U.S. insurance policy that capitalist ownership and domination of European, Asian, and African economies would continue. This also would ensure the survival of the then-extant global apartheid.

NATO is a collective security pact wherein member states pledge that an attack upon one is an attack against all. Therefore, should the Soviet Union have attacked any European Member State, the United States military shield would be activated. The Soviet Response was the Warsaw Pact that maintained a "cordon sanitaire" around the Russian Heartland should NATO ever attack. Thus, the world was broken into blocs which gave rise to the "Cold War."

Avowed "Cold Warriors" of today still view the world in these terms and, unfortunately, cannot move past Communist China and an amputated Soviet Empire as enemy states of the U.S. whose moves anywhere on the planet are to be contested. The collapse of the Soviet Union provided an accelerated opportunity to exert U.S. hegemony in an area of previous Russian influence. Africa and the Eurasian landmass containing former Soviet satellite states and Afghanistan and Pakistan along with the many other "stans" of the region, have always factored prominently in the theories of "containment" or "rollback" guiding U.S. policy up to today.

With that as background, last night's NATO rocket attack on Tripoli is inexplicable. A civilian metropolitan area of around 2 million people, Tripoli sustained 22 to 25 bombings last night, rattling and breaking windows and glass and shaking the foundation of my hotel.

I left my room at the Rexis Al Nasr Hotel and walked outside the hotel and I could smell the exploded bombs. There were local people everywhere milling with foreign journalists from around the world. As we stood there more bombs struck around the city. The sky flashed red with explosions and more rockets from NATO jets cut through low cloud before exploding.

I could taste the thick dust stirred up by the exploded bombs. I immediately thought about the depleted uranium munitions reportedly being used here–along with white phosphorus. If depleted uranium weapons were being used what affect on the local civilians?

Women carrying young children ran out of the hotel. Others ran to wash the dust from their eyes. With sirens blaring, emergency vehicles made their way to the scene of the attack. Car alarms, set off by the repeated blasts, could be heard underneath the defiant chants of the people.

Sporadic gunfire broke out and it seemed everywhere around me. Euronews showed video of nurses and doctors chanting even at the hospitals as they treated those injured from NATO's latest installation of shock and awe. Suddenly, the streets around my hotel became full of chanting people, car horns blowing, I could not tell how many were walking, how many were driving. Inside the hotel, one Libyan woman carrying a baby came to me and asked me why are they doing this to us?

Whatever the military objectives of the attack (and I and many others question the military value of these attacks) the fact remains the air attack was launched a major city packed with hundreds of thousands of civilians.

I did wonder too if the any of the politicians who had authorized this air attack had themselves ever been on the receiving end of laser guided depleted uranium munitions. Had they ever seen the awful damage that these weapons do a city and its population? Perhaps if they actually been in the city of air attack and felt the concussion from these bombs and saw the mayhem caused they just might not be so inclined to authorize an attack on a civilian population.

I am confident that NATO would not have been so reckless with human life if they had called on to attack a major western city. Indeed, I am confident that would not be called upon ever to attack a western city. NATO only attacks (as does the US and its allies) the poor and underprivileged of the 3rd world.

Only the day before, at a women's event in Tripoli, one woman came up to me with tears in her eyes: her mother is in Benghazi and she can't get back to see if her mother is OK or not. People from the east and west of the country lived with each other, loved each other, intermarried, and now, because of NATO's "humanitarian intervention," artificial divisions are becoming hardened. NATO's recruitment of allies in eastern Libya smacks of the same strain of cold warriorism that sought to assassinate Fidel Castro and overthrow the Cuban Revolution with "homegrown" Cubans willing to commit acts of terror against their former home country. More recently, Democratic Republic of Congo has been amputated de facto after Laurent Kabila refused a request from the Clinton Administration to formally shave off the eastern part of his country. Laurent Kabila personally recounted the meeting at which this request and refusal were delivered. This plan to balkanize and amputate an African country (as has been done in Sudan) did not work because Kabila said "no" while Congolese around the world organized to protect the "territorial integrity" of their country.

I was horrified to learn that NATO allies (the Rebels) in Libya have reportedly lynched, butchered and then their darker-skinned compatriots after U.S. press reports labeled Black Libyans as "Black mercenaries." Now, tell me this, pray tell. How are you going to take Blacks out of Africa? Press reports have suggested that Americans were "surprised" to see dark-skinned people in Africa. Now, what does that tell us about them?

The sad fact, however, is that it is the Libyans themselves, who have been insulted, terrorized, lynched, and murdered as a result of the press reports that hyper-sensationalized this base ignorance. Who will be held accountable for the lives lost in the bloodletting frenzy unleashed as a result of these lies?

Which brings me back to the lady's question: why is this happening? Honestly, I could not give her the educated reasoned response that she was looking for. In my view the international public is struggling to answer "Why?".

What we do know, and what is quite clear, is this: what I experienced last night is no "humanitarian intervention."

Many suspect it is about all the oil under Libya. Call me skeptical but I have to wonder why the combined armed sea, land and air forces of NATO and the US costing billions of dollars are being arraigned against a relatively small North African country and we're expected to believe its in the defense of democracy.

What I have seen in long lines to get fuel is not "humanitarian intervention." Refusal to allow purchases of medicine for the hospitals is not "humanitarian intervention." What is most sad is that I cannot give a cogent explanation of why to people now terrified by NATO's bombs, but it is transparently clear now that NATO has exceeded its mandate, lied about its intentions, is guilty of extra-judicial killings–all in the name of "humanitarian intervention." Where is the Congress as the President exceeds his war-making authority? Where is the "Conscience of the Congress?"

For those of who disagree with Dick Cheney's warning to us to prepare for war for the next generation, please support any one who will stop this madness. Please organize and then vote for peace. People around the world need us to stand up and speak out for ourselves and them because Iran and Venezuela are also in the cross-hairs. Libyans don't need NATO helicopter gunships, smart bombs, cruise missiles, and depleted uranium to settle their differences. NATO's "humanitarian intervention" needs to be exposed for what it is with the bright, shining light of the truth.

As dusk descends on Tripoli, let me prepare myself with the local civilian population for some more NATO humanitarianism.

Stop bombing Africa and the poor of the world!

DISPATCHES FROM TRIPOLI, LIBYA DURING THE NATO BOMBING CAMPAIGN OF 2011

Wayne Madsen*

June 5-6, 2011—TRIPOLI, LIBYA.
US, NATO supporting 2000 "Al Qaeda" irregulars in Benghazi

The Obama administration may have officially pronounced the assassination by US Special Operations forces of reputed "Al Qaeda" leader Osama Bin Laden in Pakistan but that has not deterred the US administration from providing over two-thousand "Al Qaeda" irregulars with weapons and other support in rebel-controlled eastern Libya.

The "Al Qaeda" guerrillas, Salafists who practice the extremist Wahhabist sect version of Islam promoted by Saudi Arabia, the United Arab Emirates, and Qatar—all three countries members of the anti-Qaddafi Arab front supporting the NATO attack on Libya—are drawn from Afghanistan, Yemen, Saudi Arabia, Egypt, Algeria, Morocco, and Tunisia, according to a group of Libyan journalists who recently reported from Benghazi and made it back to Tripoli to report on what they witnessed on the ground in rebel-held territory in eastern Libya.

This reporter was shown raw video footage of the Salafists in Benghazi cutting the throat of a Qaddafi supporter and severing his head. The footage was reminiscent of the "Al Qaeda" beheading in Pakistan of *Wall Street Journal* reporter Daniel Pearl and American Nick

---

* WayneMadsenReport (WMR)

Berg in Iraq. The Libyan journalists asked me why such footage of rebel atrocities is not being aired by CNN, Al Jazeera, or the BBC. I replied, "corporate control by the western war industry."

I also saw another video of the wounds sustained by a Libyan nurse in a Benghazi hospital who was horribly disfigured by Salafist guerrillas. The woman's head was cut in several places, her throat was cut, and she had deep gashes in her arms. The Libyan journalists also witnessed other women in Benghazi whose breasts had been cut off by Libyan rebels.

The Libyan media team was in Benghazi while French philosopher Bernard-Henri Lévy was visiting representatives of the rebel National Transitional Council in Benghazi before traveling to Jerusalem. The Libyan journalists reported that Levy told the rebels that if they wanted to see increased support from NATO, they should establish relations with Israel. After Levy met with the rebel commanders, it was announced that if victorious over Colonel Qaddafi's forces, they would proceed to establish diplomatic relations with Israel. Israeli Prime Minister Binyamin Netanyahu confirmed Levy's meeting with the Libyan rebels and the topic of their recognition of Israel.

Levy is also a supporter of former International Monetary Fund (IMF) director Dominique Strauss-Kahn. Levy has attacked the credibility of the Guinean chambermaid who charged that Strauss-Kahn sexually assaulted her in the Sofitel Hotel in Manhattan. Levy's friends in the Libyan rebel movement have been charged with raping and killing a number of workers, including women, from black African nations, including Guinea. The rebel racial-motivated attacks on black workers in Libya has resulted in a massive refugee crisis on Libya's borders with Tunisia and Egypt.

It was Levy who convinced French President Nicolas Sarkozy to be the first to recognize the Libyan rebels and commit French military force to their assistance. It is now being reported from Brega, a contested city on the battlefront, that French helicopters have entered the Libyan war on behalf of the rebel forces.

Sarkozy is said to have received substantial campaign funds for his run for the presidency of France from Qaddafi financial sources. In addition, the loss in 2008 of $1.3 billion dollars of Libyan sovereign wealth funds because of "bad investments" by Goldman Sachs reportedly involved top officials of the French government and the financial sector, including those close to Sarkozy and Strauss-Kahn, many of whom are French Jews who ardently support Israel and, now, the Libyan rebels.

WMR has also learned by informed sources in Tripoli that the former head of Liubyan intelligence under Qaddafi, Musa Kusa, was long believed to have been a double agent for the CIA in Libya. Kusa defected to Britain two weeks after the NATO attacks on Libya commenced.

Like former Egyptian intelligence chief and vice president Omar Suleiman, Kusa was a regional point man for the CIA's "extraordinary rendition" and torture program that used Middle Eastern nations like Egypt, Libya, Tunisia, Jordan, and Syria as CIA partners.

June 5-6, 2011—TRIPOLI, LIBYA.
NATO war crimes in Libya exposed

In the current NATO war on Libya, the citizens of European and North American NATO countries are being treated to the largest propaganda blitz by their governments in cahoots with corporate media outlets since the U.S.-led invasions and occupation of Iraq. The situation on the ground in Tripoli, the Libyan capital, could not be more different from what is being portrayed by Western news networks and newspapers.

The NATO missile attack that killed Muammar Qaddafi's son, Seif al Arab Qaddafi, on April 30, was an attempt to kill Muammar Qaddafi himself. This editor visited the devastated home where Seif was killed, along with his friend and three of Muammar Qaddafi's grandchildren. The only reason why Muammar Qaddafi survived the blast was that he was away from the main residence tending to some animals, including two gazelles, kept in a small petting zoo maintained

A traumatized gazelle from the children's petting zoo springs away from the DIGNITY Delegation members as they tour the bombed Qaddafi family home. (Photo courtesy of Joshalyn Lawrence, DIGNITY)

for his grandchildren. Muammar Qaddafi escaped the fate of his son and grandchildren by only about 500 feet. The residence was hit by bunker buster bombs fired from a U.S. warplane. One of the warheads did not detonate and was later removed from what remained of a bedroom in the home. Libyan authorities do not have the technical capabilities to determine if the warhead contained depleted uranium.

NATO and the Pentagon claimed the residence was a military compound, yet there is no evidence that any military assets were located in the residence that was flanked by the homes of a Libyan doctor and businessmen. The Qaddafi residence actually is owned by Qaddafi's wife. The neighbors' homes were also badly damaged in the U.S. air attack and are uninhabitable. Only a few hundred yards away from the Qaddafi compound sits the embassy of Cote d'Ivoire.

The presence of a foosball table and swing set in the yard of the Qaddafi compound belies the charge by the Pentagon that the home was a military target. However, considering that Qaddafi was present in the compound during the attack, it is clear that President Obama violated international law and three Executive Orders signed by three past presidents—Ford, Carter, and Reagan—in trying to assassinate the Libyan head of state. In fact, while Obama's order to kill Qaddafi was being carried out, the President of the United States was preparing to yuck it up with Washington's illuminati and Hollywood's glitterati at the White House Correspondents' Dinner in Washington.

Obama's order to kill Qaddafi is reminiscent of George W. Bush's order to kill Sadaam Hussein at the outset of the US war against Iraq, an assassination order that was also a violation of international and U.S. law.

Putting into context what occurred at Mrs. Qaddafi's home and the aftermath, let one say that there is an unprovoked and surprise enemy missile attack on a secondary U.S. presidential residence, say Camp David. The world's major media then claims that the attack was justified because the US president was committing unsubstantiated war crimes, all reported from sketchy sources. A group of independent journalists and human rights activists drive to Camp David and are welcomed by a plainclothes member of the Secret Service's Presidential Protective Division.

The Secret Service official then proceeds to show the delegation one of the bombed out bedrooms of the main residence and points out that one of the pulverized bedrooms is where the president's daughter was killed in the attack. The delegation is then shown the First Lady's singed handbag thrown several hundred feet away in the explosion. Although the President was taking a walk away from the main residence, the delegation is shown a windbreaker bearing the presidential seal lying on the couch of the destroyed living room. A room said contain military command and control systems is then found by the delegation to have a destroyed pool table and a shattered pinball machine. The attacking nation claims that the Camp David compound was a security threat. But the American people rally to support their president and his family after the attack. Now, you can begin to understand how the people of Libya feel after the US attack on Mrs. Qaddafi's house that killed her and her husband's son and three grand children, along with a family friend.

June 6-7, 2011—TRIPOLI, LIBYA.
Libyan rebels using Western arms, looting Libyan Central Bank in Benghazi

Shortly after Libya's rebel Interim Transitional National Council (ITNC) seized control of Benghazi, the second-largest Libyan city, they discovered the two keys for the cash vaults of the Libyan Central Bank in the city. However, because of control mechanisms, the cash vault required a third key held at the Libyan Central Bank in Tripoli, the capital. The rebel movement brought in a professional safe cracker from the United Arab Emirates who successfully opened the cash vault safe. The rebels had their hands on 900 million in Libyan dinars and $500.5 million in U.S. dollars.

According to Central Bank officials in Tripoli, the rebels have now spent or siphoned to their offshore bank accounts the entire Benghazi Central Bank cash reserves. In addition, the rebel movement has squandered millions of euros provided by the Euriopean Union. The rebel's theft of money is so great, the US Treasury has refused to provide frozen Libyan central government funds to the rebel movement.

In addition to the Libyan dinars stolen from the Benghazi Central Bank, NATO countries have printed their own Libyan dinars abroad and have made the cash available to the rebels.

Under Qaddafi's Libyan Oil Wealth program, every Libyan family received a monthly payment of 500 dinars, their share of Libya's oil revenues. With the rebels controlling the finances of eastern Libya, families in the east are no longer receiving the oil wealth-sharing payments and the looting of the Central Bank in Benghazi has resulted in no money for civil servants and pensioners.

Prior to the NATO attack on Libya, Qaddafi was working with other African nations, including that of President Laurent Gbagbo of Cote d'Ivoire, to establish an Africa-wide currency unit under the African Monetary Authority. French President Nicolas Sarkozy and his French business friends saw Qaddafi's move as threatening the collapsing CFA franc, a neo-colonial contrivance used by France to maintain control over their former colonies in Africa. With Gbagbo ousted largely by French troops and Qaddafi under attack by French-and Israeli-backed rebels, Sarkozy and his banker and business friends feel that the CFA franc is safe and plans for the African currency unit are aborted.

One of NATO's first targets in Tripoli was the Office of Investigation of Corruption in Tripoli. Several of the Qaddafi ministers who defected to the rebels, including the former Justice, Interior, Planning and Economic Development, and Trade and Industry ministers, were being investigated for fraud by the Libyan government. The documents on corruption were backed up, however, and are now stored in a safe location.

The Libyan rebels, many of whom are Libyan mujaheddin Salafists from Afghanistan and Iraq, including many Libyans captured in Afghanistan and released from detention in Guantanamo, obtained brand new weapons not found in Libyan stockpiles at the outset of their rebellion. Other Salafists crossed into Libya from neghboring Darfur in Sudan.

Some of the Salafists are members of the Islamic Combatant Group while others have established the "Emirate of Derna" in the east that is under the control of a member of "Al Qaeda" named Sheikh Abdul-Hakim. The INTC has issued Hakim a false Libyan passport. The passport photo shows Hakim with a beard and the Qaddafi government prohibits passport photos showing beards.

Many of the Islamic mujaheddin groups began their campaign to topple Qaddafi on Facebook. In November 2010, a political officer for the US embassy in Tripoli was expelled for espionage. WMR has learned the diplomat was a CIA agent who was on a liaison mission with a Libyan rebel "sleeper cell" in Ifrane, about 100 miles southwest of Tripoli, when he was caught by Libyan security. The CIA's early involvement with the Libyan rebels, along with early support for the rebels by French and British intelligence, indicates that the Libyan rebellion was not based on events in neighboring Tunisia and Egypt, but was designed to authorize the rebels to move when a favorable situation presented itself. The overthrow of the governments of Tunisia and Egypt provided just the right situation for the CIA and its French and British counterparts.

Many of the new weapons being used by the rebels are from the Belgian-based arms manufacturer Fabrique Nationale (FN), which has a CIA-connected subsidiary called FNH-USA. One FN rifle, the Fusil Automatique Léger (FAL), is the standard weapon being used by the rebels. The FAL, called the "Right Arm of the Free World" during the

Cold War, only uses NATO standard rounds. The weapon was never used by the Libyan Army, which relied on Soviet weaponry. Claims by NATO that the rebels are using Libyan weapons captured from army arsenals and caches are, therefore, false.

Libyan rebels are also using U.S.-produced machine guns chambered for NATO rounds.

There are also reports that rebels have agreed to recognize Israel and allow Israel to maintain a 30-year lease for a military base in eastern Libya that would be used to check the Egyptian military should a future breakdown in Israeli-Egyptian relations occur.

LIVING THROUGH
A FULL BLOWN
MEDIA WAR

Lizzie Phelan

Living through a full blown media war, as I did in Libya, where the excuse of protecting life is used as a pretext to cause mass death and destruction, is perhaps one of the most sinister and unfathomable experiences one can go through. When the other foreign observers in the country—western journalists—are refusing to relay the very sights they are seeing along with everyone else—an entire people—and are finding all manner of justifications for their self and collective delusion, it reminds one of the riddle: "If a tree falls in a forest, and no one is around to hear it, does it still make a sound?".

As Libya was falling, or being bombed into extermination, its people were screaming. They screamed in their millions when they filled Green Square on July 1st, 2011. They screamed when they risked their lives every day as they voluntarily gathered at their Leader Muammar Qaddafi's compound at Bab al-Aziza every evening, despite that it was being bombed every day. They screamed when they set up armed neighborhood watch duties across the country to prevent NATO's proxies from entering and terrorizing their communities. They screamed when they buried their martyrs from NATO's bombs and apache helicopters draped in green flags. Indeed they were screaming when they tried in vain to overcome the media whiteout by uploading footage and images of the crimes committed by NATO and rebels onto the internet, believing that the logic of believing the victim rather than the proven criminal would prevail with the citizens of the NATO countries that were bombing them, who would be moved to hold their governments to account.

Just because logic did not prevail and instead the people of the west blocked their ears to the screams of the Libyan people—because to do otherwise would bring their entire system based on brutality against people in the lands it once colonized into question—that would never change the fact that there were millions of Libyan people screaming to be heard.

During my stay in Libya, like all of the other western journalists in Tripoli, I was a witness to NATO crimes on a daily basis: from the hotel and shisha bar on the street next to my hotel that had been obliterated, to my frequent visits to a friend's home in the working class and densely populated Tripoli area of Salahdeen that was bombed up to 50 times a day, to the repeated bombing of the Medina area in central Tripoli, to the repeated bombing of Al Fatah University in Tripoli, to the repeated bombing next to a hotel on Tripoli's Airport Road that was housing hundreds of refugees from areas held by NATO's rebel proxies, to the massacre in Zlitan where 33 children, 32 women and 20 women were martyred by bombs dropped from British RAF planes to the NATO blitzkrieg of Tripoli during which time I was unable to move from the Rixos al-Nasr Hotel for five days as outside NATO was busy massacring anyone that moved that was not their proxy. The bloody list of crimes that NATO is responsible for unleashing has been compiled over a period, at the time of writing, nearly one year and one month long.

As well as freelancing for Press TV and later during the NATO invasion of Tripoli, for Russia Today, with all of my work facilitated by Libyans I had come to know, I was also volunteering with a group of young Libyans in the Libyan media. So not only had I made good friends with many Libyans, which was very easy to do as the Libyan people are an affectionate, welcoming and communal people, I also counted a number of Libyans as my close colleagues. While the other western journalists working for mainstream networks would spend their spare time in each others' company, I spent mine having the privilege of Libyan people sharing with me their homes and daily lives.

When NATO's intensive bombing of Tripoli began on August 19th, I could hear those daily lives being robbed by the bombs and apaches all around the hotel with the most brutal force one can imagine, while the world was being told that the Libyan people were being "liberated".

When my Libyan colleagues left the hotel after the first day of the invasion to return in most cases to their families, I would receive phone calls from them telling me how outside the hotel, the streets were lined with bodies. One of my friends and colleagues who also worked as a surgeon in Tripoli Central Hospital, who like hundreds and thousands of others has since had to flee the country, told me that when he left the hotel and immediately went on duty, the hospital was drowning with dead and injured bodies with virtually no staff present to handle the unfolding catastrophe.

This, along with the testimonies of endless other victims and eyewitnesses, corroborates the information that Moussa Ibrahim gave

Fathy Abd al Siame holding the photo of his martyred son Walid His story is available in the short Phelan video here: <http://www.youtube.com/watch?v=kN_NJJn49mM&feature=player_embedded>

Photos in this chapter contributed by Lizzie Phelan

Lizzie Phelan with Libyan girls outside a bombed girls' school in Zlitan (see page 42).

Above: The graves of the Hamedi family: Khaled al Hamedi is the son of Khweldi al Hamedi who was part of the original Revolutionary group led by Muammar Qaddafi that overthrew colonial puppet King Idris. Because of that, NATO falsely accused his son Khaled of organising a militia during the crisis and obliterated his home with 8 rockets on the night of his son's birthday party. Killing 15, including his pregnant wife and two small children. There was no basis for such claims, Khaled is an engineer who runs a UN accredited organisation the International Organisation for Peace Care and Relief, he has mediated in conflicts in Palestine, Sarajevo and elsewhere and his credentials as a man of peace are well established. Khaled continues to campaign for justice. These are his websites: www.icena.org; www.iopcr.org; www.khaleda. org;www.natocrimes.co

Right: Victims of the Zlitan massacre of the NATO bombardment that massacred 85 civilians: 33 children, 32 women and 20 men. Many were refugees who had fled areas that had already come under rebel control and had been taken in by ordinary people in areas that were still Green. NATO refused to apologise, saying that the targets were legitimate military targets and the western media questioned the number of casualties. Following the claims by NATO and the western media, many of the families of the victims, and injured came to the Rixos hotel the day after the massacre to show western journalists the photos of their loved ones who had been martyred, and to show their injuries, to try to make them understand that these were not airstrikes that targeted military sites.

Phelan with Mother and two daughters from Sudan who have been living in Libya for 17 years, forced to flee from Misrata to Tripoli following the vicious atrocities committed by the pro-NATO rebels against black skinned peoples. They are firmly standing behind their leader Muammar Qadaffi. The sisters have written on the poster, on the left: "King of Kings of Africa" and on the right: "Our souls are for you".

in his last press conference from the Rixos Hotel that was criminally ignored by the world and anyone with any power to stop the bloodbath that ensued. He relayed to the world's media the latest figures from the Ministry of Health in just 12 hours of 1,300 dead and 5,000 injured in Tripoli alone and he warned that unless it stopped immediately, "the death toll would be unimaginable." Tragically, his warning has been borne out.

Since then, those friends and colleagues of mine have seen their lives transformed terribly, although I speak to many of them frequently, I cannot tell their story because to do so would put theirs or their families lives in a danger, in a country where now one only has the freedom to live if you unquestioningly support the ever-shifting status quo. But I can tell the story of that doctor whose experience reflects that of millions. Because as unfathomable as it has been for me to witness, I cannot begin to comprehend the pain which they are experiencing having lost their homeland. He said:

> My name is Odei, I am a 27-year-old doctor who used to work in Tripoli Central Hospital. Before the war, my biggest problems were how could I improve my career, how could I help others more and which book I should read on a certain area to improve my knowledge of my profession.

> I did not get involved in anything political before. Me and many people did not realize how the world is driven by the media and that even simple issues have another point of view. I never could have believed before this that anything could happen to my beloved country because we were all living happily, as equals. There were little differences between us and we were a united people. All the different tribes lived in the same conditions. We had virtually no homeless people, free education and health and no need for any kind of social insurance. We had problems in our own way, but who in the world doesn't?

> Then this aggression started. We had no idea how big this war against us was. It was so tough the way it started through lies on the television which terrified all of us that we didn't have the time to comprehend what was really going on. The stream of lies was so great and relentless, that each time we had got to the bottom of one lie, another one came out that we had to try to work out if it was true or not. We lived

under such stress and in an environment of great fear, I tried to keep myself busy at work and by practising my usual routine to stay focused.

But then on March 19th 2011, they made the decision to enforce a no-fly-zone on our country. Still we did not expect to come under bombardment. Then just the next day after that decision was made, as I returned home at about 9pm, the earth shook and the windows flew open. My whole family freaked out and we all ran around trying to see that everyone was ok. My mum shouted for everyone to leave the house immediately. Then we began calling others to check that they were ok. Everyone was petrified, we did not sleep. The airstrikes that began with 12 bombs did not stop until the morning.

The following days were the same, and then after three days we started to hear the NATO planes flying lower and lower with each passing day of bombing. This went on for months.

We became professionals at guessing where they had bombed and what kind of bombs they were using. As time went on, the bombing continued, and more and more people were murdered, our adrenaline levels increased as we wondered if we were next and wished that we would go before those that we loved.

For me it was especially hard because I would always see the results of the bombing in the hospital and would have to deal with witnessing families crying for their lost children, mothers and fathers. The question that drove us crazy was: Why is this happening to us? And no one cared to make it stop or at least to come and see what was really happening.

I had to know why there were so many lies in the media. Because I saw how our people tried their best to show the world how much we love our country and how much we wanted the aggression to stop. That made me happy and proud, but also more scared for everyone.

As well as having to save lives and help people physically, I also had to help people psychologically which was the way in which people have been worse affected. Some people died because they could not deal with the psychological pressure. Children became unstable because of the fear which they lived with every day. Many had problems at school, couldn't control their urine and some even tried to commit suicide which was the most heartbreaking.

After so much pain and losing so many people, which doubled each day, I knew that Libya would never be the same again.

So I started volunteering to work in the media to try to show the world what was happening and challenge the way in which the mainstream media had personalized the whole of Libya in one person, Muammar Qaddafi, and tried to make it seem like it was fine to kill so many people just to get rid of him. The way that they demonized him so relentlessly made some people think that all the world's problems were down to him, even global warming.

I wanted the world to see the truth, the other side of the story that has not been invented by those who care only about their interests and not how many people die. So I took many journalists into my hospital, to show them the number of people who were murdered, injured and affected by the NATO aggression on my country. I was shocked that none of them cared or showed it on their channels. They did not even mention one or two victims that they encountered.

I was so angry and upset I wanted to do anything that I could. So I tried to reach out to people that showed they had a conscience and wanted to show the truth. So we worked together and I tried as much as I could in helping them. I contacted friends outside Libya and spent so much time emailing people, journalists and newspapers sending videos that could prove just how bad things had become because of NATO.

Some of those people knew what was happening. Most of all, Cynthia McKinney, I call her "the mother of hope". She wanted to come from the US to see with her own eyes. She did and she understood. She really gave us hope that people like her exist and maybe others would also understand.

A few journalists also knew the truth and they worked and are still working to show the world the truth. I am happy that I got the chance to meet them.

On top of volunteering with the media I was still busy at the hospital covering all the duties that I could. At night I volunteered at security checkpoints in my neighborhood with my cousins and my neighbors. I saw the unity in my country and how much people loved Libya. And I remember how when we needed blood for injured people, especially during the NATO invasion of Tripoli where there were thousands of injured, families came to give their blood and offer any help they could give.

My emotions became really unstable and my life changed after everything that I saw on the night when the rebels came into Tripoli on the back of extensive NATO bombing. I had guns pointed at me in the hospital which had become a scene of chaos. I still cannot believe and understand how people can change so easily and lose their moral values all of which have disappeared now. In Libya there is no more respect, death became easy and there is no more such a thing as law or security. I wonder how the generation that witnessed all of this will grow up, and what kind of community and country they will live in.

When I left Tripoli I had to hide in one of my friend's homes because some of our friends told us that they were targeting some houses in our neighborhood and burning people in their homes. I was so shocked when I heard they killed our family friend who was the minister of health some years ago. They killed him and his son at his house without any mercy. I was petrified for all the people who I knew and love and it made me so feel so hopeless and angry that I could not do much.

After a couple of days I went to another small city where I had friends that had known my family for a long time. They helped and supported people like me so much and did their best before I had to go to another city. I was so proud to visit and meet those people who gave me hope and a chance to share our feelings of sadness and anger.

Then I had the chance to leave the country. I was devastated and I didn't know if it was the right thing to do. But as a doctor I could not handle the idea of killing anybody, and it hurts me to see how killing has become acceptable for Libyans just because they have a difference of opinion. They say that this is freedom? I do not know what I expected, something that started with Tomahawk cruise missiles, killing and torturing, this is the freedom that they get. Freedom of killing.

I feel so sorry about the way my life has changed, now having lost my home and my country. I am away from my family, and I do not know what happened to some of them. Some of my friends died because of rebels that wanted to kill me, and others, I do not know where they are. Every day I feel dread that I will hear that someone else has died, been detained by the rebels or has been tortured to death. I am trying my best to cope, but with all of this pain and sadness unfortunately I can't. I am still working hard to show the world the truth, because I believe that is the only way that all of this can stop. People have to understand that this stupid war was for power, control and money. Knowing that this would end if they could see that is what makes me survive, and I truly believe what Martin Luther King once said, that: "Our lives begin to end the day we become silent about things that matter". So it is my mission to continue working so that the truth is known, for the people who died, the children who lost their parents and the people who lost their homes that nobody cares about.

ANATOMY
OF A MURDER

HOW NATO KILLED
QADDAFI FAMILY MEMBERS

Cynthia McKinney

How many times must a parent bury a child?

In the case of Muammar Qaddafi it's not only twice: once for his daughter, murdered by the United States bombing on his home in 1986, and again on 30 April 2011 when his youngest son, Saif al Arab was killed, but yet again for three young children, grandbabies of Muammar Qaddafi killed along with Saif at the family home.

I watched Cindy Sheehan as she bared her soul before us in her grief; I cried when Cindy cried. Now, how must Qaddafi and his wife feel? And the people of Libya, parents of all the nation's children gone too soon. I don't even want to imagine.

All my mother could say in astonishment was, "They killed the babies, they killed his grandbabies."

The news reports, however, didn't last more than one half of a news cycle because on 1 May, at a hastily assembled press conference, President Obama announced the murder of Osama bin Laden.

I haven't forgotten my empathy for Cindy Sheehan; I haven't forgotten my concern for the half million children of Iraq that Madeleine Albright said were OK to kill by U.S. sanctions if U.S. geopolitical goals were achieved. I care about the children of Palestine who throw stones at Israeli soldiers and get laser-guided bullets to their brains in return. I care about the people of North Africa and West Asia who are ready to risk their lives for freedom. In fact, I care about all of the children—from Appalachia to the Cancer Alley, from New York City to San Diego, and everywhere in-between.

On 22 May 2011, I had the opportunity to visit the residence of the Qaddafi family, bombed to smithereens by NATO. For a leader, the house seemed small in comparison, say, to the former Clinton family home in Chappaqua or the Obama family home. It was a small whitewashed suburban type house in a typical residential area in metropolitan Tripoli. It was surrounded by dozens of other family homes.

I spoke with a neighbor who described how three separate smart bombs hit the home and exploded, another one not exploding. According to the BBC, the NATO military operations chief stated that a "command and control center" had been hit. That is a lie. As anyone who visits the home can see, this home had nothing to do with NATO's war. The strike against this home had everything to do with NATO adopting a policy of targeted assassination and extra-judicial killing—clearly illegal under international law.

The neighbor said he found Saif Al-Arab in his bedroom underneath rubble; the three young grandchildren were in a different room and they were shredded to pieces. He told of how he picked up as many pieces as he possibly could. He told us that there are still pieces there that he could not get. He asked us to note the smell—not the putrid smell of rotting flesh, but a sweet smell. I did smell it and thought there was an air freshener nearby. It smelled to me of roses. He asked me why this was done and who was going to hold NATO accountable.

Muammar Qaddafi was at the house. But he was outside near where the animals are kept. It is a miracle that he survived. From the looks of that house and the small guest house beside it, the strike was a complete success if the goal was to totally and thoroughly demolish the structure and everything inside it.

NATO wants us to believe that toys, items and clothing, an opened Holy Qur'an, and a soccer board game are the appointments found in military command and control offices. I wonder if we could find similar articles in NATO's office in Brussels.

The opened Holy Qur'an seemed to be frozen in time. In fact, there was a clock dangling from its cord—dangling in space. And indeed, for the four young people in that house at the time of NATO's attack, time had stopped.

The concussion from the bombs was so great that every tile on the walls and floors of the home had been knocked from the walls. Black burn marks scorched the walls. The force broke a marble or granite countertop. The bathtub was literally split into two parts. Shards of the bomb were everywhere. I wondered if the place was now contaminated with depleted uranium.

The Qaddafi home is a crime scene—a murder scene. The United States prisons are full of men and women who are innocent—even on death row. I wonder where the guilty who are never prosecuted go.

Now, if the International Criminal Court were really a repository of justice, it would be investigating this crime. Instead, it is looking for yet another African to prosecute. We in the United States are familiar with this: on our local news every night, we are saturated with photos of Black and Brown criminals with the implication being that White people don't commit crime. The moment the face of someone arrested is not shown, then we know that the culprit is White. It's the unwritten code that we people of color all live by wherever in the world we might happen to be. Global apartheid is alive and well, and exists on many levels.

McKinney at the bombed home of Qaddafi's son and grandchildren. (Photo courtesy of Joshalyn Lawrence, DIGNITY)

I left the house sick in my heart. As I was about to depart, the neighbor begged me, asked me over and over again, why had this happened? What had they done to deserve this? He

53

seemed to not want me to leave. Honestly, I think I was his little piece of America, his little piece of President Obama, and I could help him to understand why this course of action was necessary from my President's point of view. He said NATO should just leave them alone and let them sort out their problems on their own.

I did leave his presence, but that man's face will never leave me.

Dr. Martin Luther King, Jr. warned, "History will have to record that the greatest tragedy of this period of social transition was not the strident clamor of the bad people, but the appalling silence of the good people."

In response to my previous article, "NATO, A Feast of Blood," I received the following quote about Buddha from Shiva Shankar who excerpted Walpola Rahula's "What The Buddha Taught:"

> ... The Buddha not only taught non-violence and peace, but he even went to the field of battle itself and intervened personally, and prevented war, as in the case of the dispute between the Sakyas and the Koliyas, who were prepared to fight over the question of the waters of the Rohini. And his words once prevented King Ajatasattu from attacking the kingdom of the Vajjis. ...

> ... Here is a lesson for the world today. The ruler of an empire publicly turning his back on war and violence and embraced the message of peace and non-violence. There is no historical evidence to show that any neighbouring king took advantage of Asoka's piety to attack him militarily, or that there was any revolt or rebellion within his empire during his lifetime. On the contrary there was peace throughout the land, and even countries outside his empire seem to have accepted his benign leadership. ...

Please don't allow special interest press and war mongering gatekeepers of the left to blot out the tragedy unfolding in Libya. Please don't allow them to take away our chance to live in peace throughout our land and with countries inside and outside our hemisphere. Congress should vote to end NATO's action in Libya and barring that should assert its Constitutional prerogatives and require the President to come to it for authorization of this war. And then, Congress should heed the wisdom of the people of our country who are against this war and vote for peace.

NATO BOMBS THE GREAT MAN-MADE RIVER

Mark Metcalfe*
Human Rights Investigations

It is a war crime to attack essential civilian infra-structure. 95% of Libya is desert and 70% of Libyans depend on water which is piped in from the Nubian Sandstone Aquifer System under the southern desert. The water pipe infrastructure is probably the most essential civilian infrastructure in Libya. Key to its continued function, particularly in time of war, is the Brega pipe factory which enables leaks and breaks in the system to be repaired.

NATO has admitted that its jets attacked the pipe factory on 22 July, claiming in justification that it was used as a military storage facility and rockets were launched from there.

The Great Man-Made River

Libyans like to call the Great Man-Made River "The eighth wonder of the world."

According to a March 2006 report by the BBC,[2] the industrialization of Libya following the Great Al-Fatah Revolution in 1969 put a strain on water supplies and coastal aquifers became contaminated with sea water to such an extent that the water in Benghazi was undrinkable. Finding a supply of fresh, clean water became a government priority and fortunately oil exploration in the

*Human Rights Investigations, posted July 27, 2011, see <http://humanrightsin-vestigationsorg/2011/07/27/great-man-made-river-nato-bombs/>
Reprinted with permission.

UNESCO's Great Man-Made River International Water Prize. In 1999 UNESCO accepted Libya's offer to fund an award named after the Great Man-Made River to "reward remarkable scientific research work on water usage in arid areas."[4]

1950s had revealed vast aquifers beneath Libya's southern desert.

In August 1984, Muammar Al Qaddafi laid the foundation stone for the pipe production plant at Brega. The Great Man-Made River Project had begun. Adam Kuwairi, a senior figure in the Great Man-Made River Authority (GMRA), vividly remembers the impact the fresh water had on him and his family:

> The water changed lives. For the first time in our history, there was water in the tap for washing, shaving and showering. The quality of life is better now, and it's impacting on the whole country.

On 3 April, 2011, Libya warned that NATO-led air strikes could cause a *"human and environmental disaster"* if air strikes damaged the Great Man-Made River project.[3] Engineer and project manager Abdelmajid Gahoud told foreign journalists in Tripoli: *"If part of the infrastructure is damaged, the whole thing is affected and the massive escape of water could cause a catastrophe,"* leaving 4.5 million thirsty Libyans deprived of drinking water.

The Brega Pipe-Making Plant

The Pre-Stressed Concrete Cylinder Pipe Factory at Brega is one of only two such facilities in Libya—the other being at Sarir to the east. This makes it a very important component of the Great Man-Made River[5]—with two production lines making up to 80 pipes a day.

According to the BBC:

> The engineer in charge of the Brega pipe factory is Ali Ibrahim. He is proud that Libyans are now running the factory:
>
> "At first, we had to rely on foreign-owned companies to do the work. But now it's government policy to involve Libyans in the project. Libyans are gaining experience and know-how, and now more than 70% of the manufacturing is done by Libyans. With time, we hope we can decrease the foreign percentage from 30% to 10%."

As a result, Libya is now a world leader in hydrological engineering and it wants to export its expertise to other African and Middle-Eastern countries facing similar problems with their water.

According to the official web site of the Great Man-Made River Authority:

> Approximately 500,000 pre-stressed con-crete cylinder pipes have been manufactured to date. Approximately 500,000 pipes transported to date. Pipe transportation is continuous process and the work goes on day and night, distance traveled by the transporters is equivalent to the sun and back. Over 3,700 km of haul roads was constructed alongside the pipe line trench to enable the heavy truck—trailers to deliver pipe to the installation site.[6]

NATO Attack

On 22 July, 2011, NATO warplanes attacked the pipe making plant at Brega killing six of the facility's security guards. As can be seen from Google Earth the 100s of pipes at this facility, out in the desert south of Brega, make it clear, even from the air, that this is a pipe-production plant. Video footage shows a major building within the plant has been destroyed and there is also damage to at least one of the trucks which is used to transport pipes to places where repairs are required.

According to AP, Abdel-Hakim el-Shwehdy, head of the company running the project, said "Major parts of the plant have been damaged. There could be major setback for the future projects."

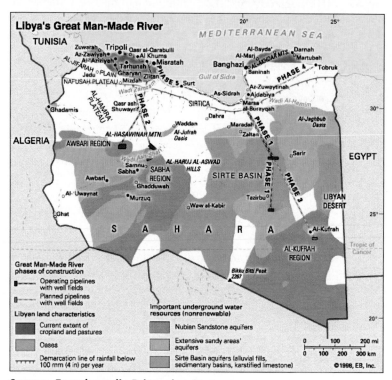

Source: Encyclopædia Britannica, Inc.

The Water Supply to Brega Is Cut

On Monday 18 July rebel spokesman Shamsiddin Abdulmolah told AFP that remnants of Gadhafi's troops were holed up among industrial facilities in Brega with supplies dwindling.Given the rebel boasts that the pro-Qaddafi forces in Brega had no water, the question has to be posed whether this attack was a deliberate attempt to prevent repair of the pipeline into Brega.

The NATO Response

In response to a Human Rights Investigations (HRI)enquiry at the 26th July NATO Press conference in Naples, the NATO press office said:

We can confirm that we targeted Brega on July 22nd and we stroke successfully: one military storage facility and four armed vehicles.

HRI requested clarification:

The building you hit (apparently in the Brega pipe factory) was being used for what kind of military storage?

What considerations were taken into account to ensure that the strikes did not damage civilian infrastructure or was damage to the civilian infrastructure considered legitimate?

Given the potential consequences to civilians of damage to the pipe factory and the ability of the engineers to be able to repair broken water pipelines I hope you will appreciate the importance of these questions.

Colonel Rolond Lavoie, neglecting to inform the assembled journalists that the "concrete factory" plays an important role in preserving Libya's water supply, said:

Now in the area of Brega, NATO strikes included armoured vehicles, rocket launchers, military storage facilities and a repurposed concrete factory from which Pro-Gaddafi forces were using multi-viral [sic] rocket launchers, exposing the population to indirect fire.

Let me show you some intelligence pictures that illustrate what we have observed at this concrete factory. By the way these pictures will be made available on the NATO site so it will be possible for the media can download them

So basically repeatedly over the last few weeks we got clear intelligence indicating that pro-Gaddafi forces are using this factory for military purposes. This factory is being used to hide military material including Multiple Rocket Launchers. These weapons have been used every day from within this factory compound and then carefully hidden after the day within or along massive pipes you can see in this picture.

Slide 1 20 July apparently shows a BM-21 rocket launcher—a model of rocket launcher widely used by both loyalist and rebel forces in Libya. Slide 2 23 July apparently shows a BM-21 rocket launcher. The slide shows black smoke in the centre of the picture which suggests two hits (possibly on vehicles) have already been made, with the BM-21 left intact.

Neither slide appears to show the building which was destroyed in the video or helps to understand when or why that was hit. So the photos lead to more questions than they answer—clearly the BM-21, spotted on the 20th, was not considered a priority target, and there is nothing in the NATO explanation which explains why the water supplies of the Libyan people have now been put at such risk.

On 27th July further enquiries by HRI elicited the additional information that:

> The factory is being used to hide military material, including multiple rocket launchers. These weapons have been used every day from within this factory compound and then carefully hidden after the day within the factory buildings and the area.

and

> All sites that could be used by the pro-Qadhafi regime forces to threaten or attack civilians can be considered as a legitimate target by NATO in full accordance with UNSCR 1973. That resolution mandates the use of all necessary measures to protect civilians in Libya from attack or threat of attacks.

According to the NATO press office, the attack was within the rules of engagement agreed upon by all 28 countries in the coalition by consensus. It seems unlikely that the rules of engagement would allow this attack or that the states in the Security Council would agree that a devious interpretation of UN Security Council Resolution 1973 should supercede international humanitarian law.

NATO have failed to provide answers to the following questions:

• *Do you have any concrete evidence that rockets were fired from inside the pipe-making plant?*

- *Can you explain the precise targeting and timing of strikes within this facility?*
- *What steps were taken to ensure collateral damage to the facility was avoided?*
- *What alternatives were considered to military strikes on this factory?*

Applicable humanitarian law

The Laws of War[7] were designed to prevent attacks on targets indispensible to the civilian population, so attacking a civilian infrastructure target such as this plant is a war crime.

Even if rockets were being fired from within the location (for which no evidence has been produced) or this facility was being used for military storage by Qaddafi forces, or housed armoured vehicles, attacking the pipe-making factory in a way that leaves it severely damaged is illegal as this facility is important to the water supplies of Libyan civilians.

The citing of UNSCR 1973 does not supercede the need for NATO forces to obey the laws of war.

Applicable humanitarian law includes (inter alia):
Rule 15. In the conduct of military operations, constant care must be taken to spare the civilian population, civilians and civilian objects. All feasible precautions must be taken to avoid, and in any event to minimize, incidental loss of civilian life, injury to civilians and damage to civilian objects. [IAC/NIAC]

Rule 16. Each party to the conflict must do everything feasible to verify that targets are military objectives. [IAC/NIAC]

Rule 17. Each party to the conflict must take all feasible precautions in the choice of means and methods of warfare with a view to avoiding, and in any event to minimizing, incidental loss of civilian life, injury to civilians and damage to civilian objects. [IAC/NIAC]

Rule 18. Each party to the conflict must do everything feasible to assess whether the attack may be expected to cause incidental loss of civilian life, injury to civilians, damage to civilian objects, or a combination thereof, which would be excessive in relation to the concrete and direct military advantage anticipated. [IAC/NIAC]

Rule 54. Attacking, destroying, removing or rendering useless objects indispensable to the survival of the civilian population is prohibited.

ENDNOTES

1   More information about the organization Human Rights Investigations is available at <http://humanrightsinvestigations.org/about/>

2   See <http://www.news.bbc.co.uk/1/hi/sci/tech/4814988.stm>

3   In a recent study conducted under the supervision of the UN Centre for Environment & Development in the Arab Region & Europe CEDARE, the Nubian Basin (of which Kufrais a part) was estimated to contain 373.3 x 1012m3. If the neighboring countries extract water at a rate of 1380 MCMY it is calculated that the reserve would last for 4860 years. See "Libya Warns Of Catastrophe If NATO Bombs Great Man-Made River", <http://wfol.tv/index.php/editorial/index.php?option=com_content&view=article&id=6519:libya-warns-of-catastrophe-if-nato-bombs-great-man-made-river&catid=55:arab-world&Itemid=54>

4   See http://unesdoc.unesco.org/images/0015/001524/ 152400e.pdf

5   See http://www.gwpmed.org/files/IWRM-Libya/Omar%20Samin%20GMMR.pdf

6   This link has now been removed. Formerly, it was at <http://www.gmmra.org/en/index.php?option=com_content&view=article&id=76&Itemid+50>

7   See <http://humanrightsinvestigations.org/the-laws-of-war/>

AMERICA'S BLACK PHAROAH AND BLACK GENOCIDE IN LIBYA

T-West

On July 1, 2011, there was a huge rally in Tripoli with a crowd of more than one million protesting the constant NATO bombings that had been occurring since mid-March, 2011. AfriSynergy depicted this in the video "July 1, 2011 Qaddafi's Speech to Libya and the World."[1] These huge demonstrations of support for the Jamahiriya government of Libya estimated to number more than 2 million inclusive of Tripoli and other cities in western Libya exemplified the massive support enjoyed by the Libyan government. It had won humanitarian accolades, was ranked number 51 in the UN Human Development Index, had virtually no foreign debt, and had the lowest divorce rate in the entire world, with no remittances: Libyans in Libya were sending more money to family members living abroad than was being sent to Libya. Most of the facts I just mentioned would be envied by the United States, Arab League countries and most of Western Europe. Women had a wide range of rights in Libya—education, driving, positions in government, media, etc. This information and far more can be found on the AfriSynergy channel on Youtube.

Today, we have President Barack Hussein Obama, a man who has cultural roots on three continents—Africa, Asia and North America—sitting at the helm of a nation with the most powerful military force in the recorded history of Earth. In 2008, he was elected with more than 92 percent of blacks who voted, voting for him. With African Americans being officially 12.2 percent of US population,[2] their voting numbers alone could not elect an American president but they certainly do have great influence with other ethnic groups, providing the collective votes to determine who will be president of the United States. Whites and other ethnic groups also played a major role in electing Barack Obama. Obama attracted the white female vote but there was no surprise there. I heard white females referring to him in glowing terms, some even saying "he's such a hunk." He attracted unparalleled crowds in most areas where he campaigned. We are talking numbers like those at the United Center for the Nation of Islam's 2012 Saviours' Day gathering where 19,000 filled the indoor sports arena. This is in contrast to the 2012 presidential candidate and Republican frontrunner, Mitt Romney, who couldn't even fill the arena's floor in Michigan, let alone the regular arena seating. In the 2008 presidential run, Barack Obama attracted a crowd of more than 75,000 in Portland, Oregon and 200,000 in Berlin. There was no doubt that he was connecting to the hearts and minds of millions, not only in the United States but around the world. I recall interviewing a young lady and her husband, who were originally from Somalia but lived in Norway prior to coming to the United States. She cried at this Obama rally after he spoke at this venue. In June, 2009, when President Obama spoke in Egypt, millions of Muslims were tuned in to the speech on their televisions and radios. Clearly, this man was connecting with people of all ethnic groups. He was a marketing phenom extraordinare.

The efficacy of the branding of Barack H. Obama has not gone unnoticed. Author and journalist Chris Hedges, interviewed by inDepth, indicated, "Obama won advertising agencies' top annual award, Marketer of The Year, because the professionals knew precisely what he had done. He beat Apple, Nike… to quote Cornell West, he became, essentially, a 'black mascot for Wall Street.'"[3] In 2007, I did a video highlighting the Democrat National Convention where there were more than 90,000 in the arena and thousands more outside the arena. In this video, I included an image of the stoned carved face of Pharaoh as the winds blew the sand away from the face. It was my way of depicting the return of the pharaohs. I had high expectations for this young president but had no illusions about the difficulties ahead of him and the choices he would be faced with, hoping that he would make the right choices and not be too influenced by the negative forces surrounding him as well as the opposition.[4]

Muammar Qaddafi has long been viewed as a Pan-Africanist, which gave rise to contention in the modern Arab leadership. He was a true revolutionary in word and deeds, unlike most of the Arab leaders. On March 19, 2011, the AfriSynergy video, "Why Has Obama Ignored Anti-Qaddafi Forces Slaughtering of Blacks"[5] posed this question at the very beginning of NATO's involvement in Libya under UN Resolutions 1970 and 1973. This shows that the targeting of blacks in Libya was the goal of those who, on March 5, 2011, became known as the National Transitional Council (NTC), a name similar to other areas in the world where Western governments, often led by the US, have become involved militarily. In Somalia it was the Somali Transitional Government. In 2000, it was the Serbia Transitional Government, the result of the Clinton Administration's manipulation to overthrow the government of the Republic of Yugoslavia in order to give NATO significance in a post-Soviet world. The Republic of Yugoslavia was made up of Croatia, Bosnia and Herzegovina, Macedonia, Montenegro, Slovenia and Serbia. The splitting of Yugoslavia started along ethnic lines in the 1980s. Today, the breakup of Yugoslavia has fostered growing resentment of the European Union and the United States in the region. Yugoslavia and later, Serbia, had close ties with the Libyan government. Therefore, it should not come as a surprise that Qaddafi's nurse was from Eastern Europe as were others who worked for him in Libya.

The same Arab states that supported and some that participated directly in the overthrow of the Jamahiriya government of Libya supported NATO's bombing of Yugoslavia in the early 1990s. When NATO was bombing civilians in Yugoslavia under the Clinton Administration, it was Muammar Qaddafi who came to the political aid of Slobodan Milosevic. It was also the daughter of Muammar Qaddafi, Aisha, who served on the legal team representing Iraqi president, Saddam Hussein, against the puppet government installed in Iraq through US and British military force. To this very day, people are killed in the streets of Iraq by bombings often attributed to al Qaeda.

There are indicators that some of the Western strategy that was used against Yugoslavia was and is being deployed in Libya. I place emphasis on the fomenting of ethnic strife because this is exactly what allied Arab and Western states and their media did in Libya. The goal of the West is to break up Libya mostly along ethnic lines, with a small group (puppets) controlling the oil. This would also mean a central bank that is Eurocentric, that ties into the stock exchange and American and European corporate banking headquarters in Qatar. What we are witnessing is the hands of monarchy at play in post-Qaddafi Libya, leading to its segmentation. [6] Any federal system would be controlled and manipulated by the monarchy of Europe with the Arab monarchies underneath such as Qatar, UAE, and Saudi Arabia. The eastern areas of Libya are more Arab-centric. They would control the oil resources. Ultimately, the NTC will outlive its usefulness to the monarchy; they are looking for a way to slide the NTC out of the equation without too much public protest about the grave crimes NATO has committed. They have foisted on Libya the pre-1969 monarchy flag representing the throne of King Idris who was then ruled by Britain, and the anthem of the monarchy of that era. Libya had a damn good governing system that benefited its people and therein is the problem. Iraq, under Saddam Hussein, had the most educated population in the Arab world, even exceeding the Persians of Iran. Women and various religious groups, generally, had good opportunities. The West fears this among non-white peoples, if they are not shaking those governments down financially. Essentially, the people who are controlling and operating key Western governments behave like gangsters.

Up until the Western-enabled coup against Qaddafi, Libya was a member of the UN Human Rights Council.

What we witnessed at the UN was unprecedented. The UN Secretary General, Ban Ki Moon, did not allow a member of the Jamahiriya government of Libya to speak in its own defense at the UN prior to the establishment of Resolutions 1970 and 1973. The Libyan UN ambassador, Abdurrahman Mohamed Shalgham, a long time close friend of Muammar Qaddafi, mutinied by jumping over to the Libyan NTC side. On February 25, 2011 Shalgham was permitted to denounce his own government at the UN. One must wonder if he would have done so, if he had known of the falsifying of news and reports about events in Libya as were proven to have happened in Syria.

American policy many years ago indicated Libya and Syria were on the list to be overthrown. This was first revealed by former NATO Secretary General, Wesley Clark.[7] The *Democracy Now* interview with General Wesley Clark went as follows:

> General Clark: "About ten days after 9/11, I went through the Pentagon and I saw Secretary Rumsfeld and Secretary (Paul D.) Wolfowitz. I went downstairs just to say hello to some of the people on the Joint Staff who used to work for me, and one of the Generals called me in. He said, 'Sir, you gotta come in and talk to me a second.' I said, well, you're too busy. He said, 'no, no'. He says, 'we've made the decision. We're going to war with Iraq.' This was on or about the 20th of September. I said, we're going to war with Iraq? Why? He said, 'I don't know.' He said, 'I guess they don't know what else to do.' So I said, well, did they find some information connecting Saddam to Al Qaida? He said, 'No, no, there's nothing new that way; they just made the decision to go to war with Iraq.' He said, 'I guess it's like, we don't know what to do about terrorists, but we've got a good military and we can take down governments.' And he said, 'I guess

if the only tool you have is a hammer, every problem has to look like a nail.' So I came back to see him a few weeks later and by that time we were bombing in Afghanistan. I said, are we still going to war with Iraq? He said, 'oh, it's worse than that.' He said—he reached over on his desk, he picked up a piece of paper. He said, 'I just got this down from upstairs (meaning the Secretary of Defense's office) today and this is a memo that describes how we're going to take out seven (7) countries in five (5) years starting with Iraq, and then Syria, Lebanon, Libya, Somalia, Sudan, and finishing off Iran.'"

There is a growing mountain of evidence that the targeting of black Libyans as well as black immigrants was as critical to the insurrectionists and mutineers as was the goal of killing Muammar Qaddafi in breaking the will of the Libyan people to fight. It would send a strong message to Africans and Pan-Africanists throughout the world that neo-colonialism was back with the US government leading it. One could also surmise that some would look upon this as another opportunity for President Obama to prove that he would serve the multinational corporate Western interests over that of Pan-African socioeconomic interests. Their concern should not be a surprise since, although Obama serves the Office of the President, that office can also be reshaped by a president. For nearly 20 years in Chicago, Barack Obama had attended a church that is considered an advocate of Black Liberation. For him, Libya therefore presented a dilemma related to principles similar to the choice he was forced to make between publicly swearing to cut all links to his pastor, Reverend Jeremiah Wright, or possibly losing the presidential election. Barack Obama chose to sever all ties with Reverend Wright. The mutinying forces within Libya, working with the French, knew black Libyans would be some of the strongest defenders of the Jamahiriya government of Libya, and rightfully so. Muammar Qaddafi identified greatly with and defended the rights of blacks as well as all citizens of Libya. Those Libyans who opposed Muammar Qaddafi's gravitation towards the African Union and movement away from the Arab League would seem to be more likely to jump at an opportunity to overthrow Qaddafi and then take their long held envy and apparent hatred out upon blacks in Libya. As Carina Ray, Assistant Professor of African and Black Atlantic History, Fordham University, wrote: "... it tapped into the smoldering resentment that many Libyans harbored against Qaddafi's gradual shift away from the Arab world in favor of Africa."[8]

When most Pan-Africans saw the old monarch flag of Libya's King Idris, they thought the rebels were the good guys because the red, black and green flag bore the same colors as the Pan-African flag. Yes, grave naivety on the part of these Pan-Africans. Therefore, most of them were slow to react in support of the Jamahiriya government. Most of them were quiet, as black Libyans were being targeted and killed, as well as black immigrants. I must sadly state that many Pan-Africans are that in name only. Prior to this Western and Arab concocted "Arab Spring", the strength of Muammar Qaddafi kept the negative effects of Arab racism in check within Libya. As a Mathaba article entitled, "Obama Bombs Africa: Targets African Unity" put it:

> If we take a cursory look at history we can see how U.S. policy and European imperialism has overtly and covertly destroyed Pan Africanist and socialist regimes in Africa. The murder of Pan Africanist Patrice Lumumba by the U.S. CIA in 1960, the CIA sponsored counter revolution leading to the overthrow of Kwame Nkrumah's government in 1966. The destabilization from 1975 onward of Mozambique by U.S. and apartheid South Africa backed RENAMO, and Angola by U.S. CIA and apartheid South Africa backed UNITA, forcing of multi party political system and preventing the development of socialism by Frelimo and the MPLA.[9]

Even though most of the Arabs reside in the Eastern portion of Libya, the fabrication of African mercenaries killing, raping and torturing other Libyans was widespread, thanks to Arab media such as Al Jazeera, headquartered in Qatar and Al Arabiya headquartered in Saudi Arabia. Qaddafi himself, not being Arab but of Berber/African heritage, embraced black Libyans as well as rights for females, unlike many of the Arab states aligned against the Jamahiriya government. He was proud of this heritage and those Libyans who hated him sometimes reflected that hatred by calling him "Friz Head"[10]. But as Qaddafi acknowledged in a satellite feed speaking to members of the Nation of Islam in the 1990s, "You see, your brother, Muammar. You see, they do not like me, see. And this is because..." [At that point, he pulled off his kufi (his African cap), grabbed some of his hair, and continued, "...my hair is like your hair. You see, they do not like this." Whoa! The joint burst out in laughter. Here was a man who knew what the score was for non-white people on this earth! And he was speaking as a head-of-state. Whoa!! God, the FEELING that that gave us!!]

In fact, among the early reasons for Western antipathy towards Qaddafi was his support for the African American struggle. In that 1990s video, Qaddafi went on to say to the NOI: "We support you to create an independent state; to create an independent black army. We are ready to train you. We give you arms because your cause is a just cause."[11] On September 22, 2009, Minister Louis Farrakhan, leader of the Nation of Islam, in honor of Muammar Qaddafi's visit to the United States to address the UN, stated, "The greatest of his efforts, in my humble opinion, has been to foster the idea of Marcus Garvey, George Padmore, Kwame Nkrumah and Gamal Abdel Nasser to move the independent states of Africa to form the United States of Africa, thus bringing Africa fully and powerfully into the 21st century as a major contributor on the World scene in all aspects of World Affairs."[12] Here you see the ongoing connection between an influential sector of Black America and the Pan-African Movement, something not looked upon favorably by the leadership within the Arab Muslim world and certainly not by American and Western European leadership. Hatred of Muammar Qaddafi festered within some Libyan circles, especially many of the wealthier and more influential residents of the port city of Misrata. Muammar Qaddafi was brutally assassinated to the great pleasure of Western European, American and Arab leaders while their leading media conducted the concert of cheers and accolades. As I articulated in the video "Crucify Him,"[13] Hillary Clinton, US Secretary of State, stated brutally and with relish, "We came, we saw, he died." Key leaders of the United States were bold and brazen about US military acts carried out in the overthrow of the legitimate and sovereign government of Libya. Never mind the open display of power in Benghazi by al Qaeda—the flying of its flag atop the Benghazi courthouse and the establishment of Hakim Belhadj as military leader in Tripoli after the fall of Tripoli.[14]

On February 28, 2011, BBC journalists interviewed Muammar Qaddafi in Tripoli. During that interview, Qaddafi talked about al Qaeda's presence in Libya being a part of the disturbance within Libya.[15] He said, "we never thought al Qaeda would come to Libya," indicating that al Qaeda took advantage of what was happening in Egypt and Tunisia and "made their presence felt" in Libya. Currently, in Nigeria, the targets of terrorist attacks are police stations and military barracks, similar to the targets in Libya in February, 2011 and for the last several months, those have also been the targets in Syria. Most recently, Senator John McCain and other Zionists in the US Senate have called for US bombing of Syria. As of the writing of this, it remains to be seen if President Obama will stand firmly against such bombing of Syria. He caved in to this pressure relative to Libya. Qaddafi indicated the target of these al Qaeda forces and misguided youth was to kill police and military personnel in al Baida and Benghazi. He indicated these al Qaeda forces and Libyan youth were stealing weapons from police stations and military barracks to kill. During this interview, Qaddafi indicated that those doing the killing are "on hallucinogenic drugs" (see below) and that the Libyan soldiers were trying to defend themselves, killing fewer "terrorists" than the number of Libyan soldiers killed. In other words, he was restraining the force the Jamahiriya military might have legitimately used against those violating the laws of sovereign, civilized societies governed by law. If the UN were an intergovernmental body truly representing international law and order, the sovereignty of nations and the prevention of wars of aggression, there should have been a full investigation prior to the passing of any resolution permitting an intervention into the conflict of any kind, including so-called "responsibility to protect" humanitarian intervention.[16] The Jamahiriya government requested an investigation. The African Union also demanded that the UN investigate. When it came at last in April, however, as Western media such as *The Guardian* headlined it, the UN investigation was focused on the Libyan government itself: "UN investigates Libya human rights violations: Inquiry team to press Libyan officials for access to prisons and hospitals as it probes alleged civilian killings by Qaddafi's forces."[17]

Qaddafi indicated that the soldiers and police were given orders not to fire upon these attackers but to evacuate to avoid more attacks. He appeared to be doing all things possible to avoid being baited into massive bloodshed. This included instruction to the Libyan Air Force pilots to avoid dropping bombs on the mutineers. To date, there are no conclusive reports showing bombs or missiles from Libyan planes killed anyone; to the contrary, there is the Russian assertion that this did not happen. Bombs were dropped in proximity of oil facilities to warn the al Qaeda forces and rebellious youth to stay away from the oil facilities. Rather than interpreting this as government restraint, the media reported Libyan pilots being very inaccurate with their bombs and missiles because they were not striking the opposing forces on the ground. The truth is that the Libyan jets have guided bombs and missiles, not the dumb bombs used in WWII or the Vietnam War. The pilots could have easily struck the belligerent forces on the ground but were instructed not to. However, at the same time, government personnel, and Libyan citizens were being killed and property was being destroyed. Naturally, in the haste to evacuate police stations and military bases, this would give al Qaeda and other foreign individuals with the intent of overthrowing the Jamahiriya government, access to any weapons left behind. As early as February, 2011, there were various foreign mercenaries operating in Libya with al Qaeda and the Libyan youth, using deadly force to steal weapons of all sorts, including tanks and even a Libyan fighter jet. The jet stolen by the belligerent rebel forces was flying over Benghazi when it was mistakenly shot down by the rebel forces.[18] However, AP falsely reported it as: "Libyan rebels shot down a warplane that was bombing their eastern stronghold Benghazi on Saturday, as the opposition accused Moammar Gadhafi's government of defying calls for an immediate cease-fire. (March 19)."

Key Libyan diplomats were quick to defy their own government and some of them stepped down from their positions. In the US, a person "not authorized" to speak, lied and stated that Libya was using aircraft to shoot Libyan protesters. Later, CNN verified that this was not the case. The National Front for the Salvation of Libya played a part in planting this lie. When the belligerent rebel forces put six badly burned bodies on display, they told the world that these were soldiers whom members of Qaddafi's government had burned alive for refusing to shoot at protesters. It is well known that Libyan rebels had attacked a military base. Did they start any fires on that base? Did they set soldiers afire?[19] Al Qaeda has a well known tactic of burning the bodies of some of those they attack.

Qaddafi told the BBC that "these people captured the positions that we had evacuated." This gave al Qaeda and the youth gangs free rein in Al Baida and Benghazi which resulted in targeted killings of Jamahiriya government representatives, and especially black Libyans working for the government. As early as February, 2011, pictures and videos were being shown over the internet of black Libyan soldiers and police being slaughtered as one would slaughter a sheep and their mangled naked bodies being paraded around the streets in Benghazi, as voices in the mobs shouted, "Allah Akbar." In an interview with Nicky Love of Love Productions in Life, I showed a young Libyan police officer who is black and how NTC Libyan forces backed by NATO and the UN slaughtered this young man, sodomized his body in the street, and then hung him upside down.[20] Neither CNN, Fox nor any of the other major television news showed or said anything about this, which was not rare. His dead body had been hanged upside down draped in a mocking way in the Jamahiriya flag of Libya. More recently, a video surfaced of blacks caged in a zoo in Misrata being forced to chew on the green Jamahiriya flag.[21] All of the major media had access to this information and were aware of it but such was not shown and hardly mentioned by television and print media. Contrast this with pictures and images these same mainstream media networks were showing of purported killings by the Libyan government, or thereafter the Syrian government, of what corporate media claimed to be peaceful demonstrators or freedom fighters. These media were even taking their pick of video from Youtube and displaying it during primetime news segments but never once did they show any of the numerous videos on the AfriSynergy and other Youtube channels showing the massive torture and killing of blacks in Libya (see the URLs in the endnotes below).

All of this was happening in the month of February 2011 while the leaders of Britain, France and the US were demanding that Muammar Qaddafi step down. In a question from Christiane Amanpour about Western media and leaders saying that he was ordering the killing of innocent people, Qaddafi indicated that "this is a lie" and that the news agencies are "not a fact finding mission" and the UN Security Council has not sent anyone to investigate. He indicated that the UN has not "seen youth with arms terrorizing in the streets." Qaddafi then mentioned some of the prisoners who were once imprisoned by the US government now operating in Benghazi and al Baida. He asked, "Has the UN Security Council seen" the members of al Qaeda released by the US government now operating within Libya? He said that he was "amazed" that given Libya has an alliance with the United States to fight al Qaeda, the United States would do what it is doing. He indicated that he had been betrayed by the United States, and that what British and others leaders are doing against Libya was "immoral." Qaddafi stated that "al Qaeda does not recognize demonstrators," and indeed as evidence after the fact, when Tawerghan women demonstrated in Tripoli in protest at treatment by NTC forces, especially those from Misrata, NTC forces were sent into a refugee camp in the Tripoli area resulting in the killing of more than ten Tawerghans, including women, youth, and an old man. When Amanpour questioned Qaddafi, asking him if he would attack oilfields, Qaddafi responded that it is al Qaeda that shoots at businesses and those working at the oilfields. Similarly now we see that in Syria, those who are attacking and blowing up oil pipelines are not members of the Syrian government but terrorists. Human logic implies that governments do not destroy their own main source of economic activity. However, those who do not benefit from that source of economic empowerment certainly would have motive to attack such infrastructure to achieve tactical advantage, which for terrorists is usually chaos. This is especially true when there are foreigners operating within the victimized country.

The full story has yet to be told about the pressure and threats against the Libyan Jamahiriya government's representatives working at the UN. When South African president, Jacob Zuma, representing the African Union, met in Libya with Qaddafi and then indicated Libya had invited UN investigators to Libya to investigate and determine the facts, this request was quickly rejected by the UN, a flaw in UN leadership that led to extensive torture and death in Libya. Instead, on the floor of the UN, the talk was about Qaddafi providing his troops with Viagra so that they could rape women. US Ambassador to the UN Susan Rice and Secretary of State Hillary Clinton echoed these unsubstantiated allegations. The UN was clearly rubber stamping the wishes of the key permanent members of the UN Security Council, namely the US, Britain and France. It appeared that claims made against the Jamahiriya government of Libya in actuality concerned things that the NATO allies, the forces of the Libyan NTC, were doing. For example, in late January, 2012, the Zintan forces who oversee the airport security in Tripoli discovered a large shipment of drugs intended for NTC forces. This included viagra and other mind altering drugs. On the AfriSynergy channel, see the video, "Viagra and Drug Shipment to NTC Rats in Libya Confiscated in Tripoli."[22] There has yet to be any proven cases of the Jamahiriya government promoting the use of viagra to Libyan troops during the Western and Arab instigated coup in Libya.

On September 27, 2011, Carina Ray wrote an article for *Huffington Post* entitled "Qaddafi and the Mercenary Myth." This article indicated: "One of the biggest headlines to emerge in the early days of the battle for Libya was that Muammar Qaddafi had unleashed Black African mercenaries to put down the revolution. This turned out to be a largely bogus claim, but it nonetheless found traction among many ordinary Libyans. Why?" [23]

In most cases, all one has to do is look at the friends, associates and allies of a nation to gain an idea of what's authentic, what's not and what's somewhere in the middle. There is absolutely no doubt that terrorist organizations were a part of the uprising in Libya and Western governments were in collusion with such organizations as al Qaeda and the non-peaceful elements of the Muslim Brotherhood. In Libya, the Libyan Islamic Fight Group (LIFG) is a known terrorist organization and is named as a terrorist organization by the UN Security Council. However, this fact did not stop permanent members of the UN Security Council from colluding with LIFG with the expressed purpose of overthrowing a sovereign member state of the UN. One could say the UN was taken aback by Muammar Qaddafi's last speech at the UN when he indicated the UN is not following its own preamble and mandate to prevent wars but instead has, at times, been a purveyor of war. Qaddafi then proceeded to rip the pages of the UN preamble to indicate the UN's disregard for its own rules.[24]

We witnessed collaboration between the Muslim, Judaic and Christian countries against one African government without representation in the UN body accept for the counterfeit hastily created Libyan NTC. It was an example of the collective strategic interests of all three groups to the detriment of the Jamahiriya government of Libya. It was the Western mainstream press controlled or influenced by Judaic individuals as well as the Qatar-based Al-Jazeera that shaped the narrative of what was happening in Libya from February, 2011 forward and encouraged the actions that would be taken. In this case, it was the Sephardim wing that was having the most influence over what was occurring in Libya. This group had a far more longstanding experience in North Africa and in the Near East among Arabs than the Ashkenazim, with the Sephardim's influence in France being equivalent to Ashkenazim influence in the United States. This included feeder organizations such as Reuters and the Associated Press. The AP is a non-profit corporation made up of board members from more than 1,500 news organizations, helping to assure one face of the news, virtually always anti-Jamahirya government and pro-rebel NTC. Richard Engel, NBC News correspondent estimated that 20 percent of those who rebelled against the Jamahiriya government bought into the propaganda of Muammar Qaddafi's supposed Jewish heritage, which in fact originated in a story on IsraelInsider on February 22, 2011.[25] Never mind it was Mustafa Jalil, Libya's Justice Minister under the Jamahiriya government who was colluding with France's Sephardic mover and shaker, Bernard Henry Levi, prior to and during the February international coup, not Muammar Qaddafi. We had two volatile lies coming together and being propelled by Western and Arab media. One was that "African Mercenaries" are killing peaceful Libyan protesters, and two, Muammar Qaddafi is "Jewish."

On June, 2011, a video posted on the AfriSynergy channel entitled, "NATO Genocide in Black Libyan Town of Tawerga"[26] showed thousands of Libyans protesting the NATO bombing of Libya. It is important to mention this protest because NATO planes were dropping leaflets on Libya warning the Libyan people to reject the Jamahiriya government, indicating NATO is stronger than the Libyan government. NATO would then continue with its terror from the skies by the dropping of bombs and missiles in those areas that were pro-Jamahiriya. The city of Tawergha was one of those areas. There had already been photos and videos of the bodies of Libyan civilians, including children, being pulled from beneath rubble of collapsed buildings struck by NATO's bombs and missiles. This included NATO's bombing of food warehouses in Libya, and bombing a vegetable market in the city of Tawergha killing at least 13, including children.[27] This aerial assault upon Libya began in March, 2011 with around the clock bombing by NATO from American and British ships in the Mediterranean Sea and French and British aircraft. There were also Western mercenary forces on the ground in Libya hiding behind dark shaded glasses and sometimes sporting beards, as well as Western forces that were not so conspicuous.

A month earlier, May, 2011, Stop The War Coalition, headquartered out of the UK wrote an article entitled, "No Boots on The Ground? Watch This and Think Again":

> There have been numerous reports in the British press that SAS soldiers are acting as spotters in Libya to help NATO warplanes target pro-Qaddafi forces. In March, six special forces soldiers and two MI6 officers were detained by rebel fighters when they landed on an abortive mission to meet rebel leaders in Benghazi, in an embarrassing episode for the SAS.[28]

The racist media reporting was quite apparent when CNN quickly reported on a Youtube video of Libyans under the NTC leadership destroying gravestones of British soldiers killed in Libya decades ago during Libya's struggle for liberation and WWII. However, I have no record of CNN doing one report on another Youtube video that has been present for months showing NTC forces firing missiles at and destroying the gravesites of Tawerghans.[29]

It is the duty of Navi Pillay, UN High Commissioner for Human Rights, to assure that the damage the UN stood by and allowed to happen in Libya does not continue to happen in Syria by some of the same players involved in the crimes committed in Libya. It is also incumbent on Mrs. Pillay to move faster in documenting and getting the international community that was so quick to wrongly judge the Jamahiriya government of Libya, to immediately end the torture and killings of Libyans who supported the Jamahiriya government. Most of those targeted by these belligerent militias are black.

It is the responsibility of President Obama to immediately end the targeting of blacks in Libya by those militias the American, European and Arab governments placed in power. Again, the emphasis on these three is because they are the ones who exploit the African/ Arab situation with the assistance of key members of the UN. Pillay is a native of South Africa of Indian decent but she should be well acquainted with tyranny steeped in the color of one's skin. The parallels of the treatment of blacks in Libya by the NATO-backed NTC forces and the treatment of blacks for hundreds of years in the United States well into the 20th century are reflected in the AfriSynergy video, "Crucify

Him"[30] and the video, "George Zimmerman, the Murderer of Trayvon Martin in Florida."[31]

Africans across the continent of Africa need to inform themselves of what their governments are doing and supporting. It is very important that African Americans do not give President Barack Obama their support for another term as president without making firm demands on him right now. There is the alternative to showing your power through a boycott of the 2012 Presidential Election. On campaign appearances, there needs to be signs in the audience that ask Mr. Obama WHAT ABOUT TAWERGHANS? There must be signs in the audience that ask WHY COMBAT TROOPS TO AFRICA? There must be a chorus asking DO YOU REMEMBER THE IVORY COAST? It is this and more that must determine whether there is or is not a deal that says "I'm In" or "I'm Not In." It comes down to the question of which Pharaoh will Mr. Obama choose to be, if he is to serve a second term? You can play a major role in helping him determine the answer to this question. The black genocide in Libya is very apparent, and our silence lessens the relevance of black life in the US. Will we allow this to happen under the watch of Barack Hussein Obama?

ENDNOTES

1   July, 2011 Rally of Millions in Libya: https://www.youtube.com/watch?v=Q0XsF03fNM4 https://www.youtube.com/watch?v=lEL76Ed0ne4

2   Overview of Race and Hispanic Origin: 2010, <http://www.census.gov/prod/cen2010/briefs/c2010br-02.pdf>

3   Chris Hedges "Brace Yourself! The American Empire Is Over & The Descent Is Going To Be Horrifying" at 6:00 mark: <http://www.youtube.com/watch?v=7zotYU21qcU&feature=g-vrec&context=G25e7d14RVAAAAAAAAAg>

4   In 1990, I had self-published the book, "New World Order—AIDS, Genocide and Theology." In this book, I indicated that the United States would have its first black president in our lifetime but it would be at a time when the country is financially bankrupt. That event turned out to be the year 2008 with the election of Barack Hussein Obama at a time when the United States acknowledged, under the outgoing president, George W. Bush, that it is experiencing the worst economic decline since the Great Depression. Included in a long list of financial issues that the incoming Obama Administration would face was the fact that the Bush Administration had hidden 2 trillion dollars from the budget—money to prosecute the wars in Iraq and Afghanistan.

5   <http://www.youtube.com/watch?v=X4tyB1-UEPU>

6   Eastern Libya Declares Semiautonomous Region: <http://www.google.com/hostednews/ap/article/ALeqM5iklOh4sVKKczlfYNiqahD915IANQ?docId=0b4e6704e5574d8bba64dc44571b9b21>

7   March 2, 2007, former 4-star General and US presidential candidate Wesley

Clark was interviewed by Democracy Now:

8   Qaddafi and the Mercenary Myth, see <http://www.huffingtonpost.com/carina-ray/Qaddafi-mercenaries_b_983506.html>

9   U.S. Imperialism Attacks Pan Africanism and Libya for Oil. <http://mathaba.net/news/?x=626291?related>

10   Frizz-Head Is Gone: <http://www.youtube.com/watch?v=jCKC-u2cB70>

11   Colonel Qaddafi Addresses the Nation of Islam. <http://www.youtube.com/watch?v=NfMDzo8TWe0>

12   The Nation of Islam Welcomes Muammar Gadhafi: <http://www.finalcall.com/artman/publish/featuredFarrakhanArticle/article_6445.shtml>

13   Crucify Him. <http://www.youtube.com/watch?v=IaJcU2Dn9Wk> – March 26, 2011

14   Hakim Belhadj and Al Qaeda flag in Benghazi (4:35 mark). <http://www.youtube.com/watch?v=IaJcU2Dn9Wk>

15   Full Colonel Qaddafi interview 02 March 2011 http://www.youtube.com/watch?v=tEq-n6ciuxc&feature=related

16   However, in January 2012, the incoming UN Security Council president called Wednesday for an investigation into human rights abuses committed during NATO's bombing campaign to oust Libyan leader Moammar Gadhafi, and demanding that all parties be investigated. South Africa's UN Ambassador Baso Sangqu, who holds the rotating Security Council presidency for January, said he believed NATO overstepped its mandate enforcing a no-fly zone, killing an untold number of innocent civilians. Michael Astor, "UN Diplomat Wants Libya Investigation," Associated Press, January 4, 2012. Note the article's deceptively low-key titling of Sangqu as a Diplomat rather than as the new UN Security Council President.

17   Reuters in Tripoli, April 27, 2011, see <http://www.guardian.co.uk/world/2011/apr/27/libya-un-investigation-human-rights>

18   Raw Video: Plane Shot Down by Libyan Rebels. <http://www.youtube.com/watch?v=Ps61IKmd1nA>

19   Libya, Africa and a Doomed Ideology Disguised as Freedom and Democracy, 1 of 3 <http://www.youtube.com/watch?v=v3PL2BC3cqo>

20   Interview with Nicky Love of Love Productions in Life, 3 of 12 - beginning at 4:37 mark: <http://www.youtube.com/watch?v=W11ARyCNQG4>

21   Shocking video: Libyan rebels cage black Africans, force-feed them flags: <http://www.youtube.com/watch?v=L4icorYD_mE>

22   Viagra and Drug Shipment to NTC Rats in Libya Confiscated in Tripoli http://www.youtube.com/watch?v=YVFEztVnY4U

23   <http://www.huffingtonpost.com/carina-ray/Qaddafi-mercenaries_b_983506.html>

24   Muammar Qaddafi Speech To United Nations Sept 23, 2009 <http://www.youtube.com/watch?v=VvOo5LK22sg>

25   See IsraelInsider, "With a Jewish Grandma, and a Jewish Mother, Qaddafi may seek refuge in Israel per its Law of Return," posted February 22, 2011, see <http://israelinsider.net/profiles/blogs/with-a-jewish-grandma-and-a>

26   NATO Genocide in Black Libyan Town of Tawergha: <https://www.youtube.com/watch?v=15Eds2B6HlU>

27   Libya—Who's Right and Who's Wrong. "http://www.youtube.com/watch?v=mRb1IPEqIBg>

28   No Boots on The Ground? Watch This and Think Again: <http://stopwar.org.

uk/index.php/middle-east-and-north-africa/532-no-ground-troops-in-libya-watch-this-and-think-again>

29   Conversation with War on The Horizon's Irritated Genie, 2 of 7—Desecrating the graves of Tawerghans by NTC forces: <https://www.youtube.com/watch?v=_67Kh2mq5tI&feature=related>

30   Parallels of lynching of Blacks in Libya and 20th and pre-20th century America - "Crucify Him" beginning at the 5:34 mark: <http://www.youtube.com/watch?v=IaJcU2Dn9Wk>

31   George Zimmerman, the Murderer of Trayvon Martin in Florida: http://www.youtube.com/watch?v=BqyUo-HmcT0 The Murder of 22 Year-Old Rekia Boyd: <http://www.youtube.com/watch?v=Xxv_uiypRGc>

NATO'S LIBYA WAR

A Nuremberg Level Crime

Stephen Lendman

The US-led NATO war on Libya will be remembered as one of history's greatest crimes, violating the letter and spirit of international law and America's Constitution.

The Nuremberg Tribunal's Chief Justice Robert Jackson (a US Supreme Court Justice) called Nazi war crimes "the supreme international crime against peace." Here are his November 21, 1945 opening remarks:

> The wrongs which we seek to condemn and punish have been so calculated, so malignant, and so devastating, that civilization cannot tolerate their being ignored, because it cannot survive their being repeated.

Jackson called aggressive war "the greatest menace of our times."

International law defines crimes against peace as "planning, preparation, initiation, or waging of wars of aggression, or a war in violation of international treaties, agreements or assurances, or participation in a common plan or conspiracy for the accomplishment of any of the foregoing."

All US post-WW II wars fall under this definition. Since then, America has waged direct and proxy premeditated, aggressive wars worldwide. It has killed millions in East and Central Asia, North and other parts of Africa, the Middle East, and Europe, as well as in Central and South America.

Arguably this ongoing slaughter exceeds the worst of Nazi and imperial Japanese crimes combined. It includes genocide, torture, mass destruction of nonmilitary related sites, colonization, occupation, plunder and exploitation. Third Reich criminals were hanged for their crimes. America's are still free to commit greater ones.

Notably today the US has been engaged against Iraq, Afghanistan, Pakistan, Somalia, Palestine, Libya, Syria, Yemen, and is implicated in numerous proxy wars. This reflects Washington's New Middle East agenda. One country at a time is being ravaged with a view to achieving America's goal of unchallenged regional dominance right up to Russia's borders. A policy of "Constructive chaos" aims to redraw regional lines according to US/Israeli/NATO geopolitical goals. All of it has been carefully planned, as US engagement shifts from one target to the next.Post-9/11, first came Afghanistan in 2001, then Iraq, Libya, and now Syria, with attacks on the territories of the other states mentioned above.

General Wesley Clark discussed it in his book *Winning Modern Wars.*[1] Shortly post-9/11, he said Pentagon sources told him that war plans were being prepared against Iraq, Syria, Lebanon, Iran, Somalia, Sudan and Libya. Months earlier, they had been finalized against Afghanistan. Clark added:

> And what about the real sources of terrorists—US allies in the region like Egypt, Pakistan, and Saudi Arabia? Wasn't it repressive policies of the first, and the corruption and poverty of the second, that were generating many of the angry young men who became terrorists? And what of the radical ideology and direct funding spewing from Saudi Arabia?
>
> It seemed that we were being taken into a strategy more likely to make us the enemy—encouraging what could look like a 'clash of civilizations'—not a good strategy for winning the war on terror.

Broadcast on FORA TV on October 3, 2007,[2] Clark said America underwent a "policy coup" post-9/11. Hardliners had co-opted power with no public debate or acknowledgement or even awareness of their role. Ten days after 9/11, he visited Defense Secretary Rumsfeld at the Pentagon. "No one will tell us where or when to bomb", Rumsfeld said. Military commanders explained that Iraq would be attacked.

"I walked out of there pretty upset," said Clark. On a second visit, he was told plans were to "destroy the governments" in the above named countries.

In addition, Pakistan and others are targeted. US Special Forces death squads operate covertly in over 120 countries. So do CIA, Mossad and MI6 operatives. No one anywhere is safe, including US citizens at home or abroad. Everyone is fair game to be targeted without any due process. So are independent nonbelligerent nations.

America's media cheerlead supportively rather than providing insight into the process. Imperial goals alone matter, not truth, full disclosure, democratic values or rule of law issues. Repeatedly Iran has been pilloried and presently it's Syria's turn. Whatever Washington says is tossed out like red meat for the media to jump on.

International law is ignored. So are imperial crimes of war and against humanity.

But US war criminals should be considered *hostis humani generis*—enemies of mankind. War crimes are against the *jus gentium*—the law of nations, an international law which natural reason establishes for all men. Established international law addresses these crimes, as does the UN Charter, which is unequivocal in delineating and restricting the conditions under which violence and coercion (by one state against another) are justified..

Article 2(3) and Article 33(1) of the UN Charter require the peaceful settlement of international disputes. Article 2(4) prohibits force or its threatened use. Only justifiable self-defense is permissible, addressed in Article 51, which allows the "right of individual or collective self-defense if an armed attack occurs against a Member....until the Security Council has taken measures to maintain international peace and security." On the other hand, Charter Articles 2(3), 2(4), and 33 absolutely prohibit any unilateral threat or use of force that is not:

- specifically allowed under Article 51;

- authorized by the Security Council.

- for the US, permitted by the US Constitution under Article I, Section 8. Only Congress can declare war provided UN Charter provisions aren't violated. Empowering presidents to do it requires an amendment ratified by three-fourths of the states.

In addition, three General Assembly resolutions also prohibit non-consensual belligerent intervention, including:

- the 1965 Declaration on the Inadmissibility of Intervention in the Domestic Affairs of States and the Protection of Their Independence and Sovereignty;

- the 1970 Declaration on Principles of International Law

Concerning Friendly Relations and Cooperation among States in Accordance with the Charter of the United Nations; and

• the 1974 Definition of Aggression, General Assembly Resolution 3314

Moreover, various post-WW II Conventions, including the four Geneva Conventions and their Common Article 1 obligate all High Contracting Parties to "respect and ensure respect for the present Convention in all circumstances." In other words, states are required to apply the principles of the Geneva Conventions universally.

They require that High Contracting Parties shall "search for persons alleged to have committed, or to have ordered to be committed, such grave breaches, and shall bring such persons, regardless of their nationality, before its own courts."

At Nuremberg, individual and command criminal responsibility was addressed. Tribunal Principles held that "(a)ny person who commits an act which constitutes a crime under international law is responsible therefor and liable to punishment....(c)rimes against international law are committed by men, not by abstract entities, and only by punishing individuals who commit (them) can the provisions of international law be enforced."

The Rome Statute's Article 25 of the International Criminal Court (ICC) codified this principle. It affirmed the culpability of individual persons committing crimes of war and against humanity.

In addition, under Article 28, commanders and their superiors are specifically culpable if any of them "either knew or, owing to the circumstances at the time, should have known that the forces were committing or about to commit such crimes, (and) failed to take all necessary and reasonable measures within his or her power to prevent or repress their commission or to submit the matter to the competent authorities for investigation and prosecutions."

Moreover, Nuremberg established that immunity is null and void, including for heads of state, other top officials, and top commanders. Further, genocide, crimes of war and against humanity are so grave that statute of limitation provisions don't apply.

As a result, every living past and present US president, top and subordinate officials, and Pentagon commanders involved in war(s) can be legally held accountable and should be prosecuted for their crimes before a special Nuremberg-type tribunal. Genocide, other forms of mass murder, targeted and indiscriminate destruction, and other crimes of war and against humanity are too intolerable to go unpunished.

Nonetheless, America and its conspiratorial allies continue to commit them. They continue, and horrifically, it remains below the radar as far as the Western masses are concerned, protected from knowing what is going on in the world and in their name by the very media that purport to inform them.. Countries like Libya are terrorized, destroyed, and occupied to be plundered in the name of "liberation" and all the Western public understands about it is that Qaddafi must have been a "bad guy."

America is the lead offender, committing what its own 1996 War Crimes Act calls "grave breaches," defined as "willful killing, torture or inhuman treatment, including biological (or other illegal) experiments, willfully causing great suffering or serious injury to body or health."

Libya is only the latest atrocity. Numerous others preceded it. More will follow. They're Nuremberg level crimes, supreme crimes against peace.

Yet on August 22, 2011 Obama outrageously said America, its "allies and partners in the international community (are committed) to protect the people of Libya, and to support a peaceful transition to democracy."

In fact, unspeakable war crimes were committed to "protect the people of Libya." Included were daily civilian terror bombings to break their morale, cause panic, weaken their resistance, and inflict mass casualties and punishment. This went on despite the fact that the Geneva Conventions and other international laws forbid targeting civilians. The Laws of War: Laws and Customs of War on Land (1907 Hague IV Convention) states:

- Article 25: "The attack or bombardment, by whatever means, of towns, villages, dwellings, or buildings which are undefended is prohibited."

- Article 26: "The officer in command of an attacking force must, before commencing a bombardment, except in cases of assault, do all in his power to warn the authorities."

- Article 27: "In sieges and bombardments, all necessary steps must be taken to spare, as far as possible, buildings dedicated to religion, art, science, or charitable purposes, historic monuments, hospitals, and places where the sick and wounded are collected, provided they are not being used at the time for military purposes."

The Fourth Geneva Convention protects civilians in time of war. It prohibits violence of any type against them and requires treatment for the sick and wounded.

As the international NGO, IHRAAM, stated in its intervention to the UN Human Rights Council on September 5, 2011 concerning the NATO bombardments undertaken under the guise of "responsibility to protect":

> The NATO assault on Libya enabled by UN Resolution 1973 (2011) has clearly gone beyond its mandate of civilian protection originally intended by the international community.
>
> Contrary to the Convention on Duties and Rights of States in the Event of Civil Strife, 1928 Art. 1, NATO has chosen sides and intervened in a civil war. It is an open secret that foreign military advisers have been working covertly inside Libya, providing guidance to rebels and giving tactical intelligence to NATO aircraft bombing government forces.
>
> Contrary to UN Charter Chapter IV, Article 33, a negotiated settlement in Libya was deliberately avoided for months while NATO illegally pursued regime change. The rebel drive to and capture of Tripoli would not have been possible without extensive NATO bombing.
>
> NATO has openly abandoned any remaining notion of "right to protect" civilians by its widespread bombing of Libyan cities such as Sirte into submission, contrary to Article 8(2)(b)(v) of the Statute of The International Criminal Court which clearly states that one criterion for indictment for war crimes is: "Attacking or bombarding, by whatever means, towns, villages, dwellings or buildings which are undefended and which are not military objectives." NATO's mandate to protect civilians under resolution 1973 cannot be interpreted so as to condone NATO's own bombing of Libyan cities as a legitimate military objective. NATO's bombings of Libyan cities are therefore war crimes.[3]

Long ago Washington trashed international and constitutional laws. As it had done in Iraq, Afghanistan and other targeted nations, America and its NATO partners waged war on Libya to conquer, colonize, occupy, and plunder another vassal state. Humanitarian intervention was mere subterfuge.

Democratic rule in Libya won't be tolerated. Servile puppets will follow the dictates of Washington. Manipulated elections will install them. This barbaric total war was planned all along, with civilians as fair game the same as combatants—if not more so.

Terror weapons are used freely in all US wars. So are weapons of mass destruction, including depleted and enriched uranium munitions. Battle plans *include* inflicting mass casualties and destroying vital civilian infrastructure such as, in the case of Libya, the Great Man-Made River (see Mark Metcalfe's article included herein).

The UN Charter's Chapter VI calls for peaceful conflict resolution. Humanitarian intervention authority not only doesn't permit, but is contrary to the very notion of the use of military force or other hostile acts—even less so when clearly exercised on behalf of one party to the conflict, as was the case in Libya.

ENDNOTES

1   Wesley K. Clark, *Winning Modern Wars: Iraq, Terrorism, and the American Empire*, Public Affairs, 2003.

2   FOR A. TV, see <http://veracitynow.com/videos/viewvideo/199/war-on-terror/general-wesley-clark-reveals-neocon-agenda-to-destroy-muslim-world>

3   The International Human Rights Association of American Minorities (IHRAAM) is an international NGO in Consultative Status with the UN. See http://www.ihraam.org/Documents/UN-18thHRC-Oral_Libya.html.

WHY QADDAFI?
WHY LIBYA?

MUAMMAR QADDAFI

MAD DOG OR BROTHER LEADER?

Mahdi Darius Nazemroaya

The flamboyant man referred to widely by African leaders and by the Libyan people themselves as "Brother Leader"—a title that that he himself was widely fond of—was even given the title "king of kings" by the tribal and village chieftains of Africa at a gathering in Benghazi in 2008 held to encourage grassroots movements in Africa working outside of governments to create a united continent. On the other hand, he was also the publicly demonized primary target of NATO's attack on Libya. Ronald Reagan called him the "mad dog of the Middle East" while a grandson of Nelson Mandela is named after him. Colonel Muammar Qaddafi, whose name can be spelt in numerous ways outside of the Arabic language, symbolized many things to many different people around the world. Although he had no official state or government position, he was an ever present force in the politics of Libya and a major figure in Africa. Over the years, he worked to cultivate a romantic figure of himself as a simple man of the people and of the desert. He travelled to meetings worldwide with his tent, pitching it in such venues as the Garden of the Elysée Palace, the French presidential residence in Paris in 2007 and in Rome's Villa Doria Pamphili in June of 2009. His reprimands of Arab dictators, such as King Abdullah of Saudi Arabia and Emir Hamad of Qatar, at Arab League meetings have made international headlines, and were relished by many Arabs. While on state visits in other countries, like France and Ukraine, he deliberately surrounded himself with an entourage of female body guards with the intent of getting heads to turn and highlighting his policy of integrating Libyan women into his country's military, police, and security infrastructure. The Brother Leader started his rise to power as a Libyan lieutenant amongst a group of Libyan military officers who carried out a bloodless coup d'état in 1969. The coup was against the young Libyan monarchy of King Idris I Al-Sanusi, a foreign puppet, and took place while King Idris was in Turkey. Many Libyans welcomed the coup. Under the Libyan monarchy the North African country had been widely acquiescent to US and Western European interests. Qaddafi would also move on to evict the US and British militaries from Libya. The Pentagon was particularly unhappy at losing Wheelus Air Base during the Cold War.

The Brother Leader was not a perfect man, but he was not the grossly depicted devil that NATO or its Libyan allies portrayed. When Nelson Mandela became the president of the Republic of South Africa, he refused the Clinton Administration's demands that South Africa cut ties with Libya and denounce Qaddafi. After all it was Qaddafi who had supported the African National Congress and Mandela against Apartheid, while countries like the United States, the United Kingdom, and France had all supported the racist government in South Africa. What the late Libyan leader did to arouse and earn the wrath of the United States and its NATO and Arab allies or clients is really what is important for analysis of NATO's war on Libya. NATO did not intervene for humanitarian reasons or to promote democracy in Libya. Love or hate the Libyan leader, under his rule Libya transformed from one of the poorest countries on the face of the planet into the country with the highest standard of living in Africa. In the words of Henri (/Henry) Habib:

> When Libya was granted its independence by the United Nations on December 24, 1951, it was described as one of the poorest and most backward nations of the world. The population at the time was not more than 1.5 million, was over 90% illiterate, and had no political experience or knowhow. There were no universities, and only a limited number of high schools which had been established seven years before independence.[1]

Despite its oil wealth, Libya under the monarchy had been in a sorry state. Like second class citizens in their own country, Libyans were not even allowed in hotels or facilities used by foreigners. Before 1969, most of the country's oil wealth was actually not being used to serve the general public. Under Qaddafi's rule this changed and the National Oil Company was founded on November 12, 1970. Libya under Qaddafi became a lucrative prize of immense economic value. When the Obama Administration and Secretary Hillary Clinton sent their ultimatums to Tripoli, the country had immense oil and gas resources, vast amounts of underground water from the Nubian Sandstone Aquifer System, great influence in Africa, important trade routes, substantial foreign investments, and large amounts of liquid capital. Up until 2011, Libya was blessed with a rare gift in regards to its national revenue and expenditures: the Jamahiriya did not spend a significant amount of its annual national income, but actually saved it. In fact Libya possessed more than $150 billion dollars (US) in overseas financial assets and had one of the largest sovereign investment funds in the world at the start of 2011. Until the conflict in Libya ignited, there was a very large foreign work force in the Jamahiriya. Thousands of foreign workers from every corner of the globe went to Libya for employment. For years, these jobs inside Libya were an important source of economic remittances in for some African economies. Moreover, many foreign workers from such places as the Philippines, Niger, Morocco, Lebanon, and Italy would even choose to make their lives in Libya and open their own businesses there.

To a great extent, the fact that Libya happened to be a rich country was one of its crimes in 2011. Oil, finance, economics, and Libyan natural resources were always tempting prizes for the United States and its allies. These were the spoils of war in Libya. While Libyan energy reserves and geo-politics played major roles in Western forces launching the war, it was also waged in part to appropriate Tripoli's vast financial holdings and to supplement and maintain the crumbling financial hegemony of Wall Street and other financial centers. Wall Street would not allow Tripoli to continue to be debt-free, to continue accumulating international financial possessions, and to be a creditor nation giving international loans and investing funds in other countries, particularly in Africa. Thus, major banks in the United States and the European Union, like the giant multinational oil conglomerates, had major roles and interests in the war on Libya.

The Colonel's Projects:
From the African Union to Wealth Redistribution

Amongst his projects, Qaddafi started the Great Man-Made River, which was a massive project to transform the Sahara Desert and reverse the desertification of Africa. The Great Man-Made River with its irrigation plans was also intended to support the agricultural sector not only in Libya, but also in other parts of Africa. This project ultimately became a military target of NATO's bombings in 2011. Claiming that Great Man-Made River infrastructure was tied to the Libyan military, NATO's bombing campaign severally damaged and destroyed important pieces and sections of the Great Man-Made River Project.

Qaddafi had many grand plans. He wanted to create a South Atlantic Treaty Organization to protect Africa and Latin America from North America and Western Europe. He advocated a gold dinar standard as the currency of Muslim countries. Many of his plans were also of a pan-African and pan-Arab nature. He was central to the creation of the African Union and in its financing. Qaddafi also envisioned the thriving of independent pan-African financial institutions. The Libyan Investment Authority and the Libyan Foreign Bank were important players in setting up these African institutions. Qaddafi, through the Libyan Foreign Bank and the Libyan Investment Authority, was instrumental in setting up Africa's first satellite network, the Regional African Satellite Communication Organization (RASCOM), to reduce African dependence on external powers.[2]

His crowning achievement would have been the creation of the United States of Africa. His ultimate objective was forming a United States of Africa with its own currency, a standing pan-African military force, and a single African passport. The supranational entity would have been created through the African Investment Bank, the African Monetary Fund, and finally the African Central Bank. These institutions were all viewed with animosity by the European Union, United States, International Monetary Fund (IMF), and World Bank.

Inside Libya, Qaddafi had a wealth redistribution project for his own citizens. US Congressional sources acknowledge this. On February 18, 2011 one Congressional report stated:

> In March 2008, [Colonel Qaddafi] announced his intention to dissolve most government administrative bodies and institute a Wealth Distribution Program whereby state oil revenues would be distributed to citizens on a monthly basis for them to administer personally, in cooperation, and via local committees. Citing popular criticism of government performance in a long, wide ranging speech, [he] repeatedly stated that the traditional state would soon be "dead" in Libya and that direct rule by citizens would be accomplished through the distribution of oil revenues. [The military], foreign affairs, security, and oil production arrangements reportedly would remain national

A massive pro-Qaddafi rally in Green Square. Only 10-30,000 as contended by western media? (Photo: Mahdi Darius Nazemroaya)

government responsibilities, while other bodies would be phased out. In early 2009, Libya's Basic People's Congresses considered variations of the proposals, and the General People's Congress voted to delay implementation.[3]

Qaddafi wanted all the people of Libya to have direct access to his nation's wealth. Maybe this was not implemented, but this is what he repeatedly promoted in words and efforts. He was also aware of the deep rooted corruption that plagued the ranks of the Libyan government and its political culture of cronyism. This was one of the reasons why he wanted to apply a model of political anarchy in Libya through progressive steps. He had been talking about both his wealth redistribution and political anarchy project for a few years before NATO engaged his country in war in 2011. The Wealth Redistribution Project, along with the establishment of an anarchist political system, were viewed as serious threats by the US, the EU, and a group of corrupt Libyan officials. If successful, the reforms could have created political unrest amongst many domestic populations around the world. Internally, many Libyan officials were working to delay the project. This included reaching out to external powers to intervene in Libya to stop Qaddafi and his projects.

Why Mahmoud Jibril Joined the Transitional Council

Amongst the Libyan officials that were heavily opposed to the Wealth Redistribution Project and viewed it with horror was Mahmoud Jibril. Jibril was put into place by Saif Al-Islam Qaddafi who, due to strong influence and advice from the US and the EU, selected him to transform the Libyan economy and impose a wave of neoliberal economic reforms that would open the Libyan market to plunder by foreign corporations under what is deceivingly called "market democracy." Jibril became the head of two government bodies in the Libyan Arab Jamahiriya, the National Planning Council of Libya and National Economic Development Board of Libya. While the National Economic Development Board was a regular ministry, the National Planning Council would actually put Jibril in a governmental position above that of the Office of the General-Secretary of the People's Committee of Libya, which is the Libyan equivalent of the post of prime minister. Jibril actually became one of the forces that opened the doors to privatization and poverty in Libya.

About six months before the conflict erupted in Libya, Mahmoud Jibril actually met with Bernard-Henri Lévy, a French intellectual who credits himself for getting France into the war against Libya, in Australia to discuss forming the Transitional Council and deposing Colonel Qaddafi.[4] He described Qaddafi's Wealth Redistribution Project as "crazy" in minutes and documents from the National Economic Development Board of the Libyan Arab Jamahiriya.[5] Moreover, he strongly believed that the Libyan masses were not fit to govern themselves and that an elite should always control the fate and wealth of any nation. What Jibril wanted to do was downsize the Libyan government and lay off a large segment of the public sector, but in exchange increase government regulations in Libya. He would also always cite Singapore as the perfect example of a neoliberal state. It is likely that he also met with Bernard-Henri Lévy while in Singapore, which he visited regularly.

When the problems erupted in Benghazi, Mahmoud Jibril immediately went to Egypt. He told his colleagues that he would be back in Tripoli soon, but he had no intention of returning. In reality, he went to Cairo to meet the leaders of the Syrian National Council (SNC) and Lévy. They were all waiting for him there to coordinate the events in Libya and Syria. This is one of the reasons that the Transitional Council has recognized the Syrian National Council as the legitimate government of Syria.

The Post-Qaddafi Era

Colonel Qaddafi nearly bested NATO. Before his capture and death in Sirte, NATO was losing steam, and facing many internal and external pressures. Italy was forced to withdraw from the war. in July.[6] Norway also announced that it would withdraw in August.[7] France was even starting to accept what Paris and NATO refused to accept from the start of the conflict, namely to end the war and to stop bombing Libya if both sides in Tripoli and Benghazi started political talks.[8] In reality, Jamahiriya officials had been calling for political dialogue with an entire international chorus for months, but it has been the Obama Administration and its Western European allies that refused to listen. There was a possibility that NATO would have settled for a divided Libya. Before the fall of Tripoli, the Transitional Council forces and NATO were offensively coordinating near the important oil city of Brega as part of a mad dash to gain as much territory and oil fields as possible before Libya could have possibly been divided.[9]

With 2011 and the death of Colonel Qaddafi, the security of the familiar is gone in Libya. Libya was never perfect under Qaddafi and many Libyans will be among the first to admit it, but the chaos that the Transitional Council and the NATO war brought has shattered their country, sending it to the edge. The "mad dog of the Middle East" is dead now. He was murdered in his hometown of Sirte. He stood his ground until the end like he said he would. The Transitional Council, which vowed to take him to court, had him murdered instead. He even reminded the men who beat him, anally raped him, mocked him, and finally murdered him that they were not following the laws of Islam about respectful treatment of prisoners. NATO played a central role and oversaw the whole sordid event. The murder was systematic, because after Qaddafi was murdered one of his sons was murdered by the Misurata Military Council and several other Libyan leaders were killed too. Colonel Qaddafi's death marks a historic milestone for Libya. An era has ended in Libya and a new chapter begins. Libya will not become a new paradise like the Transitional Council has said. In many cases the living will envy the dead, because of men like Mahmoud Jibril, Ali Tarhouni, and Sliman Bouchuiguir, who helped topple the Jamahiriya.

Mahmoud Jibril is a mere opportunist. He had no problem being a government official under the late Qaddafi. He never complained about human rights or a lack of democracy. His opposition to the late Qaddafi's Wealth Redistribution Project and his elitist attitude are amongst the reasons he conspired against Qaddafi and helped form the Transitional Council. He was also friends with Sliman Bouchiguir who helped frame Qaddafi at the UN. Jibril was the prime minister of the Transitional Council of Libya until a few days after the savage murder of Colonel Qaddafi. Is this ex-regime official, who has always been an open supporter of the Arab dictators in the Persian Gulf, really to be regarded as a representative and champion of the people? How about his colleagues in the Transitional Council who negotiated oil contracts with NATO member states, even before they held any so-called government positions in the Transitional Council? While Qaddafi supported independence and democracy movements all over the world from Africa to Latin America, many of the NATO powers opposed them. What does this say about the two respective sides in the conflict?

Qaddafi as Mere Pretext

Even if Mother Teresa or Mahatma Gandhi were the leaders of Libya, the Obama Administration, NATO, and the mainstream media in their services would have found a means to vilify them to justify intervention. NATO's war was conducted with intentions of eroding the national bonds of the Libyan people. Admiral Stavridis, the US commander in charge of NATO, told the US Senate Armed Services Committee in March 2011 that he believed that Qaddafi's support base would shrink as the tribal cleavages in Libya came "into play" as the war proceeded.[10] What Stavridis indirectly spelled out is that the NATO operations in Libya would cause further internal divisions through igniting tribal tensions that would cement regional differences inside

Libya. Italy's Prime Minister Silvio Berlusconi even admitted that the NATO bombings were not conducted as a result of a revolt in Libya, but were intended to cause a revolt against Colonel Qaddafi.[11] The Italian leader also said that he was told that the war would end when the population of Tripoli revolted against Colonel Qaddafi. This is a significant statement by the Italian Prime Minister. An analysis of cause and effect is very important here. It means that the war did not start as a result of any revolt, but was intended to instigate revolts against the Libyan government. This would explain why NATO deliberately targeted and punished the civilian population. The aim has been to instigate an uprising against Colonel Qaddafi. In other words, NATO would punish the Libyan people and make their lives so unbearable that they would opt to surrender by overthrowing Qaddafi and their government. The US and NATO knew very well that if Colonel Qaddafi was eliminated that the Libyan tribes would bicker amongst themselves for power and be politically divided. Without hesitation, it has to be said that Muammar Qaddafi guaranteed the unity of Libya in his person. This can be seen negatively or positively, but it was a political reality in Libya. This is why President Obama, Secretary Clinton, President Sarkozy, and Prime Minister Cameron were very adamant about removing Qaddafi or murdering him in breach of international law. The Obama Administration and NATO have all banked on a power vacuum that would be left in a post-Qaddafi Libya. They calculated that there would be a mad dash to fill the power vacuum that would help divide Libya further and promote more internal violence. They were also very well aware that the tribal conflicts in Libya would spread from Libya to other parts of Africa.

NATO's war in Libya was chiefly waged against the Libyan people. It was not the Libyan military that kept the country standing, but the Libyan people themselves and their resistance. Many who opposed Qaddafi even became his supporters, because they realized that the war was not waged as part of a question about the leadership of Muammar Qaddafi, but was waged for economic and strategic reasons. The war in Libya and the fall of the Libyan Arab Jamahiriya have paved the way for the re-colonization of Africa.

ENDNOTES

1   Henri Pierre Habib, *Politics and Government of Revolutionary Libya* (Québec: Le Cercle de Livre de France Ltée, 1975), p.1.

2   Regional African Satellite Communication Organization, "Launch of the Pan African Satellite," July 26, 2010:<http://www.rascom.org/info_detail2.php?langue_id=2&info_

id=120&id_sr=0&id_r=32&id_gr=3>

3   US Library of Congress, Congressional Research Service, Libya: Background and U.S. Relations, Christopher M. Blanchard and James Zanotti, CRS Report RL33412 (Washington, DC: Office of Congressional Information and Publishing, February 18, 2011), p.22.

4.   Private discussions with Mahmoud Jibril's co-workers inside and outside of Libya.

5   Internal private documents from the National Economic Development Board of the Libyan Arab Jamahiriya.

6.   "Berlusconi Opposes Libya Mission; Rome Cuts Involvement," *Voice of America*, July 7, 2011.

7   "Nato capabilities will be exhausted within 90 days in Libya," *Agence-France Presse*, July 11, 2011.

8   "France backs 'political solutions' in Libya crisis," *Agence-France Presse*, July 11, 2011.

9   Marc Champion and Joseph Parkinson, "US Recognizes Libyan Rebel Group," *Wall Street Journal*, July 16, 2011.

10   United States Senate Armed Services Committee, *US European Command and US Strategic Command in review of the Defense Authorization Request for Fiscal Year 2012 and the Future Years Defense Program*, 112th Congress, 2011, 1st Session, 29 March 2011.

11   Lamine Chikhi *et al.*, "Italy's Berlusconi exposes NATO rifts over Libya," *ed.* Elizabeth Fullerton, Reuters, July 7, 2011; As a note, Nicolas Carey, who was expelled from Tripoli and managed to immediately reappear in Misurata, also contributed to this report. As a note the reporting of Carey has to be carefully scrutinized.

WHY LIBYA
WAS ATTACKED

Stephen Lendman

Obama's March 28, 2011 address at the National Defense University was true to form. It reeked of duplicity, hypocrisy, and ball-faced lies. Obama said:

> For generations, the United States of America has played a unique role as an anchor of global security and as an advocate for human freedom.....(W)e are reluctant to use force to solve the world's many challenges. But when our interests and values are at stake, we have a responsibility to act. That's what happened in Libya....[1]

For decades, he went on, Libya was "ruled by a tyrant.... He has denied his people freedom, exploited their wealth, murdered opponents at home and abroad, and terrorized people around the world—iincluding Americans who were killed by Libyan agents."

If you substitute Washington for Libya, he got it right. America is a rogue terror state, a menacing plague on humanity.Democratic values, human and civil rights, and rule of law principles are paid lip service, but in actuality they are non-starters. Only corporate and imperial interests matter, not equity, justice, peace on earth, and government of, by and for the people with respect for the sovereign rights of other nations.

NATO's war on Libya was planned many months in advance like all wars. Why is most important, or put another way—*cui bono*?

Official accounts and the mainstream media scoundrels always leave out the "why" of the journalistic 4Ws and an H. The relevant issues are discussed below, summarizing what's most important.

Historical Facts About Libya

Like most parts of Africa for centuries, European colonial powers ravaged Libya. During the 1911 Turko/Italian war, Libya was invaded and attacked. Twenty years of resistance challenged Italian colonizers.

From 1911-1943, Italy's occupation was brutal and the Libyans never forgot it. After WW II, America, Britain and France dominated the region. In 1951, they combined three distinct regions into Libya—Cyrenaica in the east, Tripolitania in the west, and Fezzan in the south.

Britain enthroned King Idriss, who let America, Britain and France retain military bases and pursue corporate interests. America's Wheelus Air Base near Tripoli dominated the Mediterranean Basin. It's a good bet that Washington wants one or more super-bases built on Libyan land as launching pads against the region once again.

In 1955, Libyan oil was discovered. The three colonial powers controlled it until Qaddafi's bloodless September 1, 1969 coup ousted King Idris. It was an anti-imperial socialist revolution and marked the end of foreign domination. In 1977, Qaddafi transformed the Libyan Republic into the Socialist People's Libyan Arab Jamahiriya—a "state of the masses." In 1979, he established direct participatory democracy, devolving power to tribal leaders. In 1986, Libya became the Great Socialist People's Libyan Arab Jamahiriya.

Qaddafi supported pan-Africanism—a United States of Africa, free from imperial domination—a vision shared by Marcus Garvey, Kwame Kkrumah, Sekou Toure, Julius Nyerere, Jomo Kenyatta, William Tubman, Gamal Abdel Nasser, and others. Nasser said he represented Arab nationalism and unity.

He also wanted Libyans to share in the country's oil wealth, a notion foreign to America and other Western societies. Under his 1999 Decision No. 111, all Libyans received free healthcare, education, electricity, water, training, rehabilitation, housing assistance, disability and old-age benefits, interest-free state loans, as well as generous subsidies to study abroad, buy a new car, help when they marry, practically free gasoline, and more.

Literacy under Qaddafi rose from 20% to 80%. Libya's hospitals and private clinics were some of the region's best. Now they're in shambles. Some, in fact, were bombed or damaged in other fighting. NATO lied, saying only military targets were attacked.

NATO's imperial strategy involves targeting civilians and vital infrastructure, including power, communications, medical care facilities, and other essential to life sites.

Before the war began, Libyans had Africa's highest standard of living. According to David Blundy and Andrew Lycett's book titled, *Qaddafi and the Libyan Revolution*:[2]

> The young people are well dressed, well fed and well educated... Every Libyan gets free, and often excellent, education, medical and health services. New colleges and hospitals are impressive by any international standard... All Libyans have a house or a flat, a car, and most have televisions [and other conveniences]. Compared with most citizens of Third World countries, and with many [others], Libyans have it very good indeed...

including decent housing or a rent-free apartment.

Qaddafi's Green Book,[3] in fact, states, "The house is a basic need of both the individual and the family, therefore it should not be owned by others." It also covers other beneficial social policies:

> Women, like men, are human beings.

> ....(A)ll individuals have a natural right to self-expression by any means....;

> In a socialist society no person may own a private means of transportation for the purpose of renting to others, because this represents controlling the needs of others.

> The democratic system is a cohesive structure whose foundation stones are firmly laid above the other (through People's Conferences and Committees). There is absolutely no conception of democratic society other than this.

> No representation of the people—representation is a falsehood. The existence of parliaments underlies the absence of the people, for democracy can only exist with the presence of the people and not in the presence of representatives of the people.

Green Book ideology rejects Western-style democracy and predatory capitalism, especially neoliberal exploitation. It's one of many reasons why Qaddafi was ousted.

He provided other impressive social benefits, including free land, equipment, livestock and seeds for agriculture to foster self-sufficient food production. In addition, all basic food items were subsidized and sold through a network of "people's shops."

Moreover, since the 1960s, women could vote and participate politically. They could also own and sell property independently of their husbands. Under the December 1969 Constitutional Proclamation Clause 5, they had equal status with men, including in education and employment, even though the men still play leading roles in society.

Until Washington and NATO blocked its approval, the UN Human Rights Council praised Qaddafi in its January 2011 "Report of the Working Group on the Universal Periodic Review: Libya Arab Jamahiriya."[4]

It said his government protected "not only political rights, but also economic, educational, social and cultural rights." It also lauded his treatment of religious minorities, and the "human rights training" of its security forces.

In the single year of 2011, NATO's killing machine destroyed 42 years of achievements, benefitting all Libyans.

Qaddafi had overwhelming support. After NATO attacked, hundreds of thousands rallied openly for Qaddafi. On July 1, 95% of Tripoli's population (over a million strong) expressed their support in Green Square. Before the war, he felt safe enough to drive unprotected through Tripoli streets. Residents lined up to cheer him. Some despot! America and other Western societies should have such dictators. Imperial wars would end. So would homelessness, hunger and human depravation. Instead, the "new world order" imperialists want super-wealth and power to be shared only by their privileged few.

Libya was only one of many targets. Others will follow to extinguish freedom everywhere if they succeed. Universal opposition needs to stop them. Failure can't be tolerated. The alternative is too grim to imagine.

Why Qaddafi Was Targeted

Qaddafi's vision marked him for removal. It was just a matter of time, even though he tried to forestall it by cooperating with Western powers post-9/11 on matters of intelligence and terrorism. In 2003, he came in from the cold, became a valued Western ally, and had meetings and discussions with top officials like UK Prime Ministers Tony Blair and Gordon Brown, France's Nicolas Sarkozy, Italy's Silvio Berlusconi, US Secretary of State Condoleezza Rice, and others. Until vilified and targeted, he was welcomed in Western capitals.

He also participated in the 2009 G-8 Summit in L-Aquila, Italy as Chairman of the African Union. At the time, he met and shook hands with Obama.

Moreover, ABC News interviewed him live, and on January 21, 2009, *The New York Times* published his op-ed headlined, "The One-State Solution" to resolve the Israeli/Palestinian conflict. He called "living under one roof... the only option for a lasting peace."

On May 16, 2006, Washington restored full diplomatic relations. Libya was removed from its state sponsors of terrorism list. At the time, Rice called the move:

> tangible results that flow from the historic decisions taken by Libya's leadership in 2003 to renounce terrorism and to abandon its weapons of mass destruction programs....Libya is an important model as nations around the world press for changes in behavior by the Iranian and North Korean regimes.[5]

She also praised Qaddafi's "excellent cooperation" in fighting terrorism. Moreover, he opened Libya's markets to Western interests by arranging deals with Big Oil giants BP, ExxonMobil, Royal Dutch Shell, Occidental, France's Total, Italy's Eni Gas and others. By all appearances, he had joined the club, so why turn on him?

Though on board in some ways, he very much wasn't on others. He still supported Palestinian rights, opposed Israel's occupation and Gaza's siege. Earlier he backed anti-apartheid struggles in South Africa, as well as others in Northern Ireland, Spain, and elsewhere.

He had nothing to do with downing Pan Am 103 over Lockerbie, Scotland in 1988. Neither did Abdel Basset Ali al-Megrahi. The Scottish judges knew he was innocent but were pressured to convict him. When Qaddafi took responsibility solely to have international sanctions removed, he never admitted fault. To this day, he and al-Megrahi stand falsely accused. Likely CIA/MI6 and/or Mossad involvement is never mentioned.

America tried and failed numerous times to assassinate Qaddafi, including Ronald Reagan's 1986 attempt which resulted in the death of his adopted daughter. CIA covert efforts have financed opposition groups. In 1981, they helped establish the National Front for the Salvation of Libya (NFSL) and its militant wing called the Libyan National Army based in Egypt near Libya's border.Along with US and

UK Special Forces, it was directly involved in instigating insurrection last February. It wasn't homegrown. As in Syria, it was externally generated.

Qaddafi opted out of AFRICOM, one of the nine global Pentagon commands formed to control Africa and the Mediterranean Basin, including its strategic energy transit routes and choke points crucial to keep open for world economies. All African countries participate except Sudan, Zimbabwe, Eritrea, and Libya until now. He also backed an initiative to create a United States of Africa, whereas Washington wants easily exploitable divisions. More on that below.

While Libya is currently ranked ninth in the world as an oil-producing state with 42 billion proved barrels of oil reserves (and large amounts of gas), its untapped potential is believed to be much greater. Moreover, being nearly sulfur-free, Libyan oil is even more valued for its extremely high quality. Access to Libyan oil isn't at issue, rather the issue is control over who develops, produces and receives it in what amounts.

In January 2009, Qaddafi wanted to nationalize Libyan oil, but his timetable faced internal resistance. According to Pravda.ru's March 25, 2011 article titled, "Reason for war? Qaddafi wanted to nationalize oil,"[6] he considered the option because of low oil prices at the time, reasoning that:

> The oil-exporting countries should opt for nationalization because of the rapid fall in oil prices. We must put the issue on the table and discuss it seriously. Oil should be owned by the State at this time, so we could better control prices by the increase or decrease in production.

In February 2009, he asked for public support to distribute Libya's oil wealth directly to the people. However, senior officials feared losing their jobs "due to a parallel plan by Qaddafi to rid the state of corruption." Possible capital flight was also an issue. As a result, Libya's Popular Committee voted 468 - 64 to delay nationalization plans, even though a 251 majority viewed doing so as positive.

Note: Qaddafi didn't take into consideration how powerful insiders manipulate all markets up or down for profit, including oil, irrespective of demand. It's brazen fraud but goes on all the time, especially on Wall Street in collusion with Washington.

Libya's Great Man-Made River (GMMR) was developing an ocean-sized aquifer beneath the desert for irrigation, human consumption, and other uses. At 2007 consumption rates, it could last

1,000 years. No wonder Qaddafi calls his Nubian Sandstone Aquifer System (NSAS) the "Eighth Wonder of the World."

At issue now, of course, is whether it should be privatized, making water unaffordable for many, including most Libyans. But Western predators want it exploited for maximum profits, not equitable use as a public resource.

Ellen Brown's April 13, 2011 article titled, "Libya: All About Oil, or All About Banking?" raised another, easily overlooked, issue. Who controls Libya's money, the lifeblood of every economy? In 1970, Henry Kissinger said, "Control oil and you control nations. Control food and you control people." He left out money, the supreme power to control everything because without it, economies collapse.

At issue is public or private control as is the case with most nations, including America under Wall Street's owned and operated Federal Reserve.

Under Qaddafi, the Central Bank of Libya was state owned. In other words, it created its own money, the Libyan Dinar, interest free to be used productively for economic growth, not speculation, profits and bonuses for predatory bankers.

However, after the Washington-led NATO inter-ention, the privately controlled Central Bank of Benghazi was established to let Western bankers, not Libyans, run things. Money control indeed appears an important reason for intervening, perhaps most important of all.

On April 24, 2011, Manlio Dinucci's Global Research article headlined, "Financial Heist of the Century: Confiscating Libya's Sovereign Wealth Funds (SWF)," saying that besides money, oil, gas, water, and other reasons, the "Libyan Investment Authority (LIA) manages" an estimated $70 billion, "rising to more than $150 billion (including) foreign investments of the Central Bank and other bodies. But it might be more."

Confiscation gives US/NATO interests easy money for their own purposes.

Qaddafi promoted pan-African unity, a United States of Africa he hoped to lead against Western powers wanting balkanized easily-controlled states. Libya was central to Africa's independence, including its freedom from predatory central banks and international lending agencies, acting as loan sharks of last resort.

He also funded Africa's only communications satellite, thereby saving users hundreds of millions of dollars for low-cost incoming and outgoing calls.

In addition, he allocated two-thirds of the $42 billion needed to launch a public African Central Bank (headquartered in Nigeria), an African Monetary Fund based in Cameroon, and an African Investment

Bank headquartered in Libya.The Obama administration stole the money and prevented that from happening. If established, it would have provided low-cost (or perhaps interest-free) loans for health, education, and other social projects, as well as vital infrastructure development in participating African states.

He advocated a new "Gold Standard," replacing dollars with gold dinars. African and Muslim states supported it to establish real monetary wealth and value, free from predatory lending agencies and depreciating fiat currencies. Washington, however, was determined to prevent it to maintain petrodollar recycling and dollar hegemony as the world's reserve currency.

Western plans for Libya's oil excludes China and Russia. Qaddafi had granted both countries concessions, but what he gave, Washington wants revoked. America, Britain, France, Italy, and other Western partners want North African resources for themselves. They also want control of sub-Saharan Africa, depriving rivals they want excluded.

A revolutionary leader, Qaddafi was a visionary. He wanted a Libyan society based on equity, justice and fair distribution of wealth. His faults aside, Libyans supported him overwhelmingly. They still do. His spirit drives their revolutionary struggle for freedom. They won't quit until it's achieved.

Washington and its NATO partners destroyed Gadaffi's vision and raped Libya for profit and to exploit its people. That's imperialism's core element. Qaddafi wanted none of it and that's why he had to go.

ENDNOTES

1   See "Remarks by the President in Address to the Nation on Libya,National Defense University, March 28, 2011. Washington, D.C., at <www.whitehouse.gov/the-press-office/2011/03/28/remarks-president-address-nation-Libya>

2   Andrew Lycette, Qadaffi and the Libyan Revolution, Boston, Little Brown, 1987. See <.http://www.amazon.com/Qaddafi-Libyan-Revolution-David-Blundy/dp/0316100420>

3   http://911-truth.net/other-books/Muammar-Qaddafi-Green-Book-Eng.pdf

4   http://www2.ohchr.org/english/bodies/hrcouncil/docs/16session/A-HRC-16-15.pdf

5   "U.S. Restores Full Diplomatic Relations with Libya," American Forces Press Service, May 15, 2006. See <http://www.emailthepresident.com/news/2006/05-15-us-restores-full-diplomatic-relations-with-libya.html>

6   http://wikileaksdonations.wordpress.com/2011/03/28/reason-for-war-gaddafi-wanted-to-nationalise-oil/

THE US/NATO WAR IN LIBYA

A CONTINUATION OF PAST CRIMES

Sarah Flounders*

I wrote a widely circulated article on Libya a year ago, on March 2, 2011, less than three weeks before the first NATO bombs began to fall. It was at a juncture when all of the international media spoke with one voice and every major US and West European political leader was disguising the corporate drive for conquest and plunder with a call for emergency action to "save lives." A "no-fly zone" was posed as the only possible solution. My article, reprinted below, opened with the point that the worst thing that could happen to the people of Libya and the worst thing that could happen to the revolutionary upsurge shaking the Arab world is US and NATO intervention.

In order to oppose the coming war it was essential to understand US interests in Libya and in Africa, and to look at the four decades of hostility to Libya. At that time, while it may have been difficult for many observers to comprehend the full horror that lay ahead for the people of Libya, anyone truly opposed to colonial oppression and imperialist war should have been aware of the past massive destruction and dislocation of US wars in Korea, Vietnam, Yugoslavia, Iraq and Afghanistan, where the crime of military intervention was only too well known. Each of those wars was also against small countries that had no way of defending themselves against aircraft carriers, jet bombers or

*March 3, 2012

missiles that were part of the Pentagon and NATO arsenals. Each war consciously targeted the civilians and the basic infrastructure needed for survival in an effort to break their will to resist. Each of those past wars not only laid waste to the targeted country, they disrupted the stability of the entire region where these countries were located.

It's true that many may have been deceived by the overwhelming weight of propaganda disseminated by a corporate media machine as powerful as NATO›s military machine. Since that time, however, it has become apparent to anyone paying attention that what the article predicted was, if anything, an understatement of how this intervention would wreck the lives of the great mass of Libyan people and the 2 million immigrant workers dependent on their jobs in the Libyan construction, medical, service and oil industry.

Under the cover of a cynical UN Security Council vote to impose a so-called "humanitarian" no-fly zone in Libya, Washington›s goal was to systematically crush every form of resistance and reverse the policy of nationalized oil and gas wealth. US bombers had total control of the skies and everything that moved on land. With the Pentagon in the lead and the main supplier of equipment, 11 countries were dropping bombs on Libya.

From the first day of NATO bombing attacks on March 19, 2011 to the capture of Muammar Qaddafi seven months later on Oct 20, everything built in Libya over a period of 40 years—including the water supply, electric grid, national health care system and tens of thousands of modern apartment buildings and well developed infrastructure were systematically destroyed in every city in Libya. The country with the highest standard of living in Africa now lies in ruin.

The corporate media falsely reported the imminent collapse of the government from the first days of the bombing. They predicted surrender by the third day. Then the 30-day US War Powers Act came and went and so did the 90 day initial NATO order. Amazingly, the Libyan government was able to hold out through seven months of bombardment. That determination alone confirmed the deep popular support for the Qaddafi government against foreign intervention. In Tripoli huge rallies of a million and more again and again gathered to show their opposition to imperialist conquest. By every account the scattered and contending opposition militias did no fighting. They stood back until NATO bombs and missiles, unleashing destruction from the air, cleared the way. Then, like vultures, they moved in to pick up the pieces.

The responsibility of progressive intellectuals, activists and groups in the United States was to explain the corporate interests behind the cynical "humanitarian" war. The urgent need is for an antiwar movement that is determined to counter media demonization in the midst of a war mobilization and focus on the outrageous crimes being committed, while refusing to accept or give weight to any justification for them.

Despite an ocean of propaganda, poll after poll confirmed that from 60 percent to 65 percent of the US population was against the US war on Libya. But the weight of media demonization silenced too many in the anti-war movement, keeping them from speaking out.

People were able to begin to build resistance to the aggression on Libya, as former US Congresswoman Cynthia McKinney engaged them on a 23-city national speaking tour, sponsored by International Action Center in coordination with local grassroots groups in every city. Across the country there were packed meetings opposing the war where Cynthia McKinney was the featured speaker. McKinney had risked her life to visit Libya with a US delegation in the midst of the US/NATO bombing. But the corporate media was totally silent on all coverage of opposition voices.

Thousands if not tens of thousands of Libyans were killed or injured by the bombing. Black Libyans and non-Libyan Africans became the special targets of the reactionary militias that the US-NATO countries armed. Many Black Libyans and Africans from other countries are among the 8,000 prisoners of the National Transition Council regime. Even Human Rights Watch—an enemy of the Qaddafi government— reported that the Misrata rebels looted and burned homes of the Tawergha people, dark-skinned Libyans driven from their villages in the central region into Tripoli.

The videos that presented the capture and brutal execution of Qaddafi were displayed around the world, confirming the depravity not only of the opposition forces, but of their foreign masters. The African leader was burned, sodomized with a bayonet, beaten and shot, denied Muslim burial and put on display in the meat locker at a shopping center. It was the all-too-familiar treatment by the colonial oppressor of the leader a small African country that dared to defy imperialist plunder. The videos that continue to surface have recorded the torture of Black Libyans, bound, gagging and retching while forced to chew on pieces of the green Libyan flag.

As in the other US wars, once the sovereign government was smashed the colonial rulers made no effort even to rebuild what they so callously destroyed. There is no stable regime left in Libya. The colonial powers› only plans concern how to further punish and humiliate the population and get the oil flowing to Western industries and the profits flowing into Western oil companies and banks.

The corporate think tanks have praised Libya as a new model of conquest. Without casualties to the US and its NATO allies, the air war led to the seizure of all of Libya's hundreds of billions of dollars in frozen assets and control of future oil profits. These were the very funds that Libya had committed toward building a solid African currency and financing wider African development.

The imperialist powers are emboldened by their destruction in Libya. The same tactics of arming militias, sending in sabotage teams, creating social dislocation and sectarian and ethnic strife are now being attempted in Syria.

But the "model conquest" may boomerang. Consider Afghanistan. In 2001 US jets also secured Afghanistan without a single US casualty. Now they find that every Afghan soldier they train for a puppet army is capable of turning the guns against their foreign masters. No bases, roads or borders are secure.

Neighboring Pakistan, once an ally of Washington, is faced with a population so outraged at US arrogance and continuing drone attacks that the Khyber Pass and every other border crossing into Afghanistan has been closed for months, blocking the transport of hundreds of tons of supplies needed to continue the war, forcing an airlift from the north at 10 times the cost to bring in military supplies. But no provisions are made to transport basic goods for a starving and dislocated population— adding further fuel to the resistance.

In Iraq too, the plans for complete domination, the plans really to re-establish colonial rule, collapsed. The US had to abandon its grandiose plans for 14 permanent bases and withdraw its troops. The plans to staff the largest US embassy in the world in Baghdad with 2,000 officials, labeled as 'diplomats' and protected by 16,000 contractors or mercenaries, have just been downsized to less than half the original projection. The Pentagon›s invasion has destroyed Iraq in a horrendous way, killing a million people and driving four million into internal and foreign exile. But destruction alone solved none of the social problems and a new generation of resistance has taken root.

It may be hard to imagine a rapid reversal of the setback to Libya. But already there are reports of resistance and guerrilla fighting, along with armed groups operating in surrounding Mali, Chad and Niger. The war in Libya may be far from over.

Every struggle to record the crimes and demand an accounting, pursue charges of war crimes against the perpetrators and build solidarity with the people of Libya during this difficult hour must be given our greatest attention.

Warning: US Mobilization to Re-conquer Libya

By Sara Flounders, March 2, 2011

The worst thing that could happen to the people of Libya is US intervention. The worst thing that could happen to the revolutionary upsurge shaking the Arab world is US intervention in Libya.

The White House is meeting with its allies among the European imperialist NATO countries to discuss imposing a no-fly zone over Libya, jamming all communications of President Muammar Qaddafi inside Libya, and carving military corridors into Libya from Egypt and Tunisia, supposedly to "assist refugees."[1] (*The New York Times*, Feb. 27, 2011)

This means positioning US/NATO troops in Egypt and Tunisia close to Libya's two richest oil fields, in both the east and west. It means the Pentagon coordinating maneuvers with the Egyptian and Tunisian militaries. What could be more dangerous to the Egyptian and Tunisian revolutions?

Italy, once the colonizer of Libya, has suspended a 2008 treaty with Libya that includes a nonaggression clause, a move that could allow it to take part in future "peacekeeping" operations there and enable the use of its military bases in any possible intervention. Several US and NATO bases in Italy, including the US Sixth Fleet base near Naples, could be staging areas for action against Libya.

President Barack Obama has announced that "the full range of options" is under consideration. This is Washington-speak for military operations.

Secretary of State Hillary Clinton met in Geneva on Feb. 28 with foreign ministers at the UN Human Rights Council to discuss possible multilateral actions.

Meanwhile, adding to the drumbeat for military intervention is the release of a public letter from the Foreign Policy Initiative, a right-wing think tank seen as the successor to the Project for the New American Century, calling for the US and NATO to "immediately" prepare military action to help bring down the Qaddafi regime.

The public appeal's signers include William Kristol, Richard Perle, Paul Wolfowitz, Elliott Abrams, Douglas Feith and more than a dozen former senior officials from the Bush administration, plus several prominent liberal Democrats, such as Neil Hicks of Human Rights First and Bill Clinton's "human rights" chief, John Shattuck.

The letter called for economic sanctions and military action: deploying NATO warplanes and a naval armada to enforce no-fly zones and have the capability to disable Libyan naval vessels.

Senators John McCain and Joseph Lieberman while in Tel Aviv

on Feb. 25 called for Washington to supply Libyan rebels with arms and establish a no-fly zone over the country.

Not to be overlooked are calls for UN contingents of medical and humanitarian workers, human rights monitors and investigators from the International Criminal Court to be sent to Libya with an "armed escort."

Providing humanitarian aid doesn't have to include the military.

Turkey has evacuated 7,000 of its nationals on ferries and chartered flights. Some 29,000 Chinese workers have left via ferries, chartered flights and ground transportation.

However, the way in which the European powers are evacuating their nationals from Libya during the crisis includes a military threat and is part of the imperialist jockeying for position regarding Libya's future.

Germany sent three warships, carrying 600 troops, and two military planes to bring 200 German employees of the oil exploration company Wintershall out of a desert camp 600 miles southeast of Tripoli. The British sent the *HMS Cumberland* warship to evacuate 200 British nationals and announced that the destroyer York was on its way from Gibraltar.

The US announced on Feb. 28 that it was sending the huge aircraft carrier *USS Enterprise* and the amphibious assault ship *USS Kearsarge* from the Red Sea to the waters off Libya, where it will join the *USS Mount Whitney* and other battleships from the Sixth Fleet. US officials called this a "pre-positioning of military assets."

UN Vote on Sanctions

The UN Security Council—under US pressure –on Feb. 26 voted to impose sanctions on Libya despite the fact that, according to studies by the UN's own agencies, more than 1 million Iraqi children died as a result of US/UN-imposed sanctions on that country that paved the way for an actual US invasion. Sanctions are criminal and confirm that this intervention is not due to humanitarian concern.

The sheer hypocrisy of the resolution on Libya expressing concern for "human rights" is hard to match. Just four days before the vote, the US used its veto to block a mildly worded resolution criticizing Israeli settlements on Palestinian land in the West Bank. The US government blocked the Security Council from taking any action during the 2008 Israeli massacre in Gaza, which resulted in the deaths of more than 1,500 Palestinians. These international bodies, as well as the International Criminal Court, have been silent on Israeli massacres, on US drone attacks on defenseless civilians in Pakistan, and on the criminal invasions and occupation of Iraq and Afghanistan.

The fact that China went along with the sanctions vote is an unfortunate example of the government in Beijing letting its interest in trade and continued oil shipments take precedence over its past opposition to sanctions that clearly impact civilian populations.

Who Leads the Opposition?

It is important to look at the opposition movement, especially those being so widely quoted in all the international media. We must assume that people with genuine grievances and wrongs have been caught up in it. But who is actually leading the movement?

A front-page *New York Times* article of Feb. 25 described just how different Libya is from other struggles breaking out across the Arab world. "Unlike the Facebook enabled youth rebellions, the insurrection here has been led by people who are more mature and who have been actively opposing the regime for some time." The article describes how arms had been smuggled across the border with Egypt for weeks, allowing the rebellion to "escalate quickly and violently in little more than a week."

The opposition group most widely quoted is the National Front for the Salvation of Libya. The NFSL, founded in 1981, is known to be a CIA-funded organization, with offices in Washington, DC. It has maintained a military force, called the Libyan National Army, in Egypt near the Libyan border. A Google search of National Front for the Salvation of Libya and CIA will quickly confirm hundreds of references.

Also widely quoted is the National Conference for the Libyan Opposition. This is a coalition formed by the NFSL that also includes the Libyan Constitutional Union, led by Muhammad as-Senussi, a pretender to the Libyan throne. The website of the LCU calls upon the Libyan people to reiterate a pledge of allegiance to King Idris El-Senusi as historical leader of the Libyan people. The flag used by the coalition is the flag of the former Kingdom of Libya.

Clearly these CIA-financed forces and old monarchists are politically and socially different from the disenfranchised youth and workers who have marched by the millions against US-backed dictators in Egypt and Tunisia and are today demonstrating in Bahrain, Yemen and Oman.

According to the *Times* article, the military wing of the NFSL, using smuggled arms, quickly seized police and military posts in the Mediterranean port city of Benghazi and nearby areas that are north of Libya's richest oil fields where most of its oil and gas pipelines, refineries and its liquefied natural gas port are located. The *Times* and other Western media claim that this area, now under "opposition control," includes 80 percent of Libya's oil facilities.

The Libyan opposition, unlike the movements elsewhere in the Arab world, from the beginning appealed for international assistance. And the imperialists quickly responded.

For example, Mohammed Ali Abdallah, deputy secretary general of the NFSL, sent out a desperate appeal: "We are expecting a massacre." "We are sending an SOS to the international community to step in." Without international efforts to restrain Qaddafi, "there will be a bloodbath in Libya in the next 48 hours."

The *Wall Street Journal*, the voice of big business, in a Feb. 23 editorial wrote that "The US and Europe should help the Libyans overthrow the Qaddafi regime."

US Interests—OIL

Why are Washington and the European powers willing and anxious to act on Libya?

When a new development arises it is important to review what we know of the past and to always ask, what are the interests of US corporations in the region?

Libya is an oil-rich country—one of the world's 10 richest. Libya has the largest proven oil reserves in Africa, at least 44 billion barrels. It has been producing 1.8 million barrels of oil a day—light crude that is considered top quality and needs less refining than most other oil. Libya also has large deposits of natural gas that is easy to pipe directly to European markets. It is a country large in area with a small population of 6.4 million people.

That is how the powerful US oil and military corporations, banks and financial institutions who dominate global markets see Libya.

Oil and gas are today the most valuable commodities and the largest source of profits in the world. Gaining control of oil fields, pipelines, refineries and markets drives a great part of US imperialist policy.

During two decades of US sanctions on Libya, which Washington had calculated would bring down the regime, European corporate interests invested heavily in pipeline and infrastructure development there. Some 85 percent of Libya's energy exports presently go to Europe.

European transnationals—in particular BP, Royal Dutch Shell, Total, Eni, BASF, Statoil and Rapsol—have dominated Libya's oil market. The giant US oil corporations were left out of these lucrative deals. China has been buying a growing amount of oil produced by Libya's National Oil Corp. and has built a short oil pipeline in Libya.

The huge profits that could be made by controlling Libya's oil and natural gas are what is behind the drum roll of the US corporate media's call for "humanitarian intervention to save lives."

Manlio Dinucci, an Italian journalist writing for Italy's *Il Manifesto*, explained on Feb. 25 that "If Qaddafi is overthrown, the US would be able to topple the entire framework of economic relations with Libya, opening the way to US-based multinationals, so far almost entirely excluded from exploitation of energy reserves in Libya. The United States could thus control the tap for energy sources upon which Europe largely depends and which also supply China."

Libya Background

Libya was a colony of Italy from 1911 until Italy's defeat in World War II. After the war, the Western imperialist powers set up regimes across the region that were called independent states but were headed by appointed monarchs with no democratic vote for the people. Libya became a sovereign country in name, but was firmly tied to the US and Britain under a new monarch—King Idris.

In 1969 as a wave of anti-colonial struggles swept the colonized world, revolutionary-minded Pan-Arab nationalist junior military officers overthrew Idris, who was vacationing in Europe. The leader of the coup was 27-year old Muammar Qaddafi.

Libya changed its name from the Kingdom of Libya to the Libyan Arab Republic and later to the Great Socialist People's Libyan Arab Jamahiriya.

The young officers ordered the US and British bases in Libya closed, including the Pentagon's large Wheelus Air Base. They nationalized the oil industry and many commercial interests that had been under US and British imperialist control. These military officers did not come to power in a revolutionary upheaval of the masses. It was not a socialist revolution. It was still a class society. But Libya was no longer under foreign domination.

Many progressive changes were carried out. New Libya made many economic and social gains. The conditions of life for the masses radically improved. Most basic necessities—food, housing, fuel, health care and education—were either heavily subsidized or became entirely free. Subsidies were used as the best way to redistribute the national wealth.

Conditions for women changed dramatically. Within 20 years Libya had the highest Human Development Index ranking in Africa—a UN measurement of life expectancy, educational attainment and adjusted real income. Through the 1970s and 1980s, Libya was internationally known for taking strong anti-imperialist positions and supporting other revolutionary struggles, from the African National Congress in South Africa to the Palestine Liberation Organization and the Irish Republican Army.

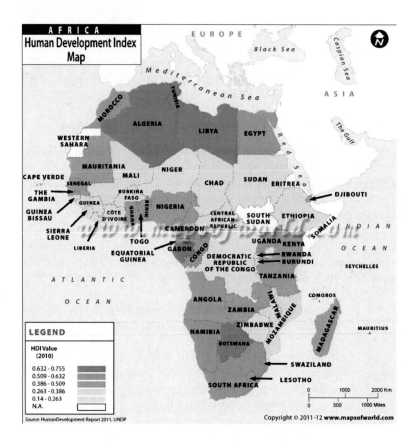

The US carried out numerous assassination and coup attempts against the Qaddafi regime and financed armed opposition groups, such as the NFSL. Some US attacks were blatant and open. For example, without warning 66 US jets bombed the Libyan capital of Tripoli and its second-largest city, Benghazi, on April 15, 1986. Qaddafi's home was bombed and his infant daughter killed in the attack, along with hundreds of others.

Throughout the 1980s and 1990s the US succeeded in isolating Libya through severe economic sanctions. Every effort was made to sabotage the economy and to destabilize the government.

Demonization of Qaddafi

It is up to the people of Libya, of Africa and of the Arab World to evaluate the contradictory role of Qaddafi, the chair of

Libya's Revolutionary Command Council. People here, in the center of an empire built on global exploitation, should not join in the racist characterizations, ridicule and demonization of Qaddafi that saturate the corporate media.

Even if Qaddafi were as quiet and austere as a monk and as careful as a diplomat, as president of an oil-rich, previously underdeveloped African country, he still would have been hated, ridiculed and demonized by US imperialism if he resisted US corporate domination. That was his real crime and for that he has never been forgiven.

It is important to note that degrading and racist terms are never used against reliable US pawns or dictators, regardless of how corrupt or ruthless they may be to their own people.

US Threats Force Concessions

It was after the US war crime billed as "shock and awe," with its massive aerial bombardment of Iraq followed by a ground invasion and occupation, that Libya finally succumbed to US demands. After decades of militant, anti-imperialist solidarity, Libya dramatically changed course. Qaddafi offered to assist the US in its "war on terror."

Washington's demands were onerous and humili-ating. Libya was forced to accept full responsibility for the downing of the Lockerbie aircraft and pay $2.7 billion in indemnities. That was just the beginning. In order for US sanctions to be lifted, Libya had to open its markets and "restructure" its economy. It was all part of the package.

Regardless of Qaddafi's many concessions and the subsequent grand receptions for him by European heads of state, US imperialism was planning his complete humiliation and downfall. US think tanks engaged in numerous studies of how to undermine and weaken Qaddafi's popular support.

IMF strategists descended on Libya with programs. The new economic advisors prescribed the same measures they impose on every developing country. But Libya did not have a foreign debt; it has a positive trade balance of $27 billion a year. The only reason the IMF demanded an end to subsidies of basic necessities was to undercut the social basis of support for the regime.

Libya 's "market liberalization" meant a cut in $5 billion worth of subsidies annually. For decades, the state had been subsidizing 93 percent of the value of several basic commodities, notably fuel. After accepting the IMF program, the government doubled the price of electricity for consumers. There was a sudden 30 percent hike in fuel prices. This touched off price increases in many other goods and services as well.

Libya was told to privatize 360 state-owned companies and enterprises, including steel mills, cement plants, engineering firms, food factories, truck and bus assembly lines and state farms. This left thousands of workers jobless.

Libya had to sell a 60-percent stake in the state-owned oil company Tamoil Group and privatize its General National Company for Flour Mills and Fodder.

The Carnegie Endowment Fund was already charting the impact of economic reforms. A 2005 report titled "Economic Reforms Anger Libyan Citizens" by Eman Wahby said that "Another aspect of structural reform was the end of restrictions on imports. Foreign companies were granted licenses to export to Libya through local agents. As a result, products from all over the world have flooded the previously isolated Libyan market." This was a disaster for workers in Libya's factories, which are unequipped to face competition.

More than $4 billion poured into Libya, which became Africa's top recipient of foreign investment. As the bankers and their think tanks knew so well, this did not benefit the Libyan masses, it impoverished them.

But no matter what Qaddafi did, it was never enough for US corporate power. The bankers and financiers wanted more. There was no trust. Qaddafi had opposed the US for decades and was still considered highly "unreliable."

The magazine *US Banker* in May 2005 ran an article titled "Emerging Markets: Is Libya the Next Frontier for US Banks?" It said that "As the nation passes reforms, profits beckon. But chaos abounds." It interviewed Robert Armao, president of the New York City-based US-Libya Trade and Economic Council: "All the big Western banks are now exploring opportunities there." said Armao. "The political situation with [Qaddafi] is still very suspect." The potential "looks wonderful for banks. Libya is a country untouched and a land of opportunity. It will happen, but it may take a little time."

Libya has never been a socialist country. There has always been extensive inherited wealth and old privileges. It is a class society with millions of workers, many of them immigrants.

Restructuring the economy to maximize profits for Western bankers destabilized relations, even in the ruling circles. Who gets in on the deals to privatize key industries, which families, which tribes? Who is left out? Old rivalries and competitions surfaced.

Just how carefully the US government was monit-oring these

imposed changes can be seen in recently released Wikileaks cables from the US Embassy in Tripoli, reprinted in the Britain-based *Telegraph* of Jan. 31. A cable titled "Inflation on the rise in Libya" and sent on Jan. 4, 2009, described the impact of "a radical program of privatization and government restructuring."

"Particular increases were seen," the cable said, "in prices for foodstuffs—the price of previously subsidized goods such as sugar, rice, and flour increased by 85 percent in the two years since subsidies were lifted. Construction materials have also increased markedly: prices for cement, aggregate, and bricks have increased by 65 percent in the past year. Cement has gone from 5 Libyan dinars for a 50-kilogram bag to 17 dinars in one year; the price of steel bars has increased by a factor of ten.

> The [Libyan government's] termination of subsidies and price controls as part of a broader program of economic reform and privatization has certainly contributed to inflationary pressures and prompted some grumbling. ...

> The combination of high inflation and diminishing subsidies and price controls is worrying for a Libyan public accustomed to greater government cushioning from market forces.

These US Embassy cables confirm that while continuing to maintain and finance Libyan opposition groups in Egypt, Washington and London were also constantly taking the temperature of the mass discontent caused by their policies.

Today millions of people in the US and around the world are deeply inspired by the actions of millions of youths in the streets of Egypt, Tunisia, Bahrain, Yemen and now Oman. The impact is felt even in the sit-in in Wisconsin.

It is vital for the US political and class-conscious movement to resist the enormous pressure of a US-orchestrated campaign for military intervention in Libya. A new imperialist adventure must be challenged. Solidarity with the peoples' movements! US hands off!

QADDAFI LYNCHED BY US-NATO

Abayomi Azikiwe*

Col. Muammar Qaddafi, leader of the Libyan people for 42 years, was brutally targeted, tortured and executed in a series of events on Oct. 20, 2011 in the coastal city of Sirte. The city had been a bastion of resistance to the US -NATO war in Libya.

Qaddafi, 69, was there directing resistance fighters who were defending the country against an imperialist-engineered civil war and bombing campaign. The war resulted in the deaths of tens of thousands of Libyans and other foreign nationals. The Libyan state and its supporters heroically held out for eight months in a struggle to reverse the counterrevolution financed and coordinated by the US -NATO governments.

Just two days prior to Qaddafi's assassination, US Secretary of State Hillary Clinton was in Libya, meeting with the "rebel" National Transitional Council regime and calling for his capture and, in flagrant contravention of international law, particularly as it concerns one whom the West had recognized as the leader of a sovereign state, his extra-judicial killing. There have been several attempts on Qaddafi's life since the beginning of the March 19 bombing campaign. Qaddafi's son and three grandchildren were killed in one of them, when their residence came under attack by imperialist warplanes. It has been reported that another one of Qaddafi's sons, Mo'tassim, was captured and executed, purportedly by the NTC rebels, on Oct. 20.

Stories reported by the NTC spokesperson illustrated the inherently dishonest character of the US-NATO rebels. They initially said Qaddafi was killed in a crossfire involving loyalist forces and the NTC rebels. However, this fabrication quickly evaporated when a video

*Slightly abridged from the original article published October 25, 2011 on Pan-African News Wire, <http://panafricannews.blogspot.ca/2011/10/gaddafi-assassinated-by-us-nato-lynch.html>

shot by someone in the lynch mob showed that Qaddafi was alive when apprehended and was killed.

Various reports indicate that the convoy Qaddafi was travelling in was tracked by a US Predator drone. Another account suggests that French Mirage fighter jets were also involved.

The video shows people who appear to be NTC rebels beating and torturing Qaddafi, we hear a series of gunshots and, later, see the dead body being thrown onto a truck. Those in the crowd cheer and celebrate at the carnage.

Again in contravention of Islamic law and international norms, Qaddafi's remains were put on display in a meat storage facility. People claiming to be rebellion supporters were allowed to view the body and take photographs. Qaddafi's remains were not turned over to his family for a proper burial within the time period required by his religious and cultural traditions.

A massive cover-up has since attempted to deflect responsibility for his death away from US imperialist forces and its collaborators in Libya. After international outrage over Qaddafi's assassination escalated, the UN, the US and the NTC client regime called for an investigation into the circumstances of his death

The US supported the anti-Qaddafi rebels for more than three decades. The UN Security Council voted to impose a so-called "no-fly zone" over Libya despite the fact that there was no evidence that alleged massacres had occurred in areas retaken by the government from the NTC forces.

The "no-fly zone" itself was a pretext to permit the commencement of total war against the state of Libya. A naval blockade was imposed by the NATO countries; more than $120 billion in foreign assets belonging to the government were frozen; the NTC rebels were armed, financed, promoted politically and given military cover by the US -NATO countries and their allies in the region; the Pentagon-NATO air and naval forces conducted more than 20,000 sorties and 9,500 bombings; and corporate-government media campaigns were conducted against the Libyan government to justify the deliberate destruction of the most prosperous country on the African continent.

Despite the objection of the 53-member African Union, the US -NATO states refused to negotiate and demanded that the government resign. The International Criminal Court in the Netherlands rushed to issue unsubstantiated charges and indictments against the Libyan leadership to further isolate the government amid a massive military invasion and bombing campaign.

Qaddafi's assassination must be viewed within the broader context of the atrocities engineered against the Libyan people by the

US -NATO alliance and their NTC rebels. A systematic racist campaign targeting Black Libyans and other Africans living and working inside the country has exposed the true nature of the opposition to Qaddafi.

Hundreds of dark-skinned people and other presumed and actual supporters of the Qaddafi government have been persecuted by the rebels. Numerous people have been beaten, tortured, driven out of their home towns and cities, imprisoned and lynched in the same fashion as Qaddafi and other high-ranking officials.

The US-NATO air campaign was specifically designed to destroy the national wealth and infrastructure of the country, which had achieved tremendous progress since the Al-Fateh Revolution of 1969 and the assumption of People's Power in 1977.

In the same city where Qaddafi was assassinated, a massacre of 53 pro-government supporters at a hotel was reported. According to Human Rights Watch, "The hotel is in an area of the city that was under the control of anti-Qaddafi fighters from Misrata before the killings took place." (Afrique en ligne, October 24)

HRW called upon the NTC to conduct an immediate investigation into the massacre. In a statement, HRW said: "We found 53 decomposing bodies, apparently Qaddafi supporters, at an abandoned hotel in Sirte, and some had their hands bound behind their backs when they were shot. ... This latest massacre seems part of a trend of killings, looting and other abuses committed by armed anti-Qaddafi fighters who consider themselves above the law."

Qaddafi's contributions to the African Revolution

Despite the imperialist-controlled media assertions that Qaddafi's rule was solely characterized by undemocratic processes, many throughout the world admired the leader and paid tribute.

Venezuelan President Hugo Chávez called the fallen leader a martyr who died a hero. The Global Alternative Agenda African youth organization, based in Nigeria, called Qaddafi's assassination "highly irresponsible, a breach of all international laws. It was barbaric and humiliating to all Africans. It must be condemned in the strongest terms." (GAA Statement)

The Zimbabwe state newspaper Sunday Mail said on Oct. 23: "Qaddafi's heroic last stand against NATO hegemony is a defining moment in this era of U.N.-backed imperialism. He could have fled Libya, but he did not. Col. Qaddafi chose to fight alongside his people in Libya, to his last breath. He stood his ground until the end, refusing to flee, choosing to be martyred on African soil."

The paper noted that "Qaddafi's legacy speaks for itself. He guaranteed the right to free education for everyone from elementary school right up to university and post-graduate studies, at home or abroad; free health care; 1:673 doctor-patient ratio, free electricity for all citizens; interest-free housing loans; and free land for farmers."

The African National Congress, the ruling party in South Africa that gained tremendous support from the people of Libya during and after their struggle for national liberation, said: "It is regrettable that the Libyan conflict ended with the gruesome killing of the Libyan Leader Muammar Qaddafi. ... We once again call on western countries under the command of NATO to stop the bombardment of Libya and its people." (ANC statement, Oct. 21)

A statement from the ANC Youth League calls Qaddafi an anti-imperialist martyr: "The ANCYL salutes Colonel Muammar Qaddafi, a brave soldier and fighter against the recolonization of the African continent. Brother Leader was ruthlessly killed by rebels armed by NATO forces who invaded Libya because of its natural resources. Brother Leader resisted imperialist domination of the African continent and never agreed to the continued draining of natural resources from beneath Africa's soil. He understood and appreciated that Africa's natural resources should be economically used to benefit the people of Africa."

In the East African state of Uganda, 30,000 people attended a memorial service in honor of Qaddafi. In Nigeria, a former militia leader said that the Libyan leader would be avenged...

Why Was Qaddafi killed?

Qaddafi was lynched in a vain attempt to end the resistance of the Libyan people against imperialist aggression. The extrajudicial killing is also designed to send a message to other opponents of imperialism in Africa, where the US and NATO states are intervening at a rapid rate.

Africa is increasingly supplying larger amounts of oil and other strategic resources to the US and Western European states. This attempt at regime change in Libya is also designed to impede the increasing cooperation between the People's Republic of China and the African continent.

If the social justice and anti-war movements inside the US and Europe are going to achieve any results aimed at ending militarism and austerity imposed by the banks and transnational corporations, they must seriously address the escalating imperialist aggression against the African continent, its people and leaders. The massacre of Libyan people and the attacks upon their government must be viewed by the oppressed peoples within the imperialist states as a setback to their struggles against low-wage capitalism and wars of occupation abroad.

ORCHESTRATING CONSENT TO REGIME CHANGE

(Photo courtesy of Mahdi Darius Nazemroaya)

THE BIG LIE AND LIBYA

USING HUMAN RIGHTS NGOS AND HUMANITARIANISM TO LAUNCH WARS

Mahdi Darius Nazemroaya

In the course of the war on Libya waged by the North Atlantic Treaty Organization (NATO) a series of human rights organizations and think-tanks were utilized for preparing the stage for the conflict in and the toppling of the Jamahiriya. These organizations were mostly part of a network that had been working to establish the mechanisms for justifying interventionism and creating the net of individuals needed for creating a proxy government in Libya. When the time came these bodies coordinated with the NATO powers and the mainstream media in the project to isolate, castrate, and subjugate the Libyan Arab Jamahiriya. These so-called human rights organizations and the media worked together to propagate the lies about African mercenaries, Libyan military jet attacks on civilians, and civilian massacres by Muammar Qaddafi. International news networks would quote these human rights organizations in what would amount to a self-fuelled cycle of misinformation, while the human rights organizations would then continue to make claims on the basis of the media's reports. This web of lies was presented at the Human Rights Council in the United Nations Office at Geneva and then presented to the United Nations Security Council in New York City as the basis for the war in Libya. These lies were accepted without any investigation being launched by the United Nations or any other international bodies. Any Libyan requests for international investigation teams were also ignored. It was from this point onward that NATO used the UN Security Council to launch its war of aggression against Libya under the pretext of protecting civilians and enforcing a no-fly zone over the country. Although not officially accepted by the United Nations Security Council, the "Responsibility to Protect" (R2P) doctrine was being showcased as a new paradigm for military intervention by NATO.

The Libyan League for Human Rights

One of the main sources for the claim that Qaddafi was killing his own people is the Libyan League for Human Rights (LLHR). The LLHR was actually pivotal to getting the UN involved through its specific claims in Geneva. On February 21, 2011 the LLHR got seventy other non-governmental organizations (NGOs) to send letters to President Obama, EU High Representative Catherine Ashton, and the UN Secretary-General Ban-ki Moon demanding international action against Libya and invoking the "Responsibility to Protect" doctrine. Only twenty-five members of this coalition actually assert that they are human rights groups.
The letter is as follows:

We, the undersigned non-governmental, human rights, and humanitarian organiza-tions, urge you to mobilize the United Nations and the international community and take immediate action to halt the mass atrocities now being perpetrated by the Libyan government against its own people.

The inexcusable silence cannot continue. As you know, in the past several days, Colonel Moammar Gadhafi's forces are estimated to have deliberately killed hundreds of peaceful protesters and innocent bystanders across the country. In the city of Benghazi alone, one doctor reported seeing at least 200 dead bodies. Witnesses report that a mixture of special commandos, foreign mercenaries and regime loyalists have attacked demonstrators with knives, assault rifles and heavy-caliber weapons.

Snipers are shooting peaceful protesters. Artillery and helicopter gunships have been used against crowds of demonstrators. Thugs armed with hammers and swords attacked families in their homes. Hospital officials report numerous victims shot in the head and chest, and one struck on the head by an anti-aircraft missile. Tanks are reported to be on the streets and crushing innocent bystanders. Witnesses report that mercenaries are shooting indiscriminately from helicopters and from the top of roofs. Women and children were seen jumping off Giuliana Bridge in Benghazi to escape. Many of them were killed by the impact of hitting the water, while others were drowned. The Libyan regime is seeking to hide all of these crimes by shutting off contact with the outside world. Foreign journalists have been refused entry. Internet and phone lines have been cut or disrupted.

There is no question here about intent. The government media has published open threats, promising that demonstrators would meet a "violent and thunderous response."

Accordingly, the government of Libya is committing gross and systematic violations of the right to life as guaranteed by the Universal Declaration of Human Rights and the International Covenant on Civil and Political Rights. Citizens seeking to exercise their rights to freedom of expression and freedom of assembly are being massacred by the government.

Moreover, the government of Libya is committing crimes against humanity, as defined by the Explanatory Memorandum to the Rome Statute of the International Criminal Court. The Libyan government's mass killing of innocent civilians amount to particularly odious offences which constitute a serious attack on human dignity. As confirmed by numerous oral and video testimonies gathered by human rights organizations and news agencies, the Libyan government's assault on its civilian population are not isolated or sporadic events. Rather, these actions constitute a widespread and systematic policy and practice of atrocities, intentionally committed, including murder, political persecution and other inhumane acts which reach the threshold of crimes against humanity.

Responsibility to Protect

*Under the 2005 World Summit Outcome Document, you
have a clear and unambiguous responsibility to protect
the people of Libya. The international community,
through the United Nations, has the responsibility to
use appropriate diplomatic, humanitarian and other
peaceful means, in accordance with Chapters VI and VIII
of the Charter, to help to protect the Libyan population.
Because the Libyan national authorities are manifestly
failing to protect their population from crimes against
humanity, should peaceful means be inadequate,
member states are obliged to take collective action,
in a timely and decisive manner, through the* **Security
Council,** *in accordance with the UN Charter, including
Chapter VII.*

In addition, **we urge you to convene an emergency
Special Session of the UN Human Rights Council,**
*whose members have a duty, under UNGA Resolution
60/251, to address situations of gross and systematic
violations of violations of human rights. The session
should:*

*—Call for the General Assembly to suspend Libya's
Council membership, pursuant to Article 8 of Resolution
60/251, which applies to member states that commit
gross and systematic violations of human rights.*

*—Strongly condemn, and demand an immediate end
to, Libya's massacre of its own citizens.*

*—Dispatch immediately an international mission
of independent experts to collect relevant facts and
document violations of international human rights
law and crimes against humanity, in order to end
the impunity of the Libyan government. The mission
should include an independent medical investigation
into the deaths, and an investigation of the unlawful
interference by the Libyan government with the access
to and treatment of wounded.*

*—Call on the UN High Commissioner of Human Rights
and the Council's relevant Special Procedures to closely
monitor the situation and take action as needed.*

—Call on the Council to remain seized of the matter and address the Libyan situation at its upcoming 16th regular session in March.

Member states and high officials of the United Nations have a responsibility to protect the people of Libya from what are preventable crimes. We urge you to use all available measures and levers to end atrocities throughout the country.

We urge you to send a clear message that, collectively, the international community, the Security Council and the Human Rights Council will not be bystanders to these mass atrocities. The credibility of the United Nations—and many innocent lives—are at stake.[1]

The letter's signatories included Francis Fukuyama, B'nai B'rith Human Rights Commission, the Cuban Democratic Directorate, and a set of organizations at odds with the governments of Nicaragua, Cuba, Sudan, Russia, Venezuela, and Libya. Some of these organizations are viewed with hostility as organizations created to wage demonization campaigns against countries at odds with the US, Israel, and the European Union.

According to Physicians for Human Rights:

[This letter] prepared under the guidance of Mohamed Eljahmi, the noted Libyan human rights defender and brother of dissident Fathi Eljahmi, asserts that the widespread atrocities committed by Libya against its own people amount to war crimes, requiring member states to take action through the Security Council under the responsibility to protect doctrine.[2]

LLHR is tied to the International Federation for Human Rights (FIDH), which is based in France and has ties to the National Endowment for Democracy (NED). FIDH is active in many places in Africa and in activities involving the National Endowment for Democracy in the African continent. Both the FIDH and LLHR also released a joint communiqué on February 21, 2011. In the communiqué both organizations asked for the international community to "mobilize" and mention the International Criminal Court while also making a contradictory claim that over 400 to 600 people had died since February 15, 2011.[3] This was about 5,500 short of the claim that 6,000 people were massacred in Benghazi and the rest of the Libyan Arab Jamahiriya. The joint letter also promoted the false view that 80% of the late Colonel Qaddafi's support came from foreign mercenaries, which is something that over half a year of fighting proves as untrue.

According to the General-Secretary of the LLHR, Dr. Sliman Bouchuiguir, when he was challenged for proof in Geneva, the claims about the massacres in Benghazi could not be validated by the LLHR. When asked how a group of seventy non-governmental organizations in Geneva could support the LLHR's claims in Geneva without it having proof of its assertions, Dr. Buchuiguir answered that a network of close relationships was the basis for this support. This is highly improper and makes a mockery of the international NGO consultation process. Speculation is neither evidence nor grounds for starting a war with a bombing campaign that has lasted about half a year and taken many innocent civilian lives, including children and the elderly. What is important to note here is that the UN Security Council decided to sanction the Libyan Arab Jamahiriya on the basis of this letter and the claims of the LLHR. Not once did the UN Security Council and the member states pushing for war bother to even investigate the allegations. In one session in New York City, the Indian Ambassador to the UN actually pointed this out when his country abstained from voting. Thus, a so-called "humanitarian war" was launched without any evidence.

The organization UN Watch which actively promoted the LLHR statement is known to look out for Israel's best interests and according to Israeli sources organized the entire session against the Libyan Arab Jamahiriya. It also pressured the UN to prevent it from releasing a positive report about human rights in Libya that was about to be released. UN Watch also has informal ties to the US Department of State and was established during the time of the Clinton Administration in 1993 under the Chairmanship of Morris B. Abram, a former US Permanent Representative to the United Nations in Geneva. Moreover, UN Watch is formally affiliated with the American Jewish Committee (AJC), a powerful pro-Israeli political lobby organization based in New York City.

The Secret Relationship between the LLHR and the Transitional Council

The claims of the Libyan League for Human Rights (LLHR) were coordinated with the formation of the Transitional Council. This becomes clear when the close and cagey relationship of the LLHR and the Transitional Council becomes apparent. Logically, the Obama Administration and NATO also had to be a part of this. Whatever the Transitional Council is and whatever the intent of some of its supporters, it is clear that it was used as a tool by the US and other foreign governments. Moreover, key members of the LLHR were or would become members of the Transitional Council almost immediately after the claims against the Libyan Arab Jamahiriya were disseminated.

According to Bouchuguir, individuals with ties to the LLHR or who hold membership include Mahmoud Jibril and Ali Tarhouni.

Dr. Mahmoud Jibril is a Libyan regime figure brought into Libyan government circles by Saif Al-Islam Qaddafi. He would undemocratically be given the position of Transitional Council prime minister. Although not a member, Jibril's involvement with the LLHR raises some real questions about any purported objectivity on the part of this organization.

The alignment of economist Ali Tarhouni, on the other hand, who would become the minister for oil and finance for the Transitional Council, is transparent: Tarhouni is Washington's man in Libya. He was groomed in the United States and was present at all the major meetings about plans for regime change in Libya. As Minister of Oil and Finance the first acts he undertook were to privatize and virtually hand over Libya's energy resources and economy to the foreign corporations and governments of the NATO-led coalition against Libya.

The General-Secretary of the LLHR, Sliman Bouchuiguir, has even privately admitted that many influential members of the Transitional Council are his friends. A real question of their private interests arises. But the secret relationship between the LLHR and the Transitional Council is far more than a question of conflict of interest. It is a question of justice and manipulation, and indeed, of the legitimacy of the NATO military action against Libya and more generally, of the R2P project of humanitarian intervention, overall.

Who is Sliman Bouchuiguir?

Sliman Bouchuguir, a dual citizen of Libya and Switzerland, is an unheard of figure for most, but he has authored a doctoral thesis that has been widely quoted and used in strategic circles in the United States. This thesis was published in 1979 as a book, *The Use of Oil as a Political Weapon: A Case Study of the 1973 Arab Oil Embargo*. The thesis is about the use of oil as an economic weapon by Arabs, but can easily be applied to its use by the Russians, the Iranians, the Venezuelans, and others. It examines economic development and economic warfare and can also be applied to vast regions, including all of Africa.

Bouchuguir's analytical thesis reflects an important line of thinking in Washington, as well as in London and Tel Aviv. It is both the embodiment of a pre-existing mentality, which includes US National Security Advisor George F. Kennan's arguments for maintaining a position of disparity through a constant multi-faceted war between the US and its allies on one hand and the rest of the world on the other hand. The thesis can be drawn on for preventing the Arabs, or others, from becoming economic powers or threats. In strategic terms, rival economies are pinned as threats and as "weapons." This has serious connotations.

Moreover, Bouchuiguir did his thesis at George Washington University under Bernard Reich, a political scientist and professor of international relations who has worked and held positions at places like the US Defense Intelligence College, the United States Air Force Special Operations School, the Marine Corps War College, and the Shiloah Center at Tel Aviv University. He has consulted on the Middle East for the Foreign Service Institute of the US State Department and received grants such as the Defense Academic Research Support Program Research Grant and the German Marshall Fund Grant. Reich also was or is presently on the editorial boards of journals such as *Israel Affairs* (1994-present), *Terrorism: An International Journal* (1987-1994), and *The New Middle East* (1971-1973).

It is also clear that Reich is tied to Israeli interests. He has even written a book about the special relationship between the US and Israel. He has also been an advocate for a "New Middle East" which would be favourable to Israel. This includes careful consideration of North Africa. His work has also focused on the important strategic interface between the Soviet Union and the Middle East, and also on Israeli policy in the continent of Africa.

It is clear why Bouchuiguir had his thesis supervised by Reich. On October 23, 1973, Reich gave testimony to the US Congress titled "The Impact of the October Middle East War," which was clearly tied to the 1973 oil embargo and Washington's aim of pre-empting or managing any similar events in the future. It has to be asked, how much did Reich influence Bouchuiguir and whether Bouchuiguir espouses the same strategic views as Reich? Later, on September 29, 2011, Bouchiguir would be rewarded for his part in the plot at the UN in Geneva by being appointed the new Libyan ambassador to Switzerland in Bern.

The Orwellian Responsibility to Protect (R2P): Libya Déjà Vu in Syria

R2P was not used in Libya, but it was mentioned a lot. The frequent mentioning of R2P served as a trial run for future wars under its aegis, and also as a threat—now directed at the Syrian Arab Republic. What has stood in the way of R2P being used against Syria are the Chinese and the Russians at the UN Security Council and an Iranian threat to go to war with any country that attacks its Syrian ally.

R2P is being prepped to be wielded as a weapon by Washington and the Atlantic Alliance. It is a neo-imperialist device in sheepskin cover that appropriates the language of humanitarianism. Where is R2P against Israel in Palestine or when Tel Aviv attacked Lebanon in 2006? Where is R2P against the foreign-imposed dictators of Bahrain and Saudi Arabia as they kill their citizens in front of the whole world? Where is R2P when it comes to the brutal Moroccan occupation of Western Sahara? Where was R2P in Rwanda? These are all places where R2P will never even come to be mentioned, because it is against the interests of the United States and its allies to intervene.

R2P is a diplomatic concept constructed in Canada by the Department of Foreign Affairs and International Trade (DFAIT) through the International Commission on Intervention and State Sovereignty (ICISS) in 2000. The concept essentially posits that a country's independence is not a right and can be taken away by the international community when the need arises. The international community under the R2P paradigm has the responsibility to intervene in any independent country in order to protect that country's citizens. This subject brings a whole series of questions into mind. Who can decide when to use R2P? Also, what is this "international community" that gives these actions legitimacy and what countries form this international community? How is the international community defined and who defines it?

The international community is much more than the countries of NATO and the dictatorial Arab petro-sheikhdoms in the Persian Gulf. Clearly, most of the world was against the Anglo-American invasion of Iraq in 2003, but Washington and London claimed that the "international community" was on their side. The term "international community" is actually a grossly misrepresented concept and term. Washington continuously gets a series of small states that are virtual dependencies and satellites or unrepresentative governments to add their names to all the lists it constantly produces for its military coalitions and initiatives, and calls them the "international community." These lists on the surface can sound impressive, but in reality they are hollow mirages meant to produce a deceiving appearance of international support and consensus. It is a smokescreen and part of a grand illusion. For example, Washington's "Coalition of the Willing," which was forged to invade Iraq in 2003 included Columbia, NATO-occupied Afghanistan's Hamid Karzai, Georgia, El Salvador, and Iceland. If not US satellites, the governments of these countries were either bribed or coerced into joining against the wishes of their populations.

Both universities and civil society in the form of NGOs inside NATO countries have a big role to play in the dissemination of the R2P paradigm. They are pushing for its normalization in international relations and its use in Syria. Together with the recognition of the unrepresentative Syrian National Council (SNC) and the mirage of Arab legitimacy provided by the undemocratic collection of GCC despots that have hijacked the Arab League, R2P will be utilized to create an international legal regime that will work to isolate, cripple, and subjugate the Syria. At the same time, under the mask of human rights, organizations like the Syrian Observatory for Human Rights, which has absurdly saluted the King of Saudi Arabia as a democrat, are propagating a wide series of lies about the events in Syrian Arab Republic.

The War in Libya is a Fraud
That Has Opened the Doors of Africa

A "New Africa" is in the works, which will have its borders redrawn in blood like in the past. The Obama Administration and its allies have opened the gateway for a new invasion of Africa. United States Africa Command (AFRICOM) opened the salvos of the war through Operation Odyssey Dawn, before the war on Libya was transferred to NATO's Operation Unified Protector. The US has used NATO to continue the occupation of post-Second World War Europe. It will now use AFRICOM to occupy Africa and create an African NATO. It is clear the US wants an expanded military presence in Libya and Africa under the disguise of humanitarian aid missions and fighting terrorism—the same terrorism that it is actually fanning in Libya and Africa vis-à-vis its policies in the African continent.

The way is being paved for more intervention in Africa under the guise of fighting terrorism. General Carter Ham has stated: "If we were to launch a humanitarian operation, how do we do so effectively with air traffic control, airfield management, [and] those kind of activities?"[4] General Ham's question is actually a sales pitch for fashioning African military partnerships and integration, as well as new bases that could include the use of more military drones against Libya and other African countries. The *Washington Post* and the *Wall Street Journal* have both made it clear that the Pentagon is actively trying to establish more drone bases in Africa and the Arabian Peninsula to expand its wars.[5] In this context, the AFRICOM Commander says that there are ties between the Al-Shabaab in Somalia, Al-Qaeda in the Islamic Maghreb in North Africa, and the Boko Harem in Nigeria.[6]

During the war General Ham stated: "I remain confident that had the UN not made the decision, had the US not taken the lead with great support, I'm absolutely convinced there are many, many people in Benghazi alive today who would not be [alive]."[7] This is not true and a far stretch from reality. The war has cost more lives than it could have ever saved. It has ruined a country and opened the door into Africa for a neo-colonial project.

There were no jet attacks by the Libyan military on civilians, and long after this has become widely known, the media and NATO have remained silent about this. Nor were the stories about mercenaries from sub-Saharan Africa true. In grossly racist terms black-skinned Libyans in their country's national military and security forces were vilified and presented to the outside world as foreigners in their own country. Moreover, the claims of the Libyan League for Human Rights (LLHR) were never supported or verified. The credibility of the United Nations must be questioned as well as the credibility of many humanitarian and human rights organizations that have virtually pushed for a war. The using of human rights as pretext via NGOs in Geneva has set a precedent that endangers the credibility of human rights organizations and NGOs. In regard to the UN Security Council, at best the UN body is irresponsible, but it has clearly acted outside of due legal process and the spirit and intent of the UN Charter. This pattern now appears to be repeating itself against the Syrian Arab Republic as unverified claims are being made by individuals and organizations supported by foreign powers that care nothing for authentic democratic reforms or liberty.

ANNEX
SIGNATORIES OF THE URGENT GENEVA LETTER
FOR ACTION ON LIBYA

February 12, 2011 – Geneva, Switzerland

1. Hillel C. Neuer, United Nations Watch, Switzerland
2. Dr. Sliman Bouchuiguir, Libyan League for Human Rights, Switzerland
3. Mary Kay Stratis, Victims of Pan Am Flight 103, Inc., USA
4. Carl Gershman, President, The National Endowment for Democracy, USA
5. Yang Jianli, Initiatives for China, USA - Former prisoner of conscience and survivor of Tiananmen Square massacre
6. Yang Kuanxing, YIbao - Chinese writer, original signatory to Charter 08, the manifesto calling for political reform in China
7. Matteo Mecacci, MP, Nonviolent Radical Party, Italy
8. Frank Donaghue, Physicians for Human Rights, USA
9. Nazanin Afshin-Jam, Stop Child Executions, Canada
10. Bhawani Shanker Kusum, Gram Bharati Samiti, India
11. G. Jasper Cummeh, III, Actions for Genuine Democratic Alternatives, Liberia
12. Michel Monod, International Fellowship of Reconciliation, Switzerland
13. Esohe Aghatise, Associazione Iroko Onlus, Italy
14. Harris O. Schoenberg, UN Reform Advocates, USA
15. Myrna Lachenal, World Federation for Mental Health, Switzerland
16. Nguyên Lê Nhân Quyên, Vietnamese League for Human Rights, Switzerland
17. Sylvia G. Iriondo, Mothers and Women against Repression (M.A.R. Por Cuba), USA
18. David Littman, World Union for Progressive Judaism, Switzerland

19. Barrister Festus Okoye, Human Rights Monitor, Nigeria
20. Theodor Rathgeber, Forum Human Rights, Germany
21. Derik Uya Alfred, Kwoto Cultural Center, Juba – Southern Sudan
22. Carlos E Tinoco, Consorcio Desarrollo y Justicia, A.C., Venezuela
23. Abdurashid Abdulle Abikar, Center for Youth and Democracy, Somalia
24. Dr. Vanee Meisinger, Pan Pacific and South East Asia Women's Association, Thailand
25. Simone Abel, René Cassin, United Kingdom
26. Dr. Francois Ullmann, Ingenieurs du Monde, Switzerland
27. Sr Catherine Waters, Catholic International Education Office, USA
28. Gibreil Hamid, Darfur Peace and Development Centre, Switzerland
29. Nino Sergi, INTERSOS – Humanitarian Aid Organization, Italy
30. Daniel Feng, Foundation for China in the 21st Century
31. Ann Buwalda, Executive Director, Jubilee Campaign, USA
32. Leo Igwe, Nigerian Humanist Movement, Nigeria
33. Chandika Gautam, Nepal International Consumers Union, Nepal
34. Zohra Yusuf, Human Rights Commission of Pakistan, Pakistan
35. Sekou Doumbia, Femmes & Droits Humains, Mali
36. Cyrille Rolande Bechon, Nouveaux Droits de l'Homme, Cameroon
37. Zainab Al-Suwaij, American Islamic Congress, USA
38. Valnora Edwin, Campaign for Good Governance, Sierra Leone
39. Patrick Mpedzisi, African Democracy Forum, South Africa
40. Phil ya Nangoloh, NamRights, Namibia
41. Jaime Vintimilla, Centro Sobre Derecho y Sociedad (CIDES), Ecuador
42. Tilder Kumichii Ndichia, Gender Empowerment and Development, Cameroon
43. Amina Bouayach, Moroccan Organisation for Human Rights, Morocco
44. Abdullahi Mohamoud Nur, CEPID-Horn Africa, Somalia
45. Delly Mawazo Sesete, Research Center on Environment, Democracy & Human Rights, DR Congo
46. Joseph Rahall, Green Scenery, Sierra Leone
47. Arnold Djuma, Solidarité pour la Promotion Sociale et la Paix, Rwanda
48. Panayote Dimitras, Greek Helsinki Monitor, Greece
49. Carlos E. Ponce, Latina American and Caribbean Network for Democracy, Venezuela
50. Fr. Paul Lansu, Pax Christi International, Belgium
51. Tharsika Pakeerathan, Swiss Council of Eelam Tamils, Switzerland
52. Ibrahima Niang, Commission des Droits Humains du Mouvement Citoyen, Senegal
53. Virginia Swain, Center for Global Community and World Law, USA
54. Dr Yael Danieli, International Society for Traumatic Stress Studies, USA
55. Savita Gokhale, Loksadhana, India
56. Hasan Dheeree, Biland Awdal Organization, Somalia
57. Pacifique Nininahazwe, Forum pour le Renforcement de la Société Civile, Burundi
58. Derik Uya Alfred, Kwoto Cultural Center, Southern Sudan
59. Michel Golubnichy, International Association of Peace Foundations, Russia
60. Edward Ladu Terso, Multi Media Training Center, Sudan
61. Hafiz Mohammed, Justice Africa Sudan, Sudan
62. Sammy Eppel, B'nai B'rith Human Rights Commission, Venezuela
63. Jack Jeffery, International Humanist and Ethical Union, United Kingdom
64. Duy Hoang, Viet Tan, Vietnam

65. Promotion de la Democratie et Protection des Droits Humains, DR Congo
66. Radwan A. Masmoudi, Center for the Study of Islam & Democracy, USA
67. María José Zamora Solórzano, Movimiento por Nicaragua, Nicaragua
68. John Suarez, Cuban Democratic Directorate, USA
69. Mohamed Abdul Malek, Libya Watch, United Kingdom
70. Journalists Union of Russia, Russia
71. Sindi Medar-Gould, BAOBAB for Women's Human Rights, Nigeria
72. Derik Uya Alfred, Kwoto Cultural Centre, Sudan
73. Sr. Anne Shaym, Presentation Sisters, Australia
74. Joseph Rahad, Green Scenery, Sierra Leone
75. Fahma Yusuf Essa, Women in Journalism Association, Somalia
76. Hayder Ibrahim Ali, Sudanese Studies Center, Sudan
77. Marcel Claude Kabongo, Good Governance and Human Rights NGO, DR Congo
78. Frank Weston, International Multiracial Shared Cultural Organization (IMSCO), USA
79. Fatima Alaoui, Maghrebin Forum for environment and development, Morocco
80. Ted Brooks, Committee for Peace and Development Advocacy, Liberia
81. Felly Fwamba, Cerveau Chrétien, DR Congo
82. Jane Rutledge, CIVICUS: World Alliance of Citizen Participation, South Africa
83. Ali Al Ahmed, The Institute for Gulf Affairs, USA
84. Daniel Ozoukou, Martin Luther King Center for Peace and Social Justice, Cote d'Ivoire
85. Dan T. Saryee, Liberia Democratic Institute (LDI), Liberia
   Individuals
   Dr. Frene Ginwala, former Speaker of the South African National Assembly
   Philosopher Francis Fukuyama
   Mohamed Eljahmi, Libyan human rights activist
   Glenn P. Johnson, Jr., Treasurer, Victims of Pan Am Flight 103,

ENDNOTES

1   United Nations Watch *et al.*, "Urgent Appeal to Stop Atrocities in Libya: Sent by 70 NGOs to the US, EU, and UN," February 21, 2011:<http://www.unwatch.org/site/apps/nlnet/content2.aspx?c=bdKKISNqEmG&b=1330815&ct=9135143>

2   Physicians for Human Rights, "PHR and Human Rights Groups Call for Immediate Action in Libya," February 22, 2011:<http://physiciansforhumanrights.org/press/press-releases/news-2011-02-22-libya.html>

3   The International Federation for Human Rights (FIDH) and the Libyan League for Human Rights (LLHR), "Massacres in Libya: The international community must urgently," respond, February 21, 2011: <http://www.fidh.org/IMG/article_PDF/article_a9183.pdf>

4   Jim Garamone, "Africa Command Learns from Libya Operations," American Forces Press Service, September 15, 2011:<http://www.defense.gov/ news/ newsarticle.aspx?id=65344&reason=1>

5   Gregory Miller and Craig Whitlock, "US US assembling secret drone bases in Africa, Arabian Peninsula, officials say," *The Washington Post,* September 20, 2011; Julian E. Barnes, "US Expands Drone Flights to Take Aim at East Africa," *The Wall Street Journal* (WSJ), September 21, 2011.

6   Garamone, "Africa Command Learns," *cit.*

7   *Ibid.*

WAS THE CASE FOR R2P BASED ON FRAUD?

THE UNIVERSAL PERIODIC REVIEW OF LIBYA

unanimously adopted March 14, 2012

Julien Teil*

UPR History and Human Rights Commission Reform

The Universal Periodic Review (UPR) was set up in 2006 following the creation of the Human Rights Council. The Council was created in response to claims that the Commission it replaced had been too political. Western states and members of the non-aligned movement shared this analysis.

However, disagreement soon broke out about the new Council too. Israel has been the object of numerous resolutions passed in the Council and in March 2012, Israel announced it was suspending all cooperation with it. This was in spite of the original plan, supported by the Americans, to make the new Council less hostile to Tel Aviv.

Initially the USA, which had been very critical of the previous Commission on Human Rights, was skeptical about the new Council. It boycotted it until the election of Barack Obama in 2009. Since then, and with the support of the American Jewish Committee and UN Watch, it has been fully engaged in the work of the Council. In some respects, indeed, the Council is seen by some in the US administration as a way of fighting multi-polarity.

Nonaligned states welcomed the reform but were afraid that the new Council would prove be a new tool in the hands of strong States

*A report by the Centre for the Study of Interventionism (CSI) www. interventionism.info

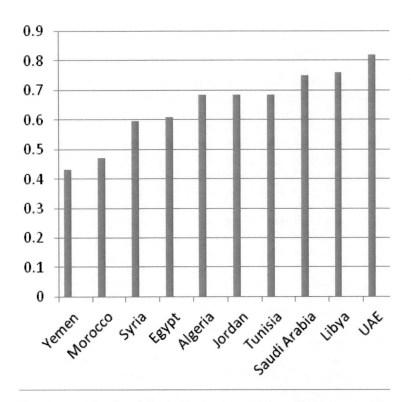

The Human Development Index is an annual ranking produced by the United Nations Development Program used to measure general well-being, and also to measure the impact of economic policies on quality of life. Based on the following rankings from the UNDP's 2011 Index, three of the four countries at the center of the Spring rank the lowest in MENA, while Saudi Arabia, Libya, and the UAE rank highest. (Source: http://en.wikipedia.org/wiki/List_of_countries_by_Human_Development_Index)

acting against weak ones. Nonaligned states and large states like Russia and China have attacked the interventionist tendencies of the new Council.

Three mechanisms contained in General Assembly Resolution 60/251, which instituted the Human Rights Council, turned out to be decisive in the Libyan case. It stated that the General Assembly:

> Paragraph 1. Decides to establish the Human Rights Council, based in Geneva, in replacement of the

Commission on Human Rights, as a subsidiary organ of the General Assembly; the Assembly shall review the status of the Council within five years;

Paragraph 8. Decides that the membership in the Council shall be open to all States Members of the United Nations; when electing members of the Council, Member States shall take into account the contribution of candidates to the promotion and protection of human rights and their voluntary pledges and commitments made thereto; the General Assembly, by a two-thirds majority of the members present and voting, may suspend the rights of membership in the Council of a member of the Council that commits gross and systematic violations of human rights;

Paragraph 10. Decides further that the Council shall meet regularly throughout the year and schedule no fewer than three sessions per year, including a main session, for a total duration of no less than ten weeks, and shall be able to hold special sessions, when needed, at the request of a member of the Council with the support of one third of the membership of the Council

The Universal Periodic Review (UPR) emerged out of the 2005 UN reform process. The UPR periodically examines the human rights performance of all 193 UN Member States. HRC Resolution 5/1 of 18 June 2007 and HRC decision 6/102 of 27 September 2007 elaborated the UPR's operation. HRC resolution 5/1 provides that the UPR should be a tool to question States regarding their Human Rights records.

Responsibility to Protect or Right to Interfere in Libya?

24 October 2005: The General Assembly votes to adopt the conclusions of the World Summit. This document, which is 38 pages long, contains two sentences which can be interpreted as providing the legal basis for a "responsibility to protect"

On 26 February and 17 March 2011, the UN Security Council votes two resolutions on Libya. The first refers the situation in Libya to the International Criminal Court, even though Libya is not a signatory state to the ICC's Rome statute. The second authorizes states to use "all necessary measures", i.e. military force, to "protect civilians" and to impose a no-fly zone.

The Libyan case provides a very good example of interference in the internal affairs of a sovereign state.

An armed opposition movement was supported from abroad and quickly recognised as the legitimate government without reference to the sovereign process inside Libya. Claims made before the Human Rights Council about massacres of civilians, later shown to be based on no evidence, were used to justify the Security Council and General Assembly resolutions.

NGOs and others invoked the responsibility to protect. But what responsibility do these bodies, and the states which use military force, bear for the consequences of their acts?

Facts Inside the Council

In May 2010, elections to the Human Rights Council took place: 47 states were elected on the basis of regional quotas. The NGOs Freedom House and UN Watch campaigned against the election of Libya but Libya was elected. UN Watch then started its campaign to get Libya expelled from the Council. It achieved its goal on 1 March 2011, when the General Assembly voted to expel the country - the first time such a decision was ever taken. The Universal Periodic Review of human rights in Libya, published on 4 January 2011, was never taken into consideration when this decision was made.

On 21 February 21, 2011 the Libyan League for Human Rights induced 70 other NGOs to send letters to President Obama, the EU High Representative, Catherine Ashton, and the UN Secretary-General, Ban Ki-moon, demanding international action against Libya and invoking the "responsibility to protect" doctrine. Only 25 members of this coalition actually assert that they are human rights groups. The signatories included Francis Fukuyama, UN Watch, the National Endowment for Democracy, B'nai B'rith Human Rights Commission, the Cuban Democratic Directorate, and a set of organizations at odds with the governments of Nicaragua, Cuba, Sudan, Russia, Venezuela, and Libya. The letter urged the following:

> We urge you to convene an emergency Special Session of the UN Human Rights Council, whose members have a duty, under UNGA Resolution 60/251, to address situations of gross and systematic violations of violations of human rights. The session should:
>
> —Call for the General Assembly to suspend Libya's Council membership, pursuant to Article 8 of Resolution 60/251, which applies to member states that commit gross and systematic violations of human rights.[1]

On 23 February 2011, Hungary, on behalf of the European Union, requested the convening of a special session of the Council on 25 February 2011 to address the situation of human rights in the Libyan Arab Jamahiriya. As required in Resolution 60/251, the request was supported by more than one third of the membership of the Council with 23 states.

The 15th Special Session took place on 25 February 2011 and hosted NGOs to hear their remarks and claims.

One of the main statements of the Session was that of Sliman Bouchuiguir, Secretary General of the Libyan League for Human Rights (LLHR). LLHR is a member organization of the International Federation for Human Rights (FIDH), which is based in France and which has ties to the National Endowment for Democracy (NED). FIDH is active in many places in Africa in cooperation with NED. The FIDH, has received direct funding, in the form of grants, from the National Endowment for Democracy for its programmes in Africa. In 2010, a NED grant of $140,186 (US) was one of the latest amounts given to the FIDH for its work in Africa.

Both the FIDH and LLHR also released a joint communiqué on 21 February 2011 in which they called on the international community to "mobilize" over Libya. They called for involvement by the International Criminal Court while claiming that 400 to 600 people had died since 15 February 2011. This was approximately 5,500 fewer than their later claim that 6,000 people had been massacred in Benghazi. The joint letter also promoted the false view that 80% of Gaddafi's military force was composed of foreign mercenaries, something which over half a year of fighting proved was untrue.

All these allegations were repeated in Bouchuiguir's statement to the 15th Special Session on 25 February, as was the call to have the situation taken up by the Security Council and the ICC, and to expel the Libyan Arab Jamahiriya from the Council.

In July 2011, Bouchuiguir admitted that those allegations were undocumented. He said they had come from the Transitional National Council. He also added that at least 3 members of the TNC were also members of the Libyan League for Human Rights.[2]

Resolution S-15/1, calling for Libya to be expelled from the Council by referring the case to the General Assembly, was adopted without a vote.

Recalling its resolution 60/251 of 15 March 2006, in particular paragraph 8, which states that the General Assembly may suspend the rights of membership in the Human Rights Council of a member of the Council that commits gross and systematic violations of human rights, the General Assembly decided to suspend the right of membership in the Human Rights Council of the Libyan Arab Jamahiriya with more than two third of the required votes to act. States such as Nicaragua and Russia were very concerned by this vote and expressed their fear regarding the procedure.

Libya's UPR: UN Watch's Fight

A member of the Council since its election in May 2010, Libya had been under the Universal Periodic Review process since November 2010. The Human Rights Council had been monitoring the human rights situation inside Libya until the process launched by UN Watch, the National Endowment for Democracy and the FIDH led to Libya's expulsion.

The Report on Libya was to have been adopted on 18 March 2011. Instead Libya was expelled on the basis of unproven claims by NGOs. Unlike those allegations, the UPR on Libya contained different views:

- Brazil noted the Libyan Arab Jamahiriya's economic and social progress and acknowledged the promotion of the rights of persons with disabilities, the free health care and the high enrolment in primary education. Brazil noted the successful cooperation with international organizations in areas such as migrant rights, judicial reform and the fight against corruption.

- Malta fully recognized the difficulties faced by the Libyan Arab Jamahiriya and welcomed the action taken at the national, bilateral and regional levels to suppress the illegal activities that gave rise to migration. Malta welcomed the cooperation of the Libyan Arab Jamahiriya with the International Organization for Migration.

- Tunisia welcomed [Libya's] national report, as well as the efforts of the National Committee, such as the website created to gather contributions. Tunisia noted progress made by the Libyan Arab Jamahiriya, such as the adoption of the Great Green Charter, which was very comprehensive and domestically enshrined fundamental freedoms and rights in Libya as they were enshrined in international human rights instruments.

UN Watch anticipated the UPR report on Libya and started on 28 February 2011 to request its cancellation by sending a letter on behalf of the Global NGO Campaign to Remove Libya from the Council created in September 2010. UN Watch was founded in 1993 by Morris Abram (1918-2000) when he was Honorary President of the American Jewish Committee

Thanks to Hillel Neuer, Chairman of UN Watch, on 1 March 2011 the Human Rights Council cancelled the consideration of the UPR report praising Libya's human rights record, which had been scheduled for 18 March, and the report's scheduled adoption by a council resolution the following week. The decision was welcomed by Eileen Chamberlain Donahoe, the US ambassador to the Human Rights Council.

On 3 March 2011, the House Foreign Affairs Committee opening statement was delivered by US Congressman Howard L. Berman. He praised UN Watch's moves inside the Council :"Hillel Neuer of the UN Watch [is] one of the strongest and most informed critics of the Human Rights Council..." [3]

The 19th Session of the Council took place from 27 February 2012 to 23 March 2012. Libya's UPR, ignored until now, was adopted on 14 March 2012. UN Watch challenged this decision but it went ahead.

Despite the protest of UN Watch, the Council finally adopted UNHRC's report praising the Libyan Arab Jamahiriya on 14 March 2012. UN Watch immediately called "on the Council president to acknowledge that the Council's review of the Qaddafi regime's record was a fraud, withdraw the report, and schedule a new session in which Council members would tell the truth about the Qaddafi regime's heinous crimes, which were committed over four decades yet ignored by the UN," said Neuer. "Libya's long-suffering victims deserve no less."

Suzanne Nossel, the new head of Amnesty USA, and previously the Obama Administration's Deputy Assistant Secretary of State for International Organizations, where she was responsible for US Engagement at the UN Human Rights Council, described the Council's report as "abhorrent" and called for a complete "redo."

Nevertheless the report was unanimously adopted.

In October 2011, Sliman Bouchuiguir was appointed the new Libyan ambassador to Switzerland. On 21 November 2011, the UN General Assembly voted to end Libya's suspension from the UN Human Rights Council.

Media Interference & NGO Communication

On 21 February 2011, the French International News Network, France 24, which is under the responsibility of the French Ministry of Foreign Affairs, broadcast a special News Show about the events in Libya. The News presenter spoke for the first time of Libyan's army planes bombing civilians in Libya, an claim which was later refuted by the French ambassador to Tripoli in a hearing in the French parliament.

At the same time, the allegations of "African mercenaries" was made. Genevieve Garrigos, head of Amnesty International in France, lent credence to these claims.

But in an interview in July 2011, Geneviève Garrigos admiited that this information "was just a rumour spread by the media".[4]

Ashur Shamis is one of the founding members of the National Front for the Salvation of Libya, which in 1981 was created in Sudan. He had been wanted by Interpol and the Libyan police for years. Ahsur has been a director of the National Endowment for Democracy in the Libyan Human and Political Development Forum. He is Editor of the Akhbar webpage, which was registered under Akhbar Cultural Limited and tied to the NED. He has also participated in key conferences for regime change in Tripoli. This includes the conference in London held by Chatham House in 2011, which discussed NATO plans for the invasion of Tripoli.[5]

The National Endowment for Democracy spent $183,900 in 2010 for its three NGOS in Libya: Akhbar Libya Cultural Limited, Transparency Libya Limited, and Libya Human and Political Development Forum. The three NGOs were registered in London.

Aly Abuzaakouk is also a member of the National Front for the Salvation of Libya and tied to the National Endowment for Democracy. He was one of the key participants and attendees at the roundtable held for the 2011 Democracy Awards by the NED. Like Ashur, he was also wanted by Interpol and serves as a director at the Libyan Human and Political Development Forum.[6] He also appeared on the News Channel Al-Jazeera during the NATO operations against Libya.

Geopolitical Keys

In 2002, the Pentagon started major operations aimed at controlling Africa militarily. This was in the form of the Pan-Sahel Initiative, which was launched by the US European Command (EUCOM) and US Central Command (CENTCOM). Under the banner of this project, the US military would train troops from Mali, Chad, Mauritania, and Niger. The plans to establish the Pan-Sahel Initiative, however, date back to 2001, when the initiative for Africa was launched following the tragic events of 11 September 2001 (9/11).

On the basis of the Pan-Sahel Initiative, the Trans-Saharan Counterterrorism Initiative (TSCTI) was launched by the Pentagon in 2005 under the command of CENTCOM. Mali, Chad, Mauritania, and Niger were joined by Algeria, Mauritania, Morocco, Senegal, Nigeria, and Tunisia in the ring of African military cooperation with the Pentagon. Later, the Trans-Saharan Counterterrorism Initiative was transferred to the command of AFRICOM on 1 October 2008, when AFRICOM was activated.[7]

The map used by Washington for combating terrorism under the Pan-Sahel Initiative says a lot. The range or area of activity for the terrorists, within the borders of Algeria, Libya, Niger, Chad, Mali, and Mauritania according to Washington's designation is very similar to the boundaries or borders of the colonial territorial entity which France attempted to sustain in Africa in 1957. Paris had planned to prop up this African entity in the western central Sahara as a French department (province) directly tied to France, along with coastal Algeria.

Libya was the only State in North Africa not to cooperate with Africom.

International Peace and Sovereign Processes

> As we insist, in the present very special circumstances, on the direct right of the Syrian people to affirm its right of self-determination before the international community, we assure that all calls based on the ground of "droit d'ingérence," "devoir d'ingérence," "humanitarian intervention" or "responsibility to protect" should not hinder the aspiration of the Syrian people to cause peaceful change by its own forces; or lead to dealing with the Syrian people as yet another sphere of influence in the game of nations
> —Political Vision of the opposition group Syrian Local Coordination Committees.

Facts that are noted in this document led the CSI to conclude that interference in the UPR mechanism was followed by the approval of undocumented claims provided by NGOS and by governmental agencies such as the National Endowment for Democracy. The lack of investigation, and the non-existence of any process to question the assertions of NGOS inside the Council are primary causes for the events which cost the lives of thousands of Libyans who died during NATO's operations in Libya.

Non-interventionism is not an abstract dogma. It is a way to guarantee Peace, Democracy and Freedom.

The Libyan case shows the reality behind the so-called Responsibility to Protect. This doctrine clearly failed to restore peace in a State where an opposition movement supported by foreign states and NGOs could have been encouraged to establish a dialogue with the authorities. Instead, those NGOs and media insisted that peace was not possible, and this in spite of the considerable efforts of by the African Union, chaired by Libya.

Resolution 1970 and 1973 of the Security Council are the direct consequences of this lack of investigation. Many international jurists have attacked these resolutions as clear violations of International Justice: from the No-Fly Zone to the Arrest warrants requested by the office of Prosecutor Luis Moreno-Ocampo and delivered in June 2011, the whole process makes it the embodiment of the negation of United Nations basic principles based on sovereignty and non-intervention.

NATO also failed in its mission, which was to protect civilians. By extension, so did the Human Rights Council, the General Assembly and the Security Council which acted in their name.

The International Criminal Court also acted fraudulently.

First, the Application Document provided by the Office of the Prosecutor of the ICC was based on the same allegations as those made by the NGOs. More than three quarters of the document was redacted (censored) or filled with Western media reports.

The Security Council's referral of the situation in Libya to the ICC was an exercise in hypocrisy. Three out of the five permanent members refuse the ICC's jurisdiction for themselves, as does Libya. The US has even signed bilateral treaties with a hundred states so that US citizens will never be transferred to The Hague.

Responsibility to Protect is but an instrument of domination. Intervention is always undertaken by strong states against weak ones. Members of the Non-Aligned Movement and some great powers, in contrast, reject this doctrine and still believe in sovereignty and non-intervention.

The CSI calls for a process similar to the UPR to be set up to review NGOs. Their right of access to state agencies and international bodies should be carefully scrutinized. The Human Rights Council should respect its own procedures, especially the UPR.

UPR should be carried out in complete accordance with the UN Charter, i.e. states subject to it should be protected from interference from outside and the inside. UPR should be consultative, not coercive.

NGOS in charge of investigations in the country should be able to demonstrate independence regarding local embassies and state agencies. NGOS should also be held to account about their allegations. Allegations should be clearly documented.

The CSI encourages Permanent Missions in Geneva to take cognizance of this problem.

This will not only protect weak states against strong; it will encourage respect for the UN Charter and encourage peace.

Time is a great healer. It is often essential for reconciliation. Russia's recent position on Syria is a step in the right direction: it has allowed a breathing space and has caused the UN to name a mediator in the person of Kofi Annan.

However, the same NGOS are taking the same position they took on Libya on Syria: supporting one side in the conflict, calling for the recognition of non-sovereign entities, providing undocumented allegations, calling for Responsibility to Protect and military involvement, and for an end to dialogue—all this with the support of government agencies.

How can such interference and lack of rigour bring peace to international relations? How can these ideas claim to be based on humanitarianism?

The CSI recalls that the United Nations was created to ensure peace, following the tragic events of the Second World War. Its Charter affirms the sovereign equality of nations precisely in order to regulate the international system and because states are the indispensable interlocutors in it. State territories are under the responsibility of state leaders; international bodies and NGOs, by contrast, never bear responsibility for the consequences of their acts.

Mrs. Rubiales de Chamorro (Nicaragua) (spoke in Spanish):

As a country that has survived several military occupations and acts of aggression by a foreign Power, for which we have paid a high price in Nicaraguan lives, Nicaragua advocates and will continue to advocate for peace and reconciliation. Wherever and under all circumstances, dialogue and negotiation among brothers is the only viable way to resolve internal conflicts and guarantee the sovereignty and integrity of a nation and its territory.

Nicaragua is extremely concerned about the loss of life among innocent civilians. In this case in particular, we profoundly regret the loss of life among the people of Libya, a country with which Nicaragua has enjoyed close links. We trust in the abilities and the wisdom of the Libyan people and its leadership, headed by Muammar Al-Qadhafi, to resolve their domestic problems and find a peaceful solution in a sovereign manner, without foreign interference, double standards or foreign military intervention of any type or under any justification.

This is why we are deeply concerned by the ferocious media campaign being waged against Libya and its people. The news is contradictory, inflated and used at the whim of the great centers of power. It serves only to incite violence and seeks to justify foreign military aggression and intervention, which would only lead to more bloodshed, chaos and destabilization, opening the way once again to those who wish to appropriate the vast oil resources of the Libyan people.

Nicaragua wishes to state for the record that it condemns all attempts by those Powers to divide Libya's territory in order to acquire its natural resources. Nicaragua would also like to state on the record that implementing this measure to suspend Libya from the Human Rights Council will not only fail to resolve the domestic crisis being experienced by the Libyan people, but will also set a bad precedent. Suspending a country's rights as a member of the Human Rights Council, precipitously and based upon the sort of information we have seen from media disseminated from the great power centers, creates a precedent for countries that use selectivity as their principal guide to foreign policy. Those countries, which turn a blind eye to their own massive human rights violations while claiming that the rest of us should ignore them as well, are the same countries that invade our peoples and set up secret prisons. Nicaragua rejects and condemns such a double standard in moral values.

Human rights violations include those perpetrated against the Arab and Palestinian peoples; against Nicaragua, as noted in the decision of the International Court of Justice; and against the five Cuban heroes.

Nicaragua calls for calm and negotiation, putting aside double standards, and the promotion of dialogue. We hold out the hope that the Libyan people will be able to achieve peace while fully exercising their national sovereignty.

Mr. Karev (Russian Federation) (spoke in Russian):

The Russian Federation firmly condemns the use of force against the peaceful protesters in Libya, which has led to great loss of life among the civilian population.

We are convinced that a solution to the current problems in that country cannot and must not lie in the use of force. A dialogue is needed to prevent any further schism in Libya's society and any interference in the country's internal affairs and sovereignty. Settling the current crisis is the prerogative of the Libyan people themselves.

The Russian delegation joined in the consensus adoption of resolution 65/265 on the suspension of the membership rights of the Libyan Arab Jamahiriya in the Human Rights Council. However, we proceed from the premise that the decision in question does not establish a precedent, including in regard to the lack of a definition of practical procedural aspects in paragraph 8 of resolution 60/251.

It is also important that the resolution refers to the suspension of rights of membership in the Human Rights Council, and not to depriving a country of its membership in the major human rights body of the United Nations; and that, as noted in the statement of the African Union, Libya's seat in the Human Rights Council is not vacant, and that there will be no additional elections to fill any such vacancy.

Ms. Zhang Dan (China) (spoke in Chinese):

In view of the extremely exceptional situation now prevailing in Libya and the views and concerns expressed by Arab and African countries, the Chinese delegation joined the consensus on resolution 65/265. At the same time, the Chinese delegation hopes that the General Assembly's suspension of Libya's membership rights in the Human Rights Council will not become a precedent.

Ms. Rice (United States of America):

For the first time ever, the General Assembly has suspended a member of the Human Rights Council. This is a harsh rebuke, but one that Libya's leaders have brought down upon themselves. The United States continues to be appalled by the situation in Libya, and our thoughts and prayers are with the families of the Libyans who have been killed.

The General Assembly has come together to speak with one voice to Libya's unrepentant rulers. This unprecedented action sends another clear warning to Mr. Al-Qadhafi and those who still stand by him. They must stop the killing. When the only way a leader can cling to power is by grossly and systematically violating his own people's human rights, he has lost any legitimacy to rule. He must go and he must go now.

The protests in Libya are being driven by the people of Libya. This is about the universal human rights of the Libyan people and all people, and about a regime that has failed to meet its responsibility to protect its own population. The United States was pleased to be a co-sponsor of resolution 65/265, along with partners from all regions of the world, which underscores the universality of this decision and the depth of our commitment to the human rights we all share.

I must add that the United States utterly rejects the wilful and ugly distortion by the Venezuelan delegation of United States policy and posture. At a time when this Assembly is acting in unison in support of the Libyan people, it is shameful that one Member State, whose own reprehensible record speaks for itself, would manipulate this occasion to spread lies, foster fear and sow hate.

The General Assembly today has, by contrast, acted in the noblest traditions of the United Nations and made it clear that Governments that turn their guns on their own people have no place on the Human Rights Council. Membership on the Human Rights Council should be earned through respect for human rights and not accorded to those who abuse them. We hope that we can work together to build on today's united, bold and principled action to defend universal human rights across the United Nations system. We applaud the members of the General Assembly for taking this historic decision.

Mr. Reuben (Israel):

Israel fully supports resolution 65/265 and Libya's suspension from membership in the Human Rights Council, which was long overdue. For years, we have been calling attention to the dire and alarming human rights situation in our region. The Libyan situation is a representative case in point. It is regrettable that such tragedies are addressed only when crises and murderous crimes unfold, such as in this case, despite the fact that such systematic and long-standing abhorrent human rights violations have been well documented throughout the years.

Under its current notorious regime, Libya should never have been elected to sit as a member of the Human Rights Council. The international community's response to this appalling human rights crisis should serve as a wake-up call as we also deliberate the future of the Council and its membership.

Mr. Valero Briceño (Bolivarian Republic of Venezuela) (spoke in Spanish):

We regret that we have to respond to the delegation of the United States, because the subject we are discussing is profoundly and universally human and thus not bilateral in nature. It is understandable that a Government with a long history of human rights violations in its own country and around the world should respond with false arguments to the self-evident references by the Venezuelan delegation to the interventionist policy of the United States.

ENDNOTES

1   Urgent Appeal to Stop Atrocities in Libya; UN Watch: 21.02.2011 <http://www.unwatch.org/site/apps/nlnet/content2.aspx?c=bdKKISNqEmG&b=1330815&ct=9135143>

2   The Humanitarian War: The Humanitarian War in Libya: There is No Evidence! <http://www.youtube.com/watch?v=pU9IzXsALwo&list=PL4A5200C8E0A38C7C&index=2&feature=plpp_video>

3   Ranking Member Howard L. Berman's Opening Statement at Hearing, "Reforming the United Nations: Lessons Learned" <http://democrats.foreignaffairs.house.gov/press_display.asp?id=808>.

4   The Humanitarian War: The Gaddafi Mercenaries and The Division of Africa <http://www.youtube.com/watch?v=opmQIkSvYgY&feature=BFa&list=PL4A5200C8E0A38C7C&lf=plpp_video>

5   America's Conquest of Africa: The roles of France and IsraelJulien Teil & Mahdi Darius Nazemroaya <http://www.globalresearch.ca/index.php?context=va&aid=26886>

6   Id.

7   Id.

RADIO PACIFICA'S DESCENT

FROM VOICE OF THE VOICELESS TO PARTNER IN THE IMPERIAL INFORMATION WAR

Don DeBar

After the 2009 April Fool's Day Coup had gutted Pacifica of its African-American members of management, its coverage of the invasion and destruction of the African nation of Libya was presented through a prism of white-led management and, in the main, white producers.

Preparing the Soil—The "April Fool's Day Coup"

In 2008, elections, litigation and the resignation of the Pacifica Foundation's CEO placed a new group in charge of the network and its operations. The new group placed Grace Aaron, one of their own, as interim executive director of Pacifica. After a sudden visit to WBAI on April 1, 2009 with a group that included a recently laid-off producer from KPFK (Tony Bates), Aaron began a purge of dissidents. Bates had presented a secret report to an executive session of the national board over the weekend of April 24, 2009 that was the basis of their actions. Claiming that the Foundation was in financial crisis and that the cause was network programming, Aaron removed Bernard White from WBAI in May, 2009, beginning what would eventually become a purge of mostly black and brown men from management positions which, ultimately, were mainly filled by white men. The new group's

156

principal public relations campaign had specifically claimed that, in particular, WBAI's programming was "too black," and scared off white listeners with "discretionary income." They painted black managers, and Bernard White in particular, as "thugs" and "black nationalists."

By 2010, the purge had been completed, and the network took on an entirely different political orientation, one less involved in, and concerned with, communities of color, and specifically less critical of US policies at home and abroad. Instead, the network's focus changed to include health guru Gary Null and "arts programming" and away from in-depth public affairs coverage. Many of the politically-oriented independent producers saw their programs moved to night or overnight time slots, obviously impacting their audiences negatively.

The Christmas Coup of 2000—A Historical Analogy

As perhaps the only media network in the US that has historically presented an alternative narrative to that presented by the national media, Pacifica Radio has often found itself a target of intrigue, particularly at times where an independent voice could present serious challenges to power. Although this intrigue has often taken the form of internal bickering and litigation, twice in a decade it took the form of a coup—literally, an insurgent group taking over the network and conducting a purge of dissenting voices.

On December 22, 2000, at its New York station, an "important alternative voice was sabotaged when the Pacifica central board carried out a coup at WBAI. They took over the station, changed the locks on the doors, fired its general manager and two reporters—then banned staff who disagreed with their actions."[1] A campaign was implemented network-wide to punish voices not considered sympathetic to Democratic Party politics, as well as a large number of Black and Hispanic producers.

In July, 2002 Fairness and Accuracy In Reporting ("FAIR") summarized the events thus:

> The crisis first gained national attention in July 1999 when Pacifica shut down KPFA for three weeks and arrested over 50 staffers before relenting in the face of massive street protests. A year and a half later, Pacifica management executed the "Christmas Coup" at WBAI in New York, firing the station's general manager and program director and then banning over two dozen producers and programmers including Amy Goodman, host of Democracy Now.

Besieged by protests, sit-ins, boycotts, email pressure campaigns and a flurry of lawsuits, the old Pacifica national board capitulated in an out-of-court settlement last December.

The people who knew how to organize were on our side," says historian Matthew Lasar, author of Pacifica Radio: Rise of an Alternative Network. "They had talkers on their side, people like Mary Frances Berry or The Nation. The people who knew how to organize demonstrations, print up T-shirts and buttons, pass out flyers were all on our side."

The dissidents consolidated control at a January (2002) board meeting in New York.

That last meeting marked the official end of the Christmas Coup. Such staff members and producers as WBAI program director Bernard White and morning show producers Sharan Harper and Errol Maitland were returned, as well as Goodman and Juan Gonzalez and their daily news program Democracy Now!

In the interim, the events of September 11, 2001 had taken place. Although located literally a few blocks from the World Trade Center site, the station played "conservatory-level jazz" in the beginning hours of the unfolding crisis. Its formerly independent voice was silenced as the national leadership began constructing its "post-9/11 world" and began its war in Afghanistan and "the war on terror."

Over the next seven years, the network rebuilt its reputation as "the voice of the voiceless," bringing independent coverage of the anti-war movement, the economic crisis and growing police violence to a national audience. All that came crashing to a halt with the advent of the 2009 takeover and the subsequent dismantling of the network's progressive base.

Enter Al Jazeera

In early February 2011, Pacifica Radio's KPFK-FM in Los Angeles issued the following statement:

February 2, 2011 – North Hollywood, CA. In light of the continuing uprising unfolding in Cairo, Egypt, Pacifica Radio KPFK 90.7 fm will carry a 30-minute news broadcast from Al Jazeera English this week from

6 to 6:30 p.m. (PST). KPFK was originally scheduled to launch Al Jazeera English starting in mid March 2011, but given the dramatic events in the Middle East, station management decided to run content from the news channel immediately to provide an additional voice and perspective from the region to the communities of Southern California. Al Jazeera English is generally not available in the United States except on Pacifica Radio.

Last December Pacifica Radio announced that it would carry news coverage from Al Jazeera English, the award-winning 24-hour international news and current affairs channel. The decision, which brings Al Jazeera English for the first time to radio audiences in North America, reinforces Pacifica's commitment to airing fresh and diverse perspectives and to presenting accurate, objective, comprehensive news on the vital issues that the world faces today. Al Jazeera English broadcasts from the four strategic locations of Doha, Qatar; Washington, DC; London, England; and Kuala Lumpur, Malaysia. Al Jazeera English has 65 bureaus around the world.

The listener-supported community radio network broadcasts one hour of news from Al Jazeera English in three markets: KPFA in Berkeley; WBAI in New York; and KPFT in Houston. Al Jazeera English will be carried by KPFK in Los Angeles starting mid March 2011, and it will subsequently be made available to Pacifica affiliates.

"Al Jazeera English's news and programming is an exciting addition to our current line-up of thought-provoking programming," said Arlene Engelhardt, executive director of the Pacifica Foundation. "It is part of our mission at Pacifica to act as a bridge between cultures and to present stories that are too often overlooked by other media in the United States. Al Jazeera English is a truly global channel, and we are pleased to provide this important news service to our dedicated listeners throughout the country."

The new content rounds out Pacifica's roster of news programs, which include "Democracy Now!" with Amy Goodman, Free Speech Radio News, local news programs, and in Houston, news from the BBC World Service.

Of course, not mentioned in any of the announcements issued by Pacifica was the fact that Al Jazeera is owned by the government of Qatar, a medieval-style absolute monarchy vested in the hands of one man, its emir, Sheik Hamad bin Khalifa al-Thani, who is credited by *The New York Times* as being the "founder of Al Jazeera."

Democracy Now!

The earliest reported reference to Libya at the Democracy Now! Web archive is from the March 27, 1998 headlines, and reads as follows:

> President Clinton toured the prison where Nelson Mandela spent nearly two decades. Mandela and Clinton discussed South Africa's relationship with Cuba and Libya. Mandela defended that relationship saying they aided the anti-apartheid efforts in South Africa when the U.S. would not.

At no time during the lead-up to the US intervention, nor during the entire military campaign, was the position of Mandela on Libya and Qaddafi mentioned, even as the African Union wrestled with the question of a war between the US and Libya.

It was in January 2011 that the program first presented Libya and Qaddafi in conjunction with the advent of the so-called "Arab Spring." The following is an excerpt from an interview by host Amy Goodman with Professor Juan Cole on January :

> **AMY GOODMAN:** And can you talk about the effects on the whole region, as you are monitoring coverage and reaction around the world? And particularly Saudi Arabia— does the regime there, the autocratic regime that has been in power for decades, have something to worry about?
>
> **JUAN COLE:** Well, I think all the regimes in the Arab world are very nervous about this development.

It is something new. I did survey the reactions. You know, interestingly, the deputy prime minister of Israel expressed concern, lest this spread and maybe regimes come to power, more democratic, but more hostile to Israel, in places like Jordan and Egypt. Libya, interestingly enough, the longtime dictator Muammar Qaddafi, who started as a revolutionary himself, condemned the Tunisian people as immature and impatient, who said, just— "You should have just waited Ben Ali out. Why would you be so eager to have a new president?" And he sounded like an old fuddy-duddy and really did himself no favors, I think. And, of course, he was mainly speaking to his own people, pleading for their patience. And other countries were much more circumspect.

The Arabs of Kirkuk in Iraq, who are now increasingly under Kurdish domination, threatened to make a Tunisian-style uprising if they didn't get their rights. So, oppressed people, people in Gaza joined in demonstrations in solidarity. Oppressed groups throughout the region were delighted. Status quo powers, whether they, you know, are old revolutionaries like Qaddafi or status quo powers like Israel, were very nervous about this.

Libya again appears on the program on February 11, in the midst of a discussion of intrigue which centers on the then-Egyptian vice president, Omar Suleiman, in a discussion with Lisa Hajjar, a professor at the University of California, Santa Barbara. She had recently written an article titled "Omar Suleiman, the CIA's Man in Cairo and Egypt's Torturer-in-Chief." While discussing the many transgressions of Suleiman, Hajjar cited the case of Ibn al-Sheikh al-Libi, who was reportedly tortured in Egypt on behalf of U.S. officials, who hoped he would link Saddam Hussein to al-Qaeda in the run-up to the Iraq invasion of 2003.

LISA HAJJAR: Al-Libi. So, al-Libi actually was, you know, a militant, had been based in Afghanistan, was someone who was a trainer or ran the al-Khaldan camp. And he was captured fleeing, in November of 2001, fleeing out of Afghanistan, picked up. He ends up in Egypt. You know, and again, many people ended up there. Al-Libi was brutally tortured...But what becomes interesting is once it's revealed that al-Libi had recanted his testimony, which — you know, once the Iraq war is going so poorly and there are no weapons of mass destruction, al-Libi is then essentially disappeared. I mean, no one knows where al-Libi went for a while. He didn't end up in Guantánamo, and— you know, because his people would have wanted to question him about the evidence he had—or the statement he had made in relation to this massively devastating war. In 2009, April 2009, several Human Rights Watch investigators were in Libya doing an investigation of Libyan prison conditions, and there they discovered al-Libi. And they saw him and spoke to him, and according to Human Rights Watch, they said he was in relatively OK health and so on. But the fact then they revealed al-Libi is alive, he's in Libya, and it immediately re-raised the questions of people wanting to speak to him.

In essence, the picture painted is that the Libyan regime was somehow connected in a covert way to the US-conducted torture of al-Libi and at least an accomplice after the fact to the US war on Iraq!

On February 16, the program gave this report which tied Libya directly to popular uprisings in the region:

AMY GOODMAN: 2011 is shaping up to be an historic year in the Middle East and North Africa with the populist uprisings in Tunisia, then Egypt, and the massive street protests that are occurring across the region. Libya, Bahrain, Iran are the latest countries to be hit by a wave of popular protest.

Demonstrations erupted in the Libyan city of Benghazi overnight. Online reports indicate two people died, many were injured. A nationwide day of protest is set to take place in Libya tomorrow.

No source was cited for this report. The following day (February 17), Goodman reported

In Libya, state forces have killed at least five people in growing rallies against Colonel Muammar Qaddafi's

41-year rule. Protesters have set fire to police stations and outposts in separate cities. The Libyan government has begun limiting internet access, and there are reports protesters have been warned they will be met with live bullets if they join another round of protests set for today.

Again, no source was cited for this report. Later in that same broadcast, Goodman said:

Meanwhile, in Libya, after hundreds protested across the country Wednesday, thousands more filled the streets today again in what's being called a "Day of Rage." Human rights observers say snipers on rooftops have killed as many as 13 protesters and wounded dozens more. The protests fall on the second anniversary of protests in Benghazi, where security forces killed several people.

The source of the report concerning the unnamed "human rights observers" was not given. The following day, on Friday, February 18, the program reported this:

Funerals are also being held in Libya today for the victims of a government crackdown on protests in several towns. At least five deaths have been confirmed, but there are reports the toll could be as high as 50. The largest rally was held in the city of Benghazi, where thousands took to the streets to denounce Colonel Muammar Qaddafi's 41-year rule.

Again, the source of the "reports" of this "government crackdown" was not given. On Monday, February 21, the rumor-mongering ended and the outright propaganda campaign began.

Human Rights Watch is reporting at least 332 people have been killed in Libya in a massive government crackdown on pro-democracy activists. Despite the violence, the protests against the 42-year reign of Muammar Qaddafi appear to be gaining steam. Civilians have reportedly taken control of Benghazi, Libya's second city. Oil workers at the Nafoora oil field have gone on strike. And protests have spread to the capital city of Tripoli. There are reports that the home of Libya's parliament in Tripoli has been set on fire. On Sunday, Qaddafi's son vowed to institute a series of reforms, but he warned that the protests could lead to a "civil war." In the United States, a group of protesters gathered outside the White House on Sunday, calling on the Obama administration to pressure the Qaddafi government.

As it turned out, there was no "government crackdown," the group that had taken Benghazi was a military force (not "civilians") and there was no protest, and no burning of government buildings, in Tripoli.

Later in the program, Goodman interviewed Khaled Mattawa, who was described as a "Libyan poet and scholar" and an associate professor in the English Language and Literature Department at the University of Michigan. Mattawa cited alleged conversations with relatives in Benghazi and reports from Al Hurra (the USIA media outlet in the region), and raised claims of government brutality and popular uprising:

I understand that Benghazi is out of the Qaddafi regime's control, and I understand that the battle for Tripoli continues. Last night, as you may—I talked to one of your staff earlier, one—I talked to one of my relatives, and he was in the city near the court building, the North Benghazi Municipal Court building, and that's where the protests were. That's where people had gathered to pray and to make speeches and so forth. And he told me that they were collecting weapons that had been left about in the clashes and that they were depositing them into the court building. There was—the demonstrations were mostly in the—by the seashore in downtown Benghazi, but also there were demonstrations, from what I could tell from the footage, near the area of Berka, which is about five kilometers south from the seashore. And it's also a kind of—it has an important square and some important buildings. And also it had a military compound, which is supposedly where Al-Saadi Qaddafi's contingent or division was stationed, and there was fighting between the military there.

And, of course, what I heard on Alhurra is that from a—I think a military officer, a colonel or higher, who had said—Colonel Saber, who said that Benghazi is completely freed from al-Qaddafi's control, and people had already declared the area or are renaming that area the name that it had from 1969 to 1978, which is the "Arab Republic of Libya," just meaning the end of the so-called Jamahiriya age, which is Qaddafi's notion of people's democracy and so forth.

Now, in Tripoli, people had come out into the streets. They were converging from Bin Ashour, which is east of Tripoli, and from Gargaresh and Hay Al-Andalus and Siyahia, west of—and Gurji. And they were trying to both meet in the—meet in Martyrs' Square, Maidan Al Shohdaa, which Qaddafi had named Green Square, and it sort of stuck, but people are coming back to call it Maidan Al Shohdaa. And they were trying to meet there, and a few—as soon as they gathered, they were shooting, and they backed off into an area called Maidan al-Jezair, or the Algeria Square, which is about less than a kilometer away. So, people are trying to converge into the center of town to protest, to celebrate the end of the Qaddafi era, but they are still fighting. They are being shot at. There was a funeral procession in Tripoli today, and the reports are that they had been shot at. And Al Jazeera, just a short while ago, reported that 60 had been perhaps shot, killed in Tripoli, which is a huge number, which is the same kind of number that we had heard about from Benghazi yesterday. The regime just sort of escalated the—its attack on civilians in Benghazi.

Again, it turns out that there were no government attacks on civilians and no protests in Tripoli. It was during this interview that the psy-op claim that Qaddafi had left the country was first floated on Democracy Now!:

AMY GOODMAN: We have 30 seconds, Professor Mattawa. Do think Qaddafi is still in the country? Do you think that these protests will overthrow Qaddafi?
KHALED MATTAWA: You know, this is the moment that

Libyans have been waiting for for a very, very, very long time. Reports that he's has flown to Venezuela, I'm not sure if that's true or not. It is really now just coming down to Tripoli. And as Saif al-Qaddafi indicated, they are trying to fight very hard, and they are fighting hard, because they're killing a lot of peoples very quickly in Tripoli.

Over the next 8 months, as the US bombs rained down on Libyans across their country, not a single voice was presented challenging the foundation of the war, although numerous "progressive" voices were presented who, nevertheless, all agreed with the basic narrative—that Qaddafi had committed war crimes against his own people. None of the relevant facts regarding Libya were presented—that all Libyans owned their own homes, free of mortgages and rent, that all had universal health care, free education, etc., etc., and, more importantly, that the US was seeking a foothold on the African continent for its AFRICOM enterprise.

Free Speech Radio News

On February 25, 2011, FSRN issued this report:

UN Human Rights Commissioner says thousands could be dead in Qaddafi crackdown

In Libya, there's growing evidence that Qaddafi's ferocious crackdown has claimed hundreds, possibly thousands of lives. There are numerous reports of militias loyal to Qaddafi opening fire on people as they left mosques after evening prayer on the way to pro-democracy rallies in the capital Tripoli. Video posted to the internet show bloodied people and loud gun fire as protesters gather in the street. Tripoli's Green Square was the site of some clashes. Pro-Qaddafi supporters gathered there early in the day, and in what appeared to be a live broadcast on State Television, Qaddafi made another defiant speech:

> I am here among you, among the public in the Green Square! And here you are the youth of Libya,

> the children and grandchildren of the battle of Jihad who crushed the Italian invasion! The Italian empire was smashed by your forefathers! We were able to crush any foreign aggression by the people's will, by our armed people! With this weapon, every Libyan individual and every Libyan tribe will be ours! So Libya will turn into a burning hell!

(Sound and translation courtesy of Al Jazeera.) As the bloodshed continues in Libya, more government officials are defecting from the Qaddafi regime, including the Libyan delegation to the Arab League, the ambassador to France, the embassy staff in India and the delegation to the UN Human Rights Council. Libyan diplomat Adel Shaltut spoke today, at an emergency meeting convened by the council.

> The young people in my country today, 100 years after the Italian fascist invasion of Libya, today are with their blood writing a new chapter in the history of struggle and resistance. Glory forever to the martyrs, victory to the heroic people of Libya. Mr President, I wish to emphasize and underscore that we in the Libyan Mission have categorically decided to serve as representatives of the Libyan people and their free will. We only represent the Libyan people. We will serve as their representative in this august body and in other international forums.

Earlier in the meeting, UN Human Rights Commissioner Navi Pillay expressed the international community's growing alarm:

Although reports are still patchy and hard to verify, one thing is painfully clear: in brazen and continuing breach of international law, the crackdown in Libya of peaceful demonstrations is escalating alarmingly with reported mass killings, arbitrary arrests, detention and torture of protestors. Tanks, helicopters and military aircraft have reportedly been used indiscriminately to attack the protestors. According to some sources, thousands may have been killed or injured.

The UN Human Rights Commissioner called for all international actors to take necessary measures now to stop the bloodshed. The UN Security Council also convened today, but is yet to announce any concrete measures. However, the US is moving forward with sanctions, according to Whitehouse spokesperson Jay Carney, who spoke to reporters today. US officials say they are also reviewing other options. At a State Department press briefing Thursday, spokesperson P J Crowley was asked if a military option was being considered:

We've had meetings constantly on this since last week when the events began to unfold in Libya. The military has been a full participant in these discussions. We are consulting broadly about steps that we can take. I'm not going to prejudge decisions that have yet to be made. But there's a lot action going on across the government. We have a full—a wide range of tools—financial sanctions, multilateral actions—and we are considering all of them. The military

> is fully involved in these discussions
> and doing its own thinking about
> options that can be presented to
> the President.

On March 4, 2011, FSRN issued the following report:

> In Libya, forces loyal to Colonel Qaddafi have been
> attacking the oil town of Zawiya. There are multiple
> reports of many dead and dozens injured. Meanwhile,
> in Tripoli today, after Friday prayers, protesters were
> dispersed with tear gas. Our sources say that most
> internet and phone communication with Libya have
> been cut off since last night. So for more we go to
> Rihab Elhaj, a Libyan American in Washington DC.
> She's co-founder of the New Libya Foundation and
> she's monitoring the situation in Libya. Her friends
> and family are in Tripoli.

During this time, I was in contact with several journalists on the ground in Libya via the internet. Two in Tripoli specifically denied the reports of protests and of the use of tear-gas.

On March 10, 2011, FSRN issued the following report:

Africans in Libya accused of being Qaddafi mercenaries

> In Libya, news reports say opposition forces are
> fleeing the oil town of Ras Lanuf and coming under
> sustained attacks at the town's western limits from
> rockets, shells, and gunboats firing at them from the
> sea. The reports quote both fleeing rebels and State
> television.
>
> As the US and the European Union continue to debate
> military intervention and whether to enforce a no-fly
> zone, France has become the first country to formally
> recognize Libya's National Council in Benghazi.
> Meanwhile, there are ongoing concerns about the
> plight of thousands of African migrant workers in
> Libya who are trying to flee the country. Some are
> being detained by rebels who accuse them of being
> mercenaries hired by Qaddafi. In comments to the

international media, Peter Bouckaert who is in Libya
with a team from Human Rights Watch, said he had
found no proof that Qaddafi was using foreign African
mercenaries and that rumors about mercenaries
were creating hysteria and even leading to lynchings
of innocent migrants. FSRN's Raphael Krafft is in
Benghazi. He's been investigating the fate of alleged
African mercenaries detained by the Libyan National
Council.

Although over time FSRN began to give some play to voices
questioning some portions of the narrative, at no time did it—or has
it—given air to those independent journalists who were actually on the
ground and challenged the factual basis of the war.

Pacifica Public Affairs Coverage

On March 9, KPFK host Ian Masters presented an interview
with Akram Ramadan, described at the program's website as a Libyan
born in the UK, and living at that time in London. According to Masters,
Ramadan's father "had been imprisoned by Qaddafi and ... just returned
to the UK from Libya." Ramadan claimed that "at least 6,000" Libyans
had been killed in the prior 18 days by "mercenaries" hired by Qaddafi,
saying "if it happened in Bosnia, if it happened in Kosovo, if it happened
God-knows-where, they would call it ethnic cleansing." He said that a so-
called "no-fly" zone "won't work" and called for direct US intervention.
He even said that, after talking with everyday Libyans, they would accept
a US base in Libya such as existed during the reign of King Idris (deposed
in 1969 by Qaddafi). Ramadan also accused Qaddafi of ruining the health
care and educational systems of Libya, in stark contrast to the official UN
and WHO statistics which showed practically unprecedented gains in
these two spheres since 1969. Far from calling Ramadan on these claims,
which were easily refuted after even a little research, Masters egged him
on to more and more absurd, yet incendiary, claims, at one point asking
him what he thought had to be done to "get rid of this monster and his
family". He also claimed that the Qaddafi family stole trillions, amplifying
Masters' goading suggestion of "billions" to "no, not billions—I think it
starts with a "T"—trillions," from the Libyan people.

Ramadan found his way onto the airwaves of Pacifica's New
York station WBAI-FM on the April 11 edition of the morning drive
time program "Wakeup Call," where host Esther Armah referred to
negotiations taking place at the time between the African Union and

the US-backed insurgents. After she referred to the insurgents as "the rebels," she was challenged by Ramadan, who said "they are not rebels, actually, they are pro-democracy fighters ... they are not rebels, there is only one rebel, which is Colonel Qaddafi, who rebelled against the whole world." Armah replied "Thank you so much, I appreciate the correction. Corrected: Pro-democracy supporters, and we shall use that term from this point on."

On June 28, Armah interviewed Phyllis Bennis of the Institute for Policy Studies, who echoed the official US position in calling the ICC warrants against Qaddafi and his family members justified, although she raised questions concerning the selective enforcement practiced by the ICC against those countries at odds with US objectives only. Bennis proceeded from the same point of assumption that the charges against the regime were valid, saying "using international law to hold dictators accountable for their crimes is a huge, important part of global mobilization against human rights violations. And I think that Muammar Qaddafi was certainly one of those dictators who has committed huge crimes against his population." Although at this point, the veracity of the claims made against the Libyan government which were presented to the UN Security Council had been proven false, and this evidence had, at this point, been forwarded on numerous occasions by me to Armah and her team, Bennis was not challenged and the naked assertion was left standing.

All in all, in the main, those programs which aired during drive-time presented a narrative that was closest to the one being peddled by the US commercial media, while those who raised factual questions which struck at the heart of that narrative were producers consigned to evening or overnight slots—many placed there by the new management.

The Facts Absent From Pacifica News Reportage on Libya: A Brief Timeline

On February 25, 2011, *The Pakistan Observer*—the largest English language daily newspaper in that former colony of Britain— reported the following:

> Islamabad—The United States, Britain and France have sent several hundred "defence advisors" to train and support the anti-Qaddafi forces in oil-rich Eastern Libya where "rebels armed groups" have apparently taken over.

According to an exclusive report confirmed by a Libyan diplomat in the region "the three Western states have landed their special forces troops in Cyrinacia and are now setting up their bases and training centres" to reinforce the rebel forces who are resisting pro-Qaddafi forces in several adjoining areas.

A Libyan official who requested not to be identified said that the U.S. and British military gurus were sent on February 23 and 24 night through American and French warships and small naval boats off Libyan ports of Benghazi and Tobruk.

The Western forces are reportedly preparing to set-up training bases for local militias set-up by the rebel forces for an effective control of the oil-rich region and counter any push by pro- Qaddafi forces from Tripoli.

Other reports claim that efforts to "neutralize" the Libyan Air Force were also underway to limit Qaddafi's rule in Tripoli if not fully uprooted from the country. Meanwhile, three Indian Navy warships are also being dispatched to be deployed in the rebel-held areas of Libya.

According to reports the Indian Navy has already sent two warships plus one its largest amphibious vessel INS Jalashwa. According to defence experts "Jalshwa" is the largest ship of Indian Navy which was delivered by the U.S. four years ago. Jalashwa, formaly the USS Trenton, has the capability to embark, transport & land various elements of an amphibious force & its equipped with mechanised landing craft, Sea King helicopters & armed with raders, ship to air missiles & rapid firing guns.

Experts say that Indian ship Jalashwa has a Landing Platform Dock with a capability 1000 fully armed troops. The warship is also used for maritime surveillance, special operations, search & rescue and to undertake other tasks. [cited as printed]

On March 1, Russia today reported:

Russian military: space satellite shows no sign of Benghazi bombings

Using its space surveillance equipment, the Russian General Staff has been closely monitoring the unrest in Libya, and cannot confirm the bombings in the city of Benghazi, a high-ranking source in the agency told Interfax. The Russian military has been closely observing the situation in Tripoli, Benghazi and other regions of Libya, engulfed in violence since strongman Muammar Qaddafi's refusal to step down in mid-February, the official said. The General Staff's data showed that the international media has often been off the mark in its accounts of the events unfolding in Libya. For instance, he said, Russia did not detect any airstrikes against civilians in Benghazi on February 21.

On March 2, Russia Today reported:

The US Sixth Fleet has begun repositioning its ships in the Mediterranean, triggering speculation of a NATO invasion of Libya.

On Wednesday (March 2) two US military ships heading towards the Libyan coast entered the Suez Canal.

The 'Telegraph' newspaper claims "British Special Forces are already in Libya."

In other words, none but a fraction of Pacifica's audience heard on the air that US forces had landed in Libya before the March Security Council meeting which imposed the "no-fly zone," that the claims that Libyan Air Force had strafed protestors were proved false by Russian satellite imagery, or that a massive invasion of Libya was imminent weeks before the Security Council actions. Instead, they were told that there was an indigenous "Arab Spring" uprising against the government that was being brutally suppressed, that only "humanitarian intervention" to remove Qaddafi could prevent a bloodbath. Without this voice of opposition being made available to anti-war activists, who were furiously attempting to organize a response and present the facts which contradicted the official story, it took many months and a national tour by former Rep. Cynthia McKinney, former US Attorney General Ramsey Clark and Sara Flounders of the International Action Center, Minister Akbar Muhammed, International Representative of the Nation of Islam, and the ANSWER Coalition, among others, to get the word out, effectively blocking opposition to this war from being organized until after it was, in the main, concluded.

ENDNOTES

1   *Revolutionary Worker,* Jan 11, 2001.

THE IMPERIALIST PLAN FOR AFRICA

Muammar Qaddaffi, King of all African Kings, a poster in the Bab Al Aziziya compound June 5th 2011. (Photo courtesy of Dr. Randy Short, DIGNITY)

THE RACIALIZATION OF THE WAR

LIBYA AND THE "CLASH OF CIVILIZATIONS"

Mahdi Darius Nazemroaya

"Identities that kill. The expression doesn't strike me as inappropriate insofar as the idea I'm challenging—the notion that reduces identity to one single affiliation—encouraging people to adopt an attitude that is partial, sectarian, intolerant, domineering, sometimes suicidal, and frequently even changes them into killers or supporters of killers. Their view of the world is biased and distorted. Those who belong to the same community as we do are "ours," we like to ourselves concerned about what happens to them, but we also allow ourselves to tyrannise over them: if they are thought to be "lukewarm" we denounce them, intimidate them, punish them as "traitors" and "renegades."As for the others, those on the opposite side, we never try to put ourselves in their place, we take good care not to ask ourselves whether on some point or other they might not be entirely in the wrong, and we won't let our hearts be softened by their complaints, their sufferings or the injustices that have been inflicted on them. The only thing that counts is the point of view of "our" side; a point of view that is often that of the most militant, the most demagogic and the most fanatical members of the community."

– Amin Maalouf, In the Name of Identity:
Violence and the Need to Belong

In the eyes of NATO and the so-called West, Libya's crime was how it distributed and used its wealth, its lack of external debts, and the key role it was attempting to play in continental development and curtailing of external influence in Africa. Tripoli was a spoiler that effectively undermined the interests of the former colonial powers. The Jamahiriya had taken on some hefty pan-African development plans intended to industrialize Africa and transform it into an integrated and assertive political entity. These initiatives conflicted with the interests of the external powers competing with one another in Africa, but it was especially unacceptable to Washington and the major EU countries. Accordingly, Libya had to be crippled and neutralized as an entity supportive of African progress and pan-African unity. As a result, today the country is essentially loosely divided along the colonial boundaries of Tripolitania, Fezzan, and Cyrenaica. Needless to say, there is much more to these events.

The narratives of the Libyan Arab Jamahiriya and the Syrian Arab Republic are intertwined as are the fates of black-skinned Arabs in and outside of Libya, and Christian Arabs in and outside of Syria. Black-skinned people and Christians are being dually targeted in the lands of Arabdom. This is not simply a routine phenomenon that is taking place because these groups are minorities in their countries or due to an inherent genetic intolerance in Arab society or societies which, to the contrary, are known for their tolerance, deriving from the principles protecting minority rights that are enshrined in their centuries-long traditions and Islam.[1] There is much more to these happenings, tied to the deliberate racialization of conflict and war. Societal identities in the Arab World have been under a continuous multi-dimensional siege. Identity has been weaponized and used to divide and conquer. This siege of identity is not new or a relic, it is actually older than both the modern states of Libya and Syria; it is part of a longstanding and continuing colonial process that has victimized Africa and other parts of the world that has helped create borders drawn in blood and genocidally erase identities while extinguishing whole cultures. It is the truly "long war" that has been waged since the first Western European colonies were established.

Colonial and neo-colonial powers have helped prop meta-myths or meta-narratives to keep entire groups of people divided that have otherwise lived with one another in relative peace for hundreds, if not thousands, of year. These colonial powers, with all the policies and devices at their disposal from the histories of empire-building, work tirelessly to reify these ideas in the minds of target populations and their own domestic populations in order to normalize the deviation—*fitna* in Arabic—from normal amicable relations that they have created or seek to create between different peoples. They popularize misconceptions such as the belief that Jews and Arabs have been at each others' throats since ancient times or that Vedicists (a much more proper name for Hindus) and Muslims could never live together in a united India because of an age-old animosity.[2] One should respond to such misconceptions by mentioning the following facts: many Jews were and are Arabs and peoples of Jewish faith have lived in Arab societies in predominately egalitarian conditions until fairly recently in history (since the implantation of Zionism as a colonial tool); in the Indian sub-continent or South Asia, Vedicists and Muslims lived together for hundreds of years in peace under such dynasties as the Mughals and it was only under British rule that tensions were deliberately promoted between them as an instrument of British rule.

Similarly, the events in Libya and Africa are part of a neo-colonial project. Under the Obama Administration the United States has expanded the Anglo-American "long war" into Africa. Barack Hussein Obama, the so-called "Son of Africa" who has hidden behind his African heritage, has actually become one of the worst enemies of Africa's peoples. Aside from his continued support of dictators in Africa, the Republic of Côte d'Ivoire (Ivory Coast) was unhinged under his watch. The division of Sudan was reprehensively publicly endorsed by the White House before that county's internal referendum on the matter, after ongoing support for secessionist South Sudan. Somalia has been further destabilized and faces daily massacres by US military drones and other US-led military operations in East Africa. US combat troops have been sent to Uganda, even before the orchestrated demands for Joseph Kony's head. US Africa Command (AFRICOM) has gone into full swing. Finally, Libya has been viciously attacked by NATO and invaded, with its leader humiliated, beaten, and murdered in cold blood under the eyes of US and NATO handlers.

The war in Libya is just the start of a new cycle of external military adventurism inside Africa. The US now wants more military bases inside Africa. France has also announced that it has the right to militarily intervene anywhere in Africa where there are French citizens and French interests are at risk. NATO is also fortifying its positions in the Red Sea and off the coast of Somalia and in the entire region of East Africa. Divide and conquer is a major dogma of this process. Many of the problems afflicting the contemporary areas of Eastern Europe, Central Asia, Southwest Asia, South Asia, East Asia, Latin America, and Africa are actually the result of the deliberate triggering of regional tensions by external powers. Sectarian division in all its forms—ethno-linguistic tension, religious differences, and internal violence—have been traditionally exploited by the US, Britain, and France in various parts of the globe. Iraq, Sudan, Rwanda, and Yugoslavia are merely a few recent examples of this strategy of "divide and conquer" being used to bring nations to their knees.

Divide and Conquer:
How the First "Arab Spring" Was Manipulated

The name "Arab Spring" is a catch phrase concocted in distant offices in Washington, London, Paris, and Brussels by individuals and groups who, other than having some superficial knowledge of the region, know very little about the Arabs. What is unfolding amongst the Arab peoples is naturally a mixed package. Insurgency is as much a part of this package as is opportunism. Where there is revolution, there is always counter-revolution.

The upheavals in the Arab World are not an Arab "awakening" either; such a term is an insult and implies that the Arabs have always been ignorant and asleep while dictatorships and injustice have been plaguing them. In reality the Arab World, which is part of the broader Turko-Arabo-Iranic World and forever tied to the continent of Africa, has been filled with frequent revolts that have been put down by the Arab dictators in coordination with countries like the United States, Britain, and France. These powers have always acted as a counter-force to democracy and are continuing to do so. Every dictator in the Arab World has either been propped up by them or has done business with them.

The plans for reconfiguring the Middle East started several years before the First World War. It was during the First World War, however, that the manifestations of these colonial designs became visible with the "Great Arab Revolt" against the Ottoman Empire. Despite the fact that the British, French, and Italians were colonial powers which had in reality prevented the Arabs from enjoying any freedom in countries like Algeria, Libya, Tunisia, Egypt, and Sudan, these colonial powers managed to portray themselves as the friends and allies of Arab liberation. The British and the French actually used the Arabs as their foot soldiers against the Ottomans to further Anglo-French geo-political schemes. The infamous and secret Sykes–Picot Agreement between London and Paris is a case in point where the British and French governments secretly planned on turning the Arab territories of the Ottoman Empire into British and French territories. France and Britain managed to use and manipulate the Arabs by selling them the idea of Arab liberation from the so-called "repression" of the Ottomans and creating ethnic tensions between the Arabs and the Turks.

In reality, the Ottoman Empire was a multi-ethnic and plural empire. It gave local and cultural autonomy to all its internal peoples, but was manipulated into becoming a Turkish entity. Even the Armenian Genocide that would ensue in Ottoman Anatolia has to be analyzed in the same context as the contemporary targeting of Christians in Iraq—as part of a sectarian scheme unleashed by external actors to divide the Ottoman Empire, Anatolia, and the citizenry of the Ottoman Empire. The Treaty of Sèvres signed between the Allies and the High Porte of Ottoman Constantinople (modern Istanbul) galvanized ethnic tensions. After the collapse of the Ottoman Empire, it was London and Paris that denied freedom to the Arabs while sowing the seeds of discord amongst the various Arab peoples. Corrupt local Arab leaders were also partners in the project and many of them were all too happy to become clients of Britain and France. In the same sense, the modern "Arab Spring" has been manipulated and hijacked. The US, Britain, France, Italy, and others are now working with the help of corrupt Arab leaders and figures to restructure the Arab World and Africa.

The Yinon Plan and Its "Clean Break" Adaptation

As disarray and turmoil are once again uprooting the Arab and African peoples fomented by external intervention, Israel sits silently in the background. Tel Aviv has actually been deeply involved in the new cycle of turmoil, which is tied to its Yinon Plan to reconfigure its strategic surroundings. This reconfiguration process is based on a well established technique of creating sectarian divisions which eventually will effectively neutralize target states or result in their dissolution. From the turmoil and chaos—ironically called "creative destruction"—new states are then fashioned. Creative destruction describes how capitalism destroys existing social systems and at the same time benefits from the economic and social systems that it sets up to take their places.[3] Mark Levine sums the proclivity of the US for using creative destruction well:

> [N]eo-liberal globalizers and neo-conservatives, and ultimately the Bush Administration, would latch on to creative destruction as a way of describing the process by which they hoped to create their new world orders.
>
> [...]
>
> For all who celebrated creative destruction, the United States was, in the words of neo-conservative philosopher and Bush adviser Michael Ledeen, "an awesome revolutionary force" for whom creative destruction was (and, we can assume, remains) "[America's] middle name.[4]

The sociology of the process takes place roughly as follows:

Sociologically speaking, the fabrics of the occupied [and targeted] countries are altered. This includes a change in societal unity/division, the social system of values, and the concept of national identity. The fabrics of national unity are weakened at every level and social anomie takes hold of the occupied country effectively creating a state of social chaos where the different groups in the occupied [or targeted] society become hostile and differential towards one another. This works as a counter-balance to internal resistance trying to fight the occupation and foreign tutelage. The same social standards and rules that were in place prior to the occupation [and targeting] no longer apply in these socially de-regulated environments. In these socially de-regulated environments Washington has attempted to engineer new social structures usually through division. These new divided societies, which are always internally weak, then are prompted to function as a part of Washington's system of global empire.[5]

In essence this is all a continuation of the British stratagem in the Middle East to create many little weak states, especially amongst the Arabs. The Yinon Plan is an Israeli strategic plan within the contours of Anglo-American designs that has the primary aim of ensuring Israeli regional superiority. This plan insists and stipulates that Israel must reconfigure its geo-political environment through the balkanization of the surrounding Arab states into smaller and weaker entities.

Israeli strategists viewed Iraq as their biggest strategic challenge from any Arab country. This is why Iraq was outlined as the centerpiece to the balkanization of the Middle East and the Arab World. On the basis of the concepts of the Yinon Plan, Israeli strategists have consistently called for the division of Iraq into a Kurdish state and two Arab states, one for Shiite Muslims and the other for Sunni Muslims. The first step towards establishing this was a war between Iraq and Iran, which the Yinon Plan discusses. The division of Iraq was regarded as an important first step needed for dividing Syria, according to another Israeli strategic document co-authored by many members of the presidential administration of George W. Bush Jr., which will be discussed later on. Aside from a divided Iraq, which the Biden Plan also calls for, the Yinon Plan calls for a divided Lebanon, Egypt, and Syria. The partitioning of

Iran, Turkey, Somalia, and Pakistan also all fall into line with these views. The Yinon Plan also calls for dissolution in North Africa and forecasts it as starting from Egypt and then spilling over into Sudan, Libya, and the rest of the region. These plans have been in continuous circulation, recycled, and modified. *The Atlantic*, in 2008, and the US military's *Armed Forces Journal*, in 2006, both published widely circulated maps of that closely followed the outline of the Yinon Plan.

Although tweaked, the Yinon Plan is in motion and coming to life under *A Clean Break: A New Strategy for Securing the Realm,* a 1996 Israel policy paper. It can be viewed as a document augmenting the Yinon Plan—as an add-on to it. This document was written by Richard Perle and the Study Group on "A New Israeli Strategy Toward 2000" for Benjamin Netanyahu, the prime minister of Israel at the time. Richard Perle was a former Pentagon under-secretary for Ronald Reagan at the time and later a US military advisor to George W. Bush Jr. and the White House. Aside from Perle, David Wurmser and Meyrav Wurmser would also author the document. The latter two figures became advisors to Vice-President Richard Cheney and admitted that Israel's attack on Lebanon in 2006 was actually intended to target Syria with a view to creating the "New Middle East." The rest of the members of the Study Group on "A New Israeli Strategy Toward 2000" consisted of James Colbert (Jewish Institute for National Security Affairs), Charles Fairbanks Jr. (Johns Hopkins University), Douglas Feith (Feith and Zell Associates), Robert Loewenberg (Institute for Advanced Strategic and Political Studies), and Jonathan Torop (The Washington Institute for Near East Policy).

In many regards, the US is executing the objectives outlined in Tel Aviv's 1996 policy paper to secure the "realm." Yet once again it has to be emphasized that Israeli geo-strategy fits within the broader contours of Anglo-American geo-strategy, which, paraphrasing Halford J. Mackinder, envisions the Arab countries being divided into little states and wants the entire geographic corridor from the Baltic Sea and the Bosporus to the Levant and the Red Sea divided and even internationalized. There is part of the convergence of Anglo-American and Israeli policy, which can be thought of as either a Venn diagram or an Euler diagram where a smaller circle representing Israel either is a contained sub-set of the larger Anglo-American circle or has a large area of overlap that represents an intersection of shared interests. Moving forward, the term "realm" is rather regal or imperial and reflects the strategic and social mentality of the authors. A realm refers to either the territory ruled by a monarch or the territories that fall under a monarch's reign, but are not physically under their control and have vassals running them in the monarch's stead. In this context, the word realm has been employed to denote the Middle East as the kingdom of Tel Aviv. The fact that Richard Perle, someone who has essentially been a career Pentagon official, and the Wurmsers helped author the Israeli paper also, makes one ask if the conceptualized sovereign of the realm is either Israel, the United States, or both?

The 1996 Israeli document calls for "rolling back Syria" sometime around the year 2000 or afterward by pushing the Syrians out of Lebanon and destabilizing the Syrian Arab Republic with the help of the Hashemite Kingdom of Jordan and Turkey. These things have respectively come into fruition in the years 2005 and 2011. The 1996 document states:

> Israel can shape its strategic environment, in cooperation with Turkey and Jordan, by weakening, containing, and even rolling back Syria. This effort can focus on removing Saddam Hussein from power in Iraq—an important Israeli strategic objective in its own right—as a means of foiling Syria's regional ambitions."[6]

As a first step towards creating an Israeli-dominated "New Middle East" and encircling Syria, the 1996 document calls for removing President Saddam Hussein from power in Baghdad and even alludes to the balkanization of Iraq and forging a strategic regional alliance against Damascus that includes a Sunni Muslim "Central Iraq." Interestingly, the authors write:

> But Syria enters this conflict with potential weaknesses: Damascus is too preoccupied with dealing with the threatened new regional equation to permit distractions of the Lebanese flank. And Damascus fears that the "natural axis" with Israel on one side, central Iraq and Turkey on the other, and Jordan, in the center would squeeze and detach Syria from the Saudi Peninsula. For Syria, this could be the prelude to a redrawing of the map of the Middle East which would threaten Syria's territorial integrity.[7]

Perle and the Study Group on "A New Israeli Strategy Toward 2000" also call for driving the Syrians out of Lebanon and destabilizing Syria by using Lebanese opposition figures. The document states: "[Israel must divert] Syria's attention by using Lebanese opposition elements to destabilize Syrian control of Lebanon."[8] This would happen in 2005 after the Hariri assassination that helped launch the so-called "Cedar Revolution" and create the vehemently anti-Syrian March 14 Alliance controlled by the corrupt Said Hariri. This movement has also currently been accused of sending arms into Syria from Lebanon. Before that it was also responsible with the US, Saudi Arabia, and Jordan for bringing foreign fighters from the Fatah Al-Islam into Lebanon in plans to use them against Hezbollah that backfired; many of whose ilk are now fighting in Syria against the Syrian military. The "Clean Break" document also calls for Tel Aviv to "take [the] opportunity to remind the world of the nature of the Syrian regime."[9] This clearly falls into the Israeli strategy of demonizing its opponents through using public relations campaigns. In 2009, Israeli news media openly admitted that Tel Aviv through its embassies and diplomatic missions had launched a global campaign to discredit the Iranian presidential elections before they even took place through a media campaign and organizing protests in front of Iranian embassies.[10]

The "Clean Break" also mentions something that resembles what is currently going on in Syria. It states:

Most important, it is understandable that Israel has an interest in supporting diplomatically, militarily and operationally Turkey's and Jordan's actions against Syria, such as securing tribal alliances with Arab tribes that cross into Syrian territory and are hostile to the Syrian ruling elite.[11]

With the 2011 upheaval in Syria, the movement of insurgents and the smuggling of weapons through the Jordanian and Turkish borders has become a major problem for the government in Damascus.

In this context, it is no surprise that Arial Sharon and Israel told Washington to attack Syria, Libya, and Iran after the Anglo-American invasion of Iraq.[12] Finally, it is worth knowing that the Israeli document also advocated a pre-emptive war to shape Israel's geo-strategic environment and to carve out the "New Middle East."[13] This is a policy that the US would also adopt in 2001.

The Eradication of the Christian Communities of the Middle East

It is no coincidence that Egyptian Christians were attacked at the same time as the South Sudan Referendum and before the crisis in Libya. Nor is it a coincidence that Iraqi Christians, one of the world's oldest Christian communities, have been forced into exile, leaving their ancestral homelands in Iraq. Coinciding with the exodus of Iraqi Christians, which occurred under the watchful eyes of the military forces of the occupying powers of the United States of America and the United Kingdom of Great Britain and Northern Ireland, the neighbourhoods in Baghdad became sectarian as Shiite Muslims and Sunni Muslims were forced by violence and death squads to form sectarian enclaves. This division is tied to doctrine coming from the Yinon Plan and other plans of its ilk, including the Biden Plan, to reconfigure Iraq and the region in the flames of sectarianism. In a manner of speaking, Zionism can be seen as on offshoot or as an ideology that became a tool of British objectives to redefine the Middle East—objectives that turned into Anglo-American plans as the US adopted them—in its own sectarian image. Israel by self-definition is an ethnocracy and a sectarian state where in practice only Jews are treated as real citizens, while Muslims, Christians, and others are not full citizens and have lesser rights.

In Iran, the Israelis have been trying in vain to get the Iranian Jewish community to leave. Iran's Jewish population is actually the second largest in the Middle East and arguably the oldest undisturbed Jewish community in the world. Iranian Jews view themselves as Iranians who are tied to Iran as their homeland, just like Muslim, Zoroastrian, and Christian Iranians. For Iranian Jews the concept that they need to relocate to Israel because they are Jewish is ridiculous.

In Lebanon, Israel and the US State Department have been working with their allies like Saudi Arabia and France to exacerbate sectarian tensions between the various Christian and Muslim confessions as well as the Druze. Lebanon is a springboard into Syria and the division of Lebanon into several states is also seen as a means for balkanizing Syria into several smaller sectarian Arab states. The objectives of the Yinon Plan are to divide Lebanon and Syria into several states on the basis of religious and confessional identities amongst Sunni Muslims, Shiite Muslims, Christians, and the Druze. There could also be objectives for a Christian exodus in Syria too. Certain elements of opposition and insurgent supporters in Syria have been chanting: "Alawaites to the grave and Christians to Lebanon."

The head of the Maronite Catholic Syriac Church of Antioch, the largest of the autonomous Eastern Catholic Churches, has expressed his fears about a purging of Arab Christians in his part of the world. Patriarch Mar Beshara Boutros Al-Rahi and many other Christian leaders in Lebanon and Syria are afraid of a takeover by the Syrian National Council (SNC), which is dominated by the Muslim Brotherhood, in Syria. Christian communities have watched the events in Libya with discomfort and they are well aware of the fate of the Iraqi Christians. Like in Iraq, armed groups have been attacking Christians in Syria. Aside from the

Eastern Catholics, the leaders of the Christian Orthodox Churches, including the Eastern Orthodox Patriarch of Jerusalem and all the patriarchs in Syria, have all publicly expressed their grave concerns and fears that Christians will face an exodus. Aside from the Christian Arabs, these fears are also shared by the Assyrian and Armenian communities, which are mostly Christian. They know that should the US and its cohorts get their way in Syria that they would be targeted in the chaos that would ensue as Syria is redesigned under the forces of creative destruction that want to break the bonds of peaceful co-existence between Muslims and Christians, which along with Jewry and a group called the Sabians are called the "People of the Book (Bible)"—*Ahl Al-Kitab* in Arabic—a people protected, if they are sincere practitioners, in the Qu'ran.

In 2011, Patriarch Al-Rahi actually went to Paris where he met President Nicolas Sarkozy, the head of France. It is reported that the Maronite Patriarch and Sarkozy had disagreements about Syria, which prompted Sarkozy to say that the Syrian regime will collapse. Al-Rahi's position was that Syria should be left alone and allowed to reform peacefully. The Maronite Patriarch also told Sarkozy that Israel needed to be dealt with as a threat if France legitimately wanted Hezbollah to disarm in Lebanon. Because of the position he took while in France, Al-Rahi was instantly thanked by the Christian and Muslim religious leaders of the Syrian Arab Republic who visited him in Lebanon upon his return. Hezbollah and its political allies in Lebanon, which include most the Christian parliamentarians in the Lebanese Parliament, also lauded the Maronite Patriarch who later went on a tour to South Lebanon. This resulted in political and verbal attack on Al-Rahi by the Hariri-led March 14 Alliance and its allies in the Tahrir Party. The Tahrir Party is an international political party with branches in Lebanon, Libya, and Syria; it has been involved in both the conflicts in Libya and Syria. Moreover, it was reported that not long after the Maronite Patriarch's opposition to attacks on Syria, high-ranking US officials cancelled their meetings with the Al-Rahi and an ecclesiastical delegation as a sign of their displeasure about the Maronite Church's positions on Lebanon's Hezbollah and Syria.

There are unknown snipers who are targeting Syrian civilians and the Syrian Army with a view to causing chaos and internal fighting. The Christian communities in Syria are also being targeted by unknown groups. Most likely the attackers include a coalition of US, French, Jordanian, Israeli, Turkish, Saudi, and Khalij (Gulf) Arab forces working with some Syrians on the inside. This is part of the reign of terror that the US and its allies are trying to spread in Syria, as they did in the Libya and elsewhere. A Christian exodus is being planned for the Middle East by Washington and its cohorts. It has been reported that Sheikh Al-Rahi was told in Paris by President Nicolas Sarkozy that the Christian communities of his region can resettle in the European Union should the need arise. This is no gracious offer at all. Behind the nice words is something more sinister and insidious. Monsieur Sarkozy's words are a slap in the face. The same powers that have deliberately and systematically created the conditions to eradicate the ancient Christian communities of the Middle East are now offering the Christians refuge. Their insidious aim appears to be either the resettling of the Christian communities outside of the region or to demarcate them into sectarian enclaves. Both are possibilities and variances of the same strategy of divide and conquer. A flood of emotional Christian refugee streaming into France and the EU as the result of a sectarian conflict could also help replenish the Christian population and re-enforce a Christian identity that could be used to support a crusade against the Middle East and North Africa with religious and civilizational undertones.

The targeting of Christians in the Middle East is a project that is meant to delineate the Arab nations as exclusively Muslim countries. It falls into accordance with both the Yinon Plan and the geo-political objectives of the US to control the World-Island, which is the combined landmass of Africa and Eurasia, as it pushes inward into Eurasia. A major war may be its outcome. It is in this context that Arab Christians have a lot in common with the targeted black-skinned Arabs of Libya.

A Modern Re-division of Africa by the US, the EU and Israel

In regard to Africa, Tel Aviv sees securing Africa as part of its broader periphery. This broader or so-called "new periphery" became an even more important basis of geo-strategy for Tel Aviv after 1979 when the "old periphery" against the Arabs that included Iran, which was one of Israel's closest allies during the reign of Mohammed-Reza Pahlavi, buckled and collapsed with the 1979 Iranian Revolution. In this context, Israel's "new periphery" was conceptualized further to include countries like Ethiopia, Uganda, and Kenya as bulwarks against the Arab states and the Islamic Republic of Iran. In part, this is why Israel has been so deeply involved in the balkanization of Sudan. Yet, it has to also be cautioned that Israel had also long been quietly involved in the African continent for years. In the Moroccan-occupied Sahrawi Arab Democratic Republic, which is known as Western Sahara, the Israelis helped build a separation security wall like the one in the Israeli-occupied West Bank. In Sudan, Tel Aviv has armed the separatist movements and insurgents. In South Africa, the Israelis supported the Apartheid regime and its occupation of Namibia. The Israelis have used Burkina Faso, Uganda, and Kenya as bases. In 2009, the Israeli Foreign Ministry outlined that Africa would be the renewed focus of Tel Aviv.

Washington has outsourced intelligence work in Africa to Tel Aviv. Tel Aviv is effectively involved as one of the parties in a broader war not just *inside* Africa, but *over* Africa. In this war, Tel Aviv is working alongside the US and the EU against China and its allies. Tehran is working alongside Beijing in a similar manner as Tel Aviv is with Washington. Iran is helping the Chinese in Africa through Iranian connections. These ties also include Tehran's ties to private Lebanese and Syrian business interests in Africa. Thus, within the broader rivalry between Washington and Beijing, an Israeli-Iranian rivalry has also unfolded within Africa.[14] Sudan is Africa's third largest weapons producer, as a result of Iranian support in weapons manufacturing. Meanwhile, while Iran provides military assistance to Khartoum, which includes several military cooperation agreements, Israel is involved in various actions directed against the Sudanese.[15]

In the same context as the sectarian divisions in the Middle East, the Israelis have outlined plans to reconfigure Africa within the contours of older divisional schemes drafted in places like London and Paris. These Israeli plans also go well with the United States and the European Union that look to securing the African continent and its vast resources for themselves. The Yinon Plan seeks to delineate Africa on the basis of three facets: (1) ethno-linguistics; (2) skin-colour and phenotype; and, finally, (3) religion. In other words, identities are being used to turn people and societies against one another in order to secure their control by outsiders. The Institute for Advanced Strategic and Political Studies (IASPS), the Israeli think-tank that published Richard Perle's "Clean Break" strategy, also advocated for the creation of the Pentagon's US Africa Command (AFRICOM) to secure the realm in Africa.

Israel must get special mention in regard to Libya. The role of Israel and the Israeli lobby was fundamental in opening the door to NATO's military intervention in Libya. It was UN Watch that actually orchestrated the events in Geneva to remove Libya from the UN Human Rights Council and to ask the U.N. Security Council to intervene militarily against Tripoli.[16] UN Watch is a part of the Israeli lobby and formally affiliated with the American Jewish Committee (AJC), which has influenced the formulation of US foreign policy since its creation. The International Federation of Human Rights (FIDH), which helped launch the unverified claims about 6,000 people being slaughtered by Qaddafi, is also tied to the Israeli lobby in France. These linkages cannot be overlooked when dealing with NATO's war on Libya.

Tel Aviv was in contact simultaneously with both the Transitional Council in Benghazi and the Libyan government in Tripoli. Mossad agents were also in Tripoli, one of whom was a former station manager. At about the same time, French members of the Israeli lobby were visiting Benghazi to secure commitments from its leaders. The Transitional Council would deceptively claim that Colonel Qaddafi was working with Israel, even as it made pledges to recognize Israel to Sarkozy's special envoy, Bernard-Henri Lévy, who would then convey the message to Israeli leaders.[17] A similar pattern to that of Israel's links to the Transitional Council had developed earlier with the leaders of South Sudan, which were armed by Tel Aviv.

Despite the Transitional Council's narrowly hidden position on Israel, its followers still demonized Qaddafi by claiming that he was secretly Jewish. Not only was this untrue, but it was also bigoted and showed the narrow-minded nature of their supporters. These accusations were intended to be a form of character assassination that equated being a Jew as being something negative. In reality, Israel and NATO are part of the same camp. Israel is actually a de facto member of NATO and has intense cooperation with NATO, even conducting naval patrols with NATO vessels in the Mediterranean Sea. Had Qaddafi been conniving with Israel while the Transitional Council was working with NATO, this would mean that both sides were actually being played like fools and marionettes against one another—not just the Transitional Council.

Colonialism and Identity Politics

What has been in motion is an attempt to separate the merging point of the Arab and African identities. This process seeks to draw dividing lines or cuts in the flesh of Africa between a so-called "Black Africa" and a supposedly "non-Black" North Africa. This is part of a scheme to create a schism in Africa between what are simplistically and wrongly assumed to be "Arabs" and so-called "Blacks." This goal is why the ridiculous identities of an "African South Sudan" and an "Arab North Sudan" have been nurtured and promoted. The alienation of South Sudan's identity from the Republic of Sudan has actually in many aspects paralleled the process under which the British alienated the identity of Sudan from Egypt. The grievances that South Sudan has had about the Republic of Sudan follow the same lines of criticisms and tensions that were nurtured amongst the Sudanese against Egyptians, which resulted in the separation of Sudan from Egypt. It is in this context that black-skinned Libyans have been targeted in a campaign to "colour cleanse"

Libya. In broader terms, the Arab identity in North Africa is being de-linked from its African identity. Simultaneously there is an attempt to marginalize and eradicate the large populations of black-skinned Arabs so that there is a clear delineation between a desired neo-colonial "Black Africa" and a desired "non-Black North Africa." North Africa in turn will further be divided as a fighting ground between those Berbers and Arabs that are not black-skinned.

There is a consistent effort to prevent people from establishing a level of consciousness about how identity is used and wielded to maintain structures of power. Any anthropologist, historian, political scientist, or sociologist can attest to the mountains of data about the manipulation of identity within a society or within colonial systems as a means of maintaining control and diluting unity amongst the oppressed and exploited. Identity has been an important device of colonial rule from Brazil and Rwanda to India and Indo-China. Identities have been lost, stolen, hidden, appropriated, transformed, and others given and naturalized through colonial processes and hegemonic cultural forces. There is a good sociological argument to be made that the racialization of identities serves something worse within a colonial discourse that not only seeks to create and preserve power structures: individual, group, and societal identities can be weaponized. Therefore, identity claims, assessments of authenticity, a sense of belonging, and identity allegiances all come into play within modern neo-colonial strategies, just as they did in the past—as a tool for the promotion of violent conflicts by external forces.

In Libya, there is a push to weaponize identity, but this identity game has also been used to justify NATO's war in Libya through underhanded reporting by the mainstream media. Racist and exaggerated reports about non-Libyan African mercenaries were disseminated by most the corporate media. These reports by networks, like the BBC and CNN, actually appropriated the identities and nationalities of black-skinned Libyans, displaying them in pictures and videos as foreigners who had come to Libya to oppress the Libyan people under Qaddafi's pay. Outside of Libya many were fooled by this, ignorantly thinking that Arabs could not be black-skinned, let alone Libyans. The media helped perpetuate these ignorant views which facilitated their lies about an army of mercenaries serving Muammar Qaddafi.

Being an Arab does not ascribe one to any particular phenotype or physical look, because it is the use of the Arabic language that defines the Arab identity and is one of the bases for the Arab culture. Arabs can be black-skinned or of an olive or fair-skinned complexion; they can have blue eyes and blond hair or brown eyes and black hair; their hair can be Afro-textured, curly, or fine and straight. The Arab identity is not a fixed ethnicity per se, but is a very open, pluralistic, and inclusive identity that has a wide embrace. In 1946, the Arab League defined and described being an Arab as follows: "An Arab is a person whose language is Arabic, who lives in an Arabic speaking country, [and] who is in sympathy with the aspirations of the Arabic speaking peoples."[18] Moreover, an Arab can physically mirror individuals that have the representative physical characteristics of the dominant phenotypes in Kenya, Nigeria, Italy, India, Turkey, Germany, or France. The same can be said about the Berbers.

This is also very true of all Libyans and other North Africans. Libya is geographically situated in a location where numerous stocks of people from Africa, Europe, and Asia have met, settled, and mixed with one another. Many Libyans are black-skinned. Amongst them are the Haratins (Harratins) and the Berber Tuareg in the south. These Libyans are as Libyan as the other inhabitants of the country. Many of the families in Libya are actually mixed in regard to their physical appearances and include family members with brown, black, and white skin. The same media networks and governments that failed to acknowledge these facts also ignored the murder and plight of black-skinned Libyans and black-skinned migrant workers from other parts of Africa. In short, as is typical of wartime (and now apparently of so-called humanitarian intervention) the Western media's coverage promoted whatever was advantageous to their governments' attack on Libya, and ignored what was not.

Identity is not a one dimensional thing, there are multiplicities to it. It is also subject to change and can become malleable under pressure, making it susceptible to change and manipulation. The assessment that a Libyan cannot be either an African or an Arab is incorrect. Identity should not be compartmentalized. Returning to our example of a Venn diagram or an Euler diagram may help conceptualize the relationship between Arabdom and Africa; both are intersecting circles in their relationship. The area where the two circles intersect one another is both mutually African and Arab as are those that people this area. Taxonomy, especially for identity, can be troubling and incomplete. In many respects the categorization or regulation of identities in Africa and elsewhere, including amongst the indigenous peoples of the America led to a process whereby key aspects of Western European race ideology have been imposed. However, we still must make reference of it to shed light on and dispel Western efforts to de-link the Arabs from the mosaic of Africa.

In ethno-linguistic terns, the tie between Arabs and Africa is also very clear when one studies the Arabic language and the family it belongs to. Arabic is a Semitic language, like Hebrew and Aramaic, and Semitic is a branch of the Afro-Asiatic language family, which is less frequently called Hamito-Semitic. The name Afro-Asiatic says something in itself too. Aside from most speakers of Arabic being located in Africa, most of the distinct members of this language family, specifically from the Hamitic side of the language family, are located in Africa. In fact, the Hamitic languages are exclusively tied to Africa and in many cases exclusively with black-skinned African ethnic groups. These languages are as listed: the Berber languages; Hausa and the other Chadic languages spoken in Chad, Niger, Nigeria, Cameroon, and the Central African Republic; and the Cushtic languages, particularly Oromo and Somali, which have a geographic range from Somalia, Djibouti, Ethiopia, Kenya, and Sudan to Tanzania and southern Egypt. Moreover, Arabs share a kinship with Ethiopians, Eritreans, and Somalis; all of which are clearly Africans.

To sever North Africa from the rest of Africa, the notion of black-skinned Arabs must be removed. Their removal does not necessarily have to be physical; their identities can be stolen and erased. They can be reduced to non-persons and denizens in their own countries and marginalized from public life and society. Black-skinned Arabs can only be severed from their lands when they no longer exist as such—as black-skinned Arabs—they are not a people in themselves, in their own minds and in the minds of others. In the same context, tensions are being fomented on a dual track between Muslims and Christians in Africa, in such places as Sudan and Nigeria, for the same ends: to further create lines and fracture points. In repetition, the fuelling of these divisions on the basis of skin-colour, religion, ethnicity, and language is intended to fuel disassociation and disunity in Africa. This is all part of a broader African strategy of cutting North Africa off from the rest of the African continent.

Preparing the Chessboard for the "Clash of Civilizations"

It is at this point that all the pieces have to be put together and the dots have to be connected. The chessboard is being staged for a clash of so-called civilizations or the "Clash of Civilizations" as envisioned by US and Israeli strategists. All the chess pieces are being lined up. The Arab World is in the process of being cordoned off and sharp delineation lines are being created. These lines of delineation are replacing the seamless and organic lines of gradual transition between different ethno-linguistic, phenotype, and religious groups. Under this design, there can no longer be a melding transition between societies and countries. This is why the Christians in the Middle East and North Africa, such as the Copts, are besieged and under attack. This is also why black-skinned Arabs and black-skinned Berbers, as well as other North African population groups which are black-skinned, are facing genocide in North Africa.

The Yinon Plan stipulates that Iraq and Egypt would be key to destabilizing the Arab World. After these two states, the Libyan Arab Jamahiriya and the Syrian Arab Republic are both important points of regional destabilization in North Africa and the Middle East respectively. What happens in Libya will have rippling effects on Africa, as what happens in Syria will have rippling effects on the Middle East and beyond. Both Iraq and Egypt, in connection with what the Yinon Plan states, have acted as primers for the destabilization of both these Arab states. What is being staged is the creation of an almost exclusively "Muslim Middle East" area, excluding Israel and possibly a few small Christian enclaves, that will see turmoil due to the exacerbation of externally-induced Shiite and Sunni fighting amongst its Muslim inhabitants. A similar scenario is being staged for a North Africa area devoid of black-skinned peoples which will be characterized by a confrontation between Arabs and Berbers. At the same time, under the "Clash of Civilizations" model of Samuel P. Huntington, the Middle East and North Africa are slated to simultaneously be in conflict with the so-called civilizations of the "West" and "Black Africa." Herein lays the crux of the matter. This "Clash of Civilizations" between so-called Islamic Civilization and all the other surrounding civilizations has been envisioned and intended for many years. In the 1990s there were continuous references by US policy makers and Pentagon officials to Islam and a coming conflict with the Muslim countries and so-called Western Civilization. Communism was replaced by Islam as the next threat within a twisted Straussian worldview of reality. The Belgian politician Willem Claes, while acting as the secretary-general of NATO before he was forced to resign after it became public that he was taking bribes, would actually say that Islam had become NATO's new threat.

In reality, there are no clear cuts between these so-called civilizations. A careful analysis will prove that Huntington's "Clash of Civilizations" theory is unsound fantasy. A Muslim country like Albania is part of so-called Western Civilization, while a pluralistic country comprised of Christians like Lebanon is branded as part of Islamic Civilization. If one agrees with the notion that Bulgaria, Romania, Serbia,

Belarus, Moldova, Georgia, Armenia, Ukraine, and Russia are part of a distinct Orthodox Civilization, where does Bosnia and Herzegovina fit with its Eastern Orthodox Serbs, Muslim Bosniaks, and Roman Catholic Croats? Moreover, countries like Russia, Kazakhstan, and Nigeria have mixed Christian and Muslim populations and regions. Where do they fit?

These so-called civilizations all actually and thoroughly overlap and it is these overlapping lines that the racialization of war and ideas like the Yinon Plan and the Biden Plan seek to erase. This is why both Nicolas Sarzoky and David Cameron made back-to-back declarations in France and Britain during the start of the conflict in Libya that multiculturalism was dead in their respective Western European societies.[19] This implies that their citizenry is homogenous, which it is not, and that their legal systems are assimilationist, which they are not. While several Western European countries have a very developed minority rights system that legally protects minority cultures as such—which these internal nationalities themselves have struggled to achieve or maintain—the cultural intolerance tacitly encouraged by the state works as a countervailing force.

The push for the drawing of dividing lines between Muslim countries and the West is also taking shape in the form of the discourse and laws banning mosques and Muslim dress in the West. Conversely, government installed and controlled puppet clerics are being used in client Muslim countries like Saudi Arabia to do the same. The so-called Grand Mufti of Saudi Arabia and other government clerics in the Gulf Cooperation Council (GCC) countries have been calling for the destruction of Christian churches in the Arabian Peninsula while they have denounced mentioning the liberation of Palestine in public sermons and prayers.[20] Both these bigoted trends are aimed at eroding multiculturalism and creating homogeneity.

Real multiculturalism threatens the legitimacy of the NATO war agenda and prevents the alienation of other regions of the world. It constitutes a real obstacle to the implementation of the "Clash of Civilizations" paradigm which constitutes the cornerstone of US foreign policy. In this regard, Zbigniew Brzezinski, former US National Security Advisor, explains why multiculturalism is a threat to the war plans of Washington and its allies:

> [A]s America becomes an increasingly multicultural society, it may find it more difficult to fashion a consensus on foreign policy issues [e.g., war with the Arab World, China, Iran, or Russia and the former

Soviet Union], except in the circumstances of a truly massive and widely perceived direct external threat. Such a consensus generally existed throughout World War II and even during the Cold War [and exists now because of the "Global War on Terror"].[21]

Brzezinski's next sentence is the qualifier of why populations would oppose or support wars:

[The public consensus in the United States] was rooted, however, not only in deeply shared democratic values, which the public sensed were being threatened, but also in a cultural and ethnic affinity for the predominantly European victims of hostile totalitarianisms [meaning Germany, Italy, and the Axis Powers].[22]

Again, it is precisely with the intention of breaking these cultural affinities between the regions of the Middle East and North Africa with the so-called Western and "Black Africa" or sub-Saharan Africa that Christians and black-skinned peoples are being targeted in Arab regions and there is a push in the so-called West to create an identity that is hostile to the Middle East and North Africa both abroad and at home.

**Meta-Myths and Ethnocentricism:
Justifying Today's "Just Wars"**

In the past, the colonial powers of Western Europe would indoctrinate their people. Their objective was the acquirement of acquiescence and popular support for their colonial conquests and occupations of other lands and peoples. They tried all means to normalize their actions to make them seem enlightened, natural, or moral. One main form this took was the pretext of spreading Christianity and promoting Christian values with the support of armed merchants and colonial armies. At the same time, racist ideologies were developed or put forth. The people whose lands were stolen and plundered were portrayed as sub-human, inferior, or soulless. The creation of the *encomienda* system in Latin America and the Atlantic slave trade that followed it were rationalized as positive.[23] As organized religion declined domestically in Western Europe, the "White Man's burden" of taking on a mission of civilizing the so-called "uncivilized peoples of the world" was used in its stead. This ideological framework was used to portray colonialism as a "just cause." The latter in turn was used to provide legitimacy to the waging of "just wars" as a means to conquering and "civilizing" foreign lands and their peoples. Unjustifiable acts were committed and wars such as the Opium Wars waged to force China into accepting British narcotics distribution to the Chinese people were moralized.

Today, the imperialist designs of the United States, Britain, and France have not changed. What has changed are their pretexts and justifications for waging their neo-colonial wars of conquest. During the colonial period, the narratives and justifications for waging war were accepted by public opinion in the colonizing countries. Today's "just wars" and "just causes" are now being conducted under the banners of women's rights, human rights, humanitarianism, and democracy. International development, for the most part, is to be added to this list as a means of colonization and invasion—after all it was under colonial administrations, the predecessors of modern development practitioners, that both the professionalization and conceptualization of development took shape. Modern development discourse is, as the post-modernists say, "nothing more than an apparatus of control and surveillance."[24]

Ethnocentricism is also part of the tool kit of waging colonial wars. Under it the different traditions and forms of governing of other peoples are demonized. In underlying terms, many of the supporters of these wars also wish to see their cultures and normative system of values imposed on the targets of these wars. This is actually genocide through not only killing, but through the erasing of entire cultures. As in the Americas with the indigenous peoples, the erasing of an identity or of multiple identities and the disruption of other peoples' way of life is actually a form of genocide. According to the meaning of the term, as coined in 1944 by the Polish lawyer Raphael Lemkin, during the discussions leading to UN Genocide Convention:

Generally speaking, genocide does not necessarily mean the immediate destruction of a nation, *except* when accomplished by mass killing of all the members of a nation. It is intended rather to signify a coordinated plan of different actions aimed at destruction of the essential foundations of the life of national groups, with the aim of annihilating the groups themselves. The objective of such a plan would be disintegration of the political and social institutions, of culture, language, national feelings, religion, and the economic existence of national groups, and the economic existence of national groups, and the destruction of personal security, liberty, health, dignity, and the lives of individuals belonging to such groups. . . . Genocide has two phases:

one, destruction of the national pattern of the oppressed group; the other, the imposition of the national pattern of the oppressor.[25]

Under the smokescreens of academic jargon and political bravado, this is what the end result of the racialization of war and the "Clash of Civilizations" paradigm are. They are a form of modern colonization and genocide that are being rationalized and sustained by the meta-myths produced by the mass media, intelligentsia, establishment institutions, and governments. While the West is painted as superior, culturally tolerant and modern, other so-called civilizations from the so-called Islamic, Orthodox, and African to the so-called Hindu and Sinic (Chinese) are portrayed as lesser, intolerant, and pre-modern. The peoples outside of the cultural and political boundaries of the West are thought of as being in need of Western—really *capitalist*—liberation, modes of production, norms, and values. In one way or another, these lands are viewed as *underdeveloped* places that are locked in a state of static and redundant traditionalism, which is ipso facto undesirable, and which only the so-called West can free. The *developed* West and its outliers are depicted as the epitome of perfect states that do not need to develop any further; they are what the *underdeveloped* and *developing* must mimic and become to succeed or progress, i.e. to be developed. At its roots Western "tolerance" of all else is conditioned as something that is necessitated toward undesirable and blemished entities and practices that would preferably not exist.

The values of "civilizational tolerance" that Huntington and US policymakers actually desire to spread are those of Western capitalist hegemony over others. The "just causes" are merely pretexts supported by cultural meta-myths to allow Western capitalism to subvert and replicate itself in different regions of the world like a virus attacking and invading living cells and then replicating itself. International development, as one of these "just causes," in many ways also serves as a force for the diffusion of Western culture and for economic domination. In many cases development assistance has worked as to continue colonial political and socio-economic relations between colonial powers and their former colonies.[26]

The tragedy in Libya of what has been happening to its black-skinned peoples and the attacks on the Christian communities of Syria, which hereto have both mostly gone unreported, remain unmentioned so that the ignorant beliefs that Arabs cannot possibly be black-skinned or Christian can go unchallenged. This facilitates the continuation of post-modern colonial domination by alienating the affinities of peoples to one another under the deceptive guise of "just wars" and Machiavellian manipulation of notions of cultural enlightenment.

ENDNOTES

1   Black-skinned Arabs are only a minority when all Arab peoples are aggregated, but in an actual country by country basis they are not a minority in Sudan, Moroccan-occupied Western Sahara, and Mauritania.

2   Sanatana Dharma or Vedic Dharma (Vedicism) is the proper name for Hinduism. The terms Hindu and Hinduism are misnomers, just as Mohammedan and Mohammedanism are misnomers respectively for Muslims and the faith of Islam. The term Hindu is originally a geographic definition used by the ancient Iranians to label all the peoples living in the lands of the Indus Valley or east of the Indus River regardless of religious affinity or faith. The term Hindu was later adopted by the Arabs who conquered Sassanid Iran and then expanded their territories towards India. As the Altaic peoples, such as the Mongolian and Turkic-speaking tribes, migrated westward in Eurasia they also adopted the term through interaction with both the Iranians and the Arabs. At this point in history, and up to the rule of the Mughal Dynasty in India, the term Hindu started gaining popular and recurrent usage, but was still used as an ethnographic term and not a religious identification label. All the Muslims, Sikhs, Christians, Buddhists, Zoroastrians, Jainists, and Vedicists of India were exclusively called Hindus by themselves and outsiders. It was during the colonial rule of the British, that colonial administrators coined the English-language word of "Hinduism" and in 1830 assigned the already existing and ancient Iranian word Hindu to describe and designate the faiths and peoples of India belonging to Vedicism. Hindus are in reality all the people of India. The term Hindi, also used to label Indians and one of the main Indic languages, comes from Hindustani which also reflects the geographic nature and origins of the term Hindu; Hindustan means land of India and Hindustani people of India.

3   Mark LeVine, "The New Creative Destruction," *Asia Times*, August 22, 2006.

4   *Ibid.*

5   Mahdi Darius Nazemroaya, "Privatizzazione e costruzione del 'impero'" ["Privatization and the construction of 'Empire'"], trans. Pietro Longo, *Eurasia: Revista di Studi Geopolitici* 23:3 (May/August 2011), p.50.

6   Richard Perle *et al.*, *A Clean Break: A New Strategy for Securing the Realm* (Tel Aviv: Institute for Advanced Strategic and Political Studies), 1996.

7   *Ibid.*

8   *Ibid.*

9   *Ibid.*

10   Barak Ravid, "Israeli diplomats told to take offensive in PR war against Iran," *Haaretz*, June 1, 2009.

11   Perle *et al.*, "Clean Break," *op. cit.*

12   Aluf Benn, "Sharon says US should also disarm Iran, Libya and Syria," *Haaretz*, September 30, 2009.

13   Richard Perle *et al.*, Clean Break, *op. cit*.

14   *The Economist*, "Israel and Iran in Africa: A search for allies in a hostile world," February 4, 2011.

15   *Ibid.*

16   Tova Lazaroff, "70 rights groups call on UN to condemn Tripoli," *Jerusalem Post*, February 22, 2011.

17   *Radio France Internationale*, "Libyan rebels will recognise Israel, Bernard-Henri Lévy tells Netanyahu," June 2, 2011.

18   William D. Wunderle, *Through the Lens of Cultural Awareness: A Primer for US Armed Forces Deploying to Arab and Middle Eastern Countries* (Washington D.C.: US Government Printing Office, 2006), p.25.

19   Robert Marquand, "Why Europe is turning away from multiculturalism," *Christian Science Monitor*, March 4, 2011

20   The number of deviations practiced by these so-called Muslim leaders is vast. Firstly, in Islam there are not to be any clerics or religious hierarchy. As a minor demonstration of the deviances of these so-called Muslim leaders from Islam, it should be mentioned that Jews and Christians lived in large numbers in both Mecca and Medina during the time of the Prophet Mohammed and well after his death for generations. The Prophet Mohammed had no problem with this and Jews and Christians were always welcome to the Mecca and Medina. Under the Al-Sauds, however, Jews and Christians are band from even stepping foot in either city, because it is supposedly against Islam. This puts the Al-Sauds in conflict with the practices of teachings of the Prophet Mohammed and Islam.

21   Zbigniew Brzezinski, *The Grand Chessboard: American Primacy and Its Geostrategic Imperatives* (New York: Basic Books October 1997), p.211.

22   *Ibid.*

23   The *encomienda* was a neo-feudal system constructed by the Spanish through a royal grant that created properties and estates in Latin America run by Spaniards who would control the indigenous peoples. The individuals who were bestowed with these lands were supposed to be helping the indigenous people in theory by "civilizing" them and protecting them. Aside from colonizing the indigenous people and instituting cultural hegemony, the system was for all intents and purposes a form of slavery used to force slave work.

24   Frederick Cooper and Randall Packard, "The History and Politics of Development Knowledge" in *The Anthropology of Development and Globalization: From Classical Political Economy to Contemporary Neoliberalism*, eds. Marc Edelman and Angelique Haugerud (Malden, MA: Blackwell Publishing, 2005), p.127.

25   Bonita Lawrence, *"Real" Indians and Others: Mixed-Blood Urban Native Peoples and Indigenous Nationhood* (Toronto: UBC Press, 2004), p.*xviii.*

26   Cooper and Packard, "Development Knowledge," *op. cit.*, pp.126-139.

NEOCOLONIALISM, SUBVERSION IN AFRICA AND GLOBAL CONFLICT

Dr. Christof Lehman

The withdrawal of the old colonial powers from Africa, in the context of a developing cold war,[1] a developing Pan-African Nationalism,[2] and the rising cost of maintaining a colonial administration system, during the 1960s, left the African nations in a euphoric state of independence. In most cases this euphoria was soon to be substituted by shocking massacres and conflict, coup d´etats, unrest and destabilization. The old colonial rulers had returned with a vengeance. Over fifty years later, most African nations are, in spite of the richness of their resources and productivity of their population, still catastrophically underdeveloped, impoverished, indebted, and plagued by conflict, unrest and instability due to the return of the colonial powers influence. Those African nations who failed to comply with their returning rulers were and are mercilessly attacked. Libya and the Ivory Coast are examples of the new colonizations' subversive influence, and a warning for African leaders to face the lion in solidarity or be devoured one by one.

Common Denominators

All conflicts in post-colonial African wars as well as internal unrest have the same common elements: the involvement of foreign nations and the instrumentalization of local elements, with the goal of controlling the resources, the economy, and geopolitically as well as strategically significant locations. Western medias' narrative of French, British, and USA involvement in Africa commonly takes the form of manufacturing popular consent by eliciting a fabled advocacy for stability, human rights, and democracy for African countries. Nothing could be farther from the truth. Stability, human rights and democracy are but the pretext for aggressive neo-colonial subversion, invasion, long-term military presence and control. This subversion and invasion has acquired an additional dimension after China began to invest massively on the African continent. While the traditional colonial powers and the USA maintained the traditional role of the supremacist usurper, China is, though resource, trade and profit oriented, taking an approach of joint ventures and contribution to the development of African nations' infrastructure.[3] After all, the Sino-African model of free market enterprise and joint venture cannot function if African nations don´t develop to such degree that they can import consumer goods that are manufactured in China. Thus, since China began investing in interests in Africa, the traditional colonial powers and the USA´s subversions and aggressions began being directed against primarily China, and secondarily Russia, which is recently re-discovering its strength as a global power after a period of restructuring and re-consolidation after the collapse of the USSR.[4]

The neo-colonial model of subversion is based on directing and co-opting local instruments, such as opposition parties, human rights organizations, and ongoing internal low intensity conflicts, as well as expatriate communities, expatriates sponsored and with ties to i.e. the National Endowment for Democracy, and other Institutes, NGOs and organizations that are notorious for their involvement in subversion.[5] These systems interface with both civilian and military intelligence services and special operations forces in a logical, systematic approach that invariably has the same outcome: the subversion of the country, and the installation of a controlled, friendly, or proxy government. Precisely the same methodology is explained in an analysis of the subversion of Syria that began with the "Arab Spring" in 2011.[6] A successful subversion without the co-conspiracy of local elements is neither viable nor desirable. A U.S. Training Manual for Unconventional Warfare is breaking such terms as feasibility for subversion down into operational details.[7] The co-opting of local opposition in African subversions has been an invariable part of neo-colonial strategy since day one of neo-colonialism, when the Congolese Government and Patrice Lumumba were overthrown by creating and aggravating internal tensions, and by the financial as well as covert military support of an armed insurgency with its basis in a local militia.[8] The function of any of these subversions is invariably the controlling of resources and wealth while keeping the African nations impoverished and indebted and, since the beginning of the rapid development of China´s economy, includes geopolitical as well as economic warfare on Russia and China.

Mercenary Armies in Colonial Warfare and Al Qaeda

Abdelhakim Belhadj LIFG

The use of local instruments in subversions has largely been based on either tribal or religious aspects. A prime example of this strategy is Angola. After the Socialist MPLA backed by Cuba and the USSR came to power in Angola, the Western Block, read NATO countries, began building and supporting two alternative movements, the NFLA in Northern Angola, and UNITA in Southern Angola. Both the NFLA and UNITA were based on the same charter, but were divided by tribal affiliation.[9] In the case of Afghanistan, the USA and NATO countries heavily supported what was then called the "Mujahideen", and a CIA-run network of Arab mercenaries, which came to become known as Al-Qaeda (10). The same network of mainly Arab and Afghan mercenaries was used by NATO in the war on Serbia, and the conquering of Kosovo,[11] and has been used against Libya by Western Intelligence Services for decades. It is currently providing the core of the so-called "rebels" in Libya.[12] How NATO is using this "network" or Al Qaeda, depending on what function it is supposed to fulfill in a given operation—as respectively purported enemy or ally—is illustrated by a West Point Study,[13] that shows that the same Al Qaeda Terrorist Network in Bengazi and Derna, Libya, the Libyan Islamic Fighting Group (LIFG), delivered the greatest per capita contribution of foreign fighters against the USA in Iraq, while the same LIFG is now providing the core around which other CIA- imported Afghan fighters[14] are installed in the theater of operations in the occupation of Libya.

At the onset of what is generally termed "The Arab Spring" in Libya, US President Barak Obama signed an order designating CIA operatives to the eastern Libyan cities of Derna and Bengazi, in preparation for the final stages of the covert, and the beginning stages of the overt subversion of the Libyan Government,[15] Publicly, Obama sent the CIA operatives to "analyze" the rebel forces. This analysis however, had been done in the West Point Study long before; how intelligence operations are performed was part of the step by step strategy for subversion explained in the TC18-01 Unconventional Warfare manual cited above. The military leadership of the Al Qaeda fraction, the Libyan Islamic Fighting group, was re labeled "the rebels" and not long after, the Tripoli Military Council.[16] Meanwhile, the corporate Western media vilified and positioned Muammar Qaddafi and the Libyan Government as dictatorial villains who indiscriminately bombed "peaceful protesters" while Al Qaeda and its associated army of mercenaries, and the political proxies Mahmud Jibril, Jalil, and a cohort of "anonymous "politicians" of the Transitional National Counsel were made into the heroes of the Libyan Revolution. The manufacturing of consent by media is one invariable element of warfare. The manufacturing of a quasi legitimate new government is an invariable element of neo-colonial strategy, as it can be observed in the example of the manufacturing of the National Counsel of Syria, which is in NATO´s sites too.[17] The main obstacle for the advance of neo-colonialism on the African Continent has never been Al Qaeda, but Muammar Qaddafi and the Libyan Government, as well as Laurent Gbagbo of Ivory Coast, and Robert Mugabe of Zimbabwe.

Do Africans Really Know What a Supreme Court Is?

Laurent Gbagbo

In Ivory Coast, the situation was not unlike the one in Libya. Ivory Coast held a Presidential election, with an apparently very close outcome. In the Western corporate media, all we heard was that the Electoral Commission of Ivory Coast had declared Outara the winner of the elections. What the Western Media failed to report was that there had been widespread election fraud, that the President of Ivory Coast and his party took the election results to the Supreme Court, and that the Supreme Court declared Laurent Gbagbo the winner of the election, and thus Laurent Gbagbo to be the lawful President Elect of Ivory Coast. What was reported, and emphatically reported, was that "security forces" clamped down on "peaceful protesters", and then that "Outara´s Army" is cornering Gbagbo "in his bunker".[18] This news coverage and manufacturing of consent is only possible in populations that are inherently racist and traditional or neo-colonial powers.[19] The important question is: where did Outara, who just claimed to have won the election, get an "Army" from? Unless a population is so used to condescending racism and colonialist thinking, one would immediately say: "But the electoral commission is not the one to approve of election results, it´s the Supreme Court". Not so, if the audience is inherently racist, and inherently thinking in a way typical of colonial powers' condescension towards the wild and uncivilized African.

To illustrate the point with a Western example: When George Bush and Al Gore had the closest ever election held in the United States of America,[20] who certified the election? The Supreme Court.[21] Even though many Americans felt utterly disenfranchised, the population respected the Supreme Court. Can you for one moment imagine that *"Al Gore cornered Bush in his bunker, with Al Gore´s Army, neglecting the Supreme Court, because an Electoral Commission had pronounced him the winner? " Where did Al Gore get an Army from anyway?"* What happened in Ivory Coast was that France and the United States backed Outara in neglecting the ruling of the Supreme Court and the Constitutional Counsel of Ivory Coast because the Supreme Court decided in favor of Laurent Gbagbo and not the Proxy President of Neo-Colonialism in Africa.

Where did Outara get an army from? Outara´s "army" consisted of a collection of *"rebel forces"* or French-backed insurgents from the Northern part of Ivory Coast, who had been convinced by the French DGSE[22] and old colonial power structures inherent in, among other French Freemasonry in Africa, to side with Outara, against Laurent Gbagbo.[23] Besides that, 2.500 French soldiers,[24] plus UN soldiers[25] were present, taking active part in the ousting of Laurent Gbagbo, and the legitimate government of Ivory Coast. That is where Outara got *"His Army"* from. Insurgents, French and UN troops were *Outara´s Army*.[26] An army that murdered thousands of Ivory Coast citizens in a neo-colonial post-modern coup d´etat. Justice on Laurent Gbagbo is then served at the United Nation´s ICC, making the UN, France and the USA the judge, the jury, and the executioner.[27]

Why Did France Have to Remove Gbagbo from Office?

The question that needs to be answered before it is possible to discern why the events in Ivory Coast and Libya occur as they do is *"why"* did the USA and France want Laurent Gbagbo and Qaddafi removed from political office. The unrests, the engineering of dissent, the alliances with armed militia, politicians and oligarchs are nothing but *"functions"* and *"instruments"*. It is comparable to a script for a play in the world political theater—the script is written, the acts planned, long before the cast of actors is chosen. The discourse of political reporting, and the manufacturing of opinion discuss the cast, seldom the playwright, almost never the playwright's motivation, and that "why" is one of the most critical functions of media with respect to social engineering. It is absolutely necessary to have an understanding of this background to understand the subversions in Ivory Coast and Libya. After World War II the European economies were scrambling to reconstitute. So was that of France, which devised long term plans for economic recovery in several phases. The traditional form of colonial control by military might and absolute political control had, in spite of the richness of African resources, become too costly, too cumbersome. In the light of the depletion of military force due to two major conflicts, it had become impossible. What is also noteworthy is that the post-war period also is the period where the development of media and public relations significantly began substituting for police and military force as instruments for social control.[28]

Laurent Gbagbo had discussions with other visionary African leaders who not only knew that the new colonization of Africa was keeping African nations impoverished and virtually enslaved, their citizens being the backbone of the new colonial powers' economy, but who had the vision, courage, and integrity to resist the usurpers of Europe, the USA, and globalized corporate influences. Most prominently, with Robert Mugabe, President of Zimbabwe, and Muammar al-Qaddafi, honorary leader of the Libyan Revolution. One of the main reasons why Laurent Gbagbo had to be replaced by France, and replaced fast, was that Gbagbo was not only seriously working towards creating Ivory Coast's own currency that would be independent of France, but that he, like Robert Mugabe and Muammar Qaddafi, actively lobbied and encouraged other African nations in the CFA region (countries that employ the franc, the Communaute Financiere Africaine) to follow suit.[29] The main reason why France *"never would allow this to happen"* in one of its old colonies is that the CFA is one of the main sources of income for the French economy. Not only does France control the value of the CFA, and thus how much it earns on trade with CFA nations, not only does France cooperate with the IMF on regular devaluations of the CFA,[30] France is printing the money for and exerts absolute control over the eight African countries' economies.

Moreover, the monetary policy of France in governing the eight nations' economies is in fact operated by the French Treasury, without any reference to the central fiscal authorities of any of these eight nations. Under the terms of the CFA Agreement, it is France that is unilaterally setting up these African nations' central banks, and each of the eight countries is obliged to keep at least 65% of its foreign exchange reserves in an "operations account" held at the French Treasury, as well as another 20% to cover financial liabilities.[31] In other words, 85% of all foreign exchange reserves of Ivory Coast, Benin, Burkina Faso, Guinea Bissau, Mali, Niger, Senegal and Togo are 100% under control of the French Treasury, with France in a position to devalue and manipulate these countries economy to its own advantage. The CFA was created to keep African nations impoverished, to maintain the plunder of their resources and wealth, while feeding the French and European economy.[32] The social unrest that follows in the wake of new devaluations,[33] is then hard-handedly suppressed by those "African Vice Roys" that are nepotist enough to co-operate with France as agents of their own nations' and peoples' enslavement. Laurent Gbagbo opposed the colonial master because Laurent Gbagbo was working for the benefit of his people and Ivory Coast; that is *why* Laurent Gbagbo had to be removed.

So Why Did the Sun Kings of Europe and the USA Hate Qaddafi?

Colonialism in Africa has changed significantly since the USA entered African politics after world war two, and very significantly, with the consolidation of the European Union. While France has particular national interests in the CFA region, most of Southern Europe's states are working towards an expansion of the European Market to the Mediterranean Basin, and a new colonization by means of economic control and military presence in Northern Africa. Seldom mentioned in the corporate media, the Royal Family of Morocco is a stern supporter of this policy. Cooperation on multiple areas, such as the control of the Mediterranean Basin states' social cconomy[34] has been implemented for years.

French President Nicolas Sarkozy made it his personal ambition to achieve what even Napoleon did not, a colonization of the entire Northern and Western African Continent. In 2008 France and the European Union had been so far in their preparations that the only remaining obstacle for their North African colonial ambitions was Libya, and Libya outright rejected to play into the hands of the want-to-be colonialists. When asked for his opinion about the Mediterranean Basin alliance, Muammar Qaddafi said: "*If Europe wants co-operation, it should go through Cairo and Addis Ababa*".[35] In 2008, President Sarkozy wanted to make the Mediterranean Alliance his contribution to the European Union, and during the six months of the French EU Presidency French Foreign Minister Bernard Kouchner only conveyed Sarkozy's "*disappointment*" but clearly indicated that Libya and Qaddafi had become "the" obstacle for further colonial expansion in Northern Africa, when he stated that "*Colonel Qaddafi is not in agreement with this vision. Neither was he in agreement with the Barcelona process which we intend to support and pursue*".

The reason why Libya opposed the Mediterranean Alliance was that it would have split, rather than united, African nations. Rather than establishing one more "*zone*" like the CFA Region in Northern Africa, Qaddafi and Libya were lobbying the African Union to abandon the CFA treaties with France, and to establish a Pan-African, gold-backed currency, which would end the usury, the robbery of African nations' resources, and the enslavement of an entire continent's population. The Libyan arguments were persuasive. Libya had the highest per capita GDP, the highest standard of living, social services, wages, job security, education program, literacy rate, and countless other "firsts" among African nations. What Qaddafi and Libya's outright rejection of the Mediterranean Alliance and success at lobbying for a Pan-African currency, with among others Laurent Gbagbo from Ivory Coast meant, was that the USA and Europe had only one option left: to topple the Libyan Government by any means necessary.

The Myth of an African Union

To understand the full range of the problem Libya created, it is necessary to understand what the African Union (AU) is. The African Union was established in 2002 by member states of the former Organization of African Unity (OAU). The OAU was established in 1963 with the function to facilitate African nations' transition to independence, to counter all forms of colonialism, and protect the independence and national integrity of African nations.[36] The transition from the OAU to the African Union in 2002 was nothing less than the European Union's co-opting the only forum that actively lobbied against neo-colonialism, substituting it with an African Union that is modeled on the European Union.[37] The African Union is but the new colonial administration of a now united Europe.

With approximately one third of the entire budget of the African Union paid for by the European Union, as alms to Africa—taken from the money that is usurped from Africa—the African Union is but the European Union's Colonial Administration: an African Court of Justice[38] modeled on the ICC, an African Investment Bank, an African Development Bank, and an African Central Bank, managed by Europe, for Europe and the USA,[39] and global finance capital.[40] The African Union did not *"cower in the light of pressure from the EU"*[41] as some interpreted its support of UNSC Resolution 1973.[42] The African Union strictly speaking functioned exactly as it was designed to do—as an instrument for the new colonization of Africa. Just like Laurent Gbagbo, who had to be removed because he wanted Ivory Coast to have its own currency or a Pan-African currency under African control rather than that of the French National Bank, Muammar Qaddafi had to be removed because he was the one obstacle that prevented the establishment of the Mediterranean Alliance, and because his ideas about a Pan-African Gold Dinar were seriously considered by many African leaders who do not dare to speak of it out loud. That is *"why"* Qaddafi had to be removed.

The Spiral Towards Global Conflict

Ivory Coast and the removal of incumbent President Laurent Gbagbo from office; the criminal war against Libya and the ousting of the legitimate Libyan Government, the aggressive expansion of the US African Command, the ongoing subversion of Syria, the manufacturing of war in Afghanistan, Pakistan, Iraq, Yugoslavia, Somalia, Sudan, Ossetia; the manufacturing of insurgencies in Chechnya, Yemen, among other, and countless Color Revolutions and Arab Spring Coup d´etats have only been possible for two reasons: the fact that Russia was severely destabilized after the collapse of the USSR and under the presidency of Boris Yeltsin, who strip sold Russian assets to global oligarchs, and which had to find its footing as a global power; and the fact that the transformation of the Chinese economy was prioritized higher by China than the defense of the nations in Africa that provide much of the resources that drive the Chinese economy.

Already at the International Security Conference in Munich, 2007, then President of The Russian Federation, Vladimir Putin, used the strongest possible words of diplomatic parlance to warn the United States of America, saying that its aggressive expansionism has brought the world closer to a third world war than it has ever been before.[43] After the absolutely criminal and shameless abuse of the United Nations Security Council Resolution 1973 and the attempt by NATO countries to abuse the UN for a similar resolution on Syria, both China and Russia responded with a veto.[44] The global danger, however, is not the fact of the veto, but the fact that the world today, with a United Nations that has utterly been co-opted by NATO countries,[45] has no forum for a peaceful resolution of what increasingly seems to develop into a global war. This is indeed an unprecedented crisis that demands unprecedented leadership, courage, and integrity.

REFERENCES

1   Cold War <https://secure.wikimedia.org/wikipedia/en/wiki/Cold_War>
2   Pan-African Nationalism <http://www.press.uchicago.edu/ucp/books/book/chicago/N/bo3645795.html>
3   The Guardian, China sais the Booming Trade with Africa is Transforming the Continent.<http://www.guardian.co.uk/world/2010/dec/23/china-africa-trade-record-transform>
4   NATO`s War on Libya is Directed Against China <http://nsnbc.wordpress.com/2011/09/26/natos-war-on-libya-is-directed-against-china/>
5   Washington is conquering Africa, using France, Human Rights, Terrorism, and The National Endowment for Democracy. <http://nsnbc.wordpress.com/2011/10/02/washington-is-

conquering-africa-using-france-human-rights-terrorism-and-the-national-endowment-for-democracy/>

6   The National Counsel of Syria and U.S. Unconventional Warfare. http://nsnbc.wordpress.com/2011/10/06/the-national-counsel-of-syria-and-u-s-unconventional-warfare/

7   TC 18-01 Special Forces and Unconventional Warfare. <http://info.publicintelligence.net/USArmy-UW.pdf>

8   New Data on Murder of Lumumba. <http://www.africawithin.com/lumumba/murder_of_lumumba.ht>

9   Frontline Vol 2. Issue 8. December 2008, How Africa Won Freedom. <http://www.redflag.org.uk/frontline/dec08/africa.html>

10 Al Qaeda: The Database <http://globalresearch.ca/index.php?context=va&aid=24738>

11 German Intelligence and CIA supported Al Qaeda Terrorists in Yugoslavia. <http://www.globalresearch.ca/articles/BEH502A.html>

12 Abdelhakim Belhadj, The Mask behind the Many Men. <http://nsnbc.wordpress.com/2011/09/25/abdelhakim-belhadj-the-mask-behind-the-many-men/>

13 Al Qa´ida´s Foreighn Fighters in Iraq. Combatting Terrorism center at West Point. <http://tarpley.net/docs/CTCForeign-Fighter.19.Dec07.pdf>

14 CIA recruits 1.500 from Mazar-e-Sharif to fight in Libya. <http://nation.com.pk/pakistan-news-newspaper-daily-english-online/Politics/31-Aug-2011/CIA-recruits-1500-from-MazareSharif-to-fight-in-Libya>

15 U.S. Sends CIA agents into Libya to analyze rebel forces. <http://www.catholic.org/international/international_story.php?id=40906>

16 Abdelhakim Belhadj, The Mask Behind the Many Men. <http://nsnbc.wordpress.com/2011/09/25/abdelhakim-belhadj-the-mask-behind-the-many-men/>

17 The National Counsel of Syria and US Unconventional Warfare. <http://nsnbc.wordpress.com/2011/10/06/the-national-counsel-of-syria-and-u-s-unconventional-warfare/>

18 Cornered in Abidjan as Fears Grow. <http://www.bbc.co.uk/blogs/thereporters/andrewharding/2011/04/cornered_in_abidjan_as_fears_g.html>

19 Libya; Just One Moment. <http://nsnbc.wordpress.com/2011/10/12/libya-just-one-moment/>

20 Gore won election by 538.948 votes; Bush won the count by

300.<http://www.leinsdorf.com/Gore%20Wins%20the%20 Election%20by%20538.htm>

21   Supreme Court of the United States; George W. Bush, et al., Petitioners v. Albert Gore, Jr., et al. <http://www.law.cornell. edu/supct/html/00-949.ZPC.html>

22   DGSE   <http://www.globalsecurity.org/intell/world/france/ dgse.htm>

23   West African Leaders On The Sqare Against Gbagbo. <http:// www.ocnus.net/artman2/publish/Editorial_10/West-African- Leaders-On-The-Square-Against-Gbagbo.shtml>

24   Ivory Coast´s Gbagbo held after French tRoops move in. <http:// af.reuters.com/article/topNews/idAFJOE73A01F20110411>

25   Ivory Coast´s Gbagbo Captured at Presidential Compound. <http://www.voanews.com/english/news/africa/west/ Fresh-Clashes-Erupt-in-Ivory-Coast-After-UN-French-At- tacks-119588724.html>

26   UN forces launch assault on Gbagbo stronghold in Abidjan. <http://www.telegraph.co.uk/news/worldnews/africaandindi- anocean/cotedivoire/8442953/UN-forces-launch-assault-on- Gbagbo-stronghold-in-Abidjan.html>

27   ICC Prosecutor requests judges for authorization to open an investigation in Cote d´Ivoire.

28   History is a Weapon, Propaganda, E. Bernaise. <http://www. historyisaweapon.com/defcon1/bernprop.html>

29   Laurent Gbagbo wants Ivory Coast to leave CFA and create Ivoryan Currency. <http://www.africanews.com/site/I_Coast_ contemplate_new_currency/list_messages/36877>

30   IMF, France and Devaluation of CFA. <http://www.imf.org/ex- ternal/pubs/ft/fabric/backgrnd.htm>

31   French Treasure controlls 8 African Nations Central Bank <http://saoti.over-blog.com/article-17347736.html>

32   CFA Created To Keep African States Poor. <http://www.panafri- canvisions.com/old/9/development.htm>

33   CFA Devaluations, Poverty and Social Unrest. <http://www.ny- times.com/1994/02/23/world/french-devaluation-of-african- currency-brings-wide-unrest.html?pagewanted=all&src=pm>

34   The Euro-mediterranean Network of Social Economy. <http:// www.ces.es/TRESMED/docum/esmed_en.pdf >

35   Libya rejects mediterranean Alliance. <http://www.france24. com/en/20080615-libya-rejects-mediterranean-alliance-libya- france>

36   InfoPlease   OAU.   <http://www.infoplease.com/ce6/history/

A0836842.html>

38   InfoPlease African Union. <http://www.infoplease.com/ce6/history/A0921480.html>

39   African Court of Justice. <http://www.aict-ctia.org/courts_conti/acj/acj_home.html>

40   Financial Institutions of the A-U. <http://www.au.int/en/organs/fi>

41   GIGA EU-African Economic Relations. <https://www.econstor.eu/dspace/bitstream/10419/47856/1/60872808X.pdf>

42   The African Unions Mistake of Policy and Principle. <http://www.finalcall.com/artman/publish/Perspectives_1/article_7931.shtml>

43   UNSC Resolution 1973. <http://www.un.org/News/Press/docs/2011/sc10200.doc.htm#Resolution>

44   ISC Munich 2007 – Punin, Full Text of Speech <http://www.securityconference.de/Putin-s-speech.381+M52087573ab0.0.html>

45   Russia, A Force to be recogned with..... <http://nsnbc.wordpress.com/2011/10/15/russia-a-force-to-be-reckogned-with-in-the-coming-years/>

46   UN DONE. <http://nsnbc.wordpress.com/2011/09/28/un-done-the-66th-session-of-the-general-assembley-reflections-by-dr-christof-lehmann/>

ENDNOTES

1   Posted on October 16, 2011 at <http://nsnbc.wordpress.com/2011/10/16/neo-colonialism-subversion-in-africa-and-global-conflict/>

PETROLEUM & EMPIRE IN NORTH AFRICA

NATO PROPAGANDA AND THE BETRAYAL OF MUAMMAR QADDAFI

Keith Harmon Snow*

I arrived in Tripoli in October 2009, one of the 13 members of the US delegation chosen by former Congresswoman Cynthia McKinney and invited by the Government of Libya to attend the *First International Conference for the Supporters of the Green Book* in Tripoli, Libya. I was not a supporter of Qaddafi's Green Book, I had hardly heard of it and had never read it. I went because I was honored to be invited, because I could, and because I am an independent journalist. Here was a chance to see Libya for myself.

Most of the five days we were there were spent in meetings and conferences halls, and we hardly left our hotel. One day I slipped off to the city by myself for a few hours. What I saw was a vibrant city in the throes of capitalist expansion. It was reasonably clean, the little I saw, but the coastline suffered from your usual unregulated development and environmental destruction – it was no better or worse than cities I have seen on the coast of Italy or Spain. So there was nothing beautiful about most of what I saw, which wasn't much, except for the people, who were lovely.

*Keith Harmon Snow traveled to Tripoli, Libya in 2009 and stayed five days while attending the "2009 International Conference of the Green Book Supporters" as a member of the US DIGNITY Delegation invited by former US Congresswoman Cynthia McKinney (D-GA). Keith regretfully declined the second invitation to travel to Libya with the DIGNITY Delegation in 2011 for personal reasons. This chapter is based on reportage published on 3 March 2011, revised on 4 March 2011 and 19 March 2011; additional background and explanation was provided in March 2012 in preparation for this DIGNITY publication.

I wandered on foot for hours, until I found the old city and its cobblestoned alleys and intricate tunnels and a big mosque. It was all one big market, and there were all sorts of goods offered for sale, new and old, and all sorts of people. It's very hard to imagine that everything I saw has been destroyed, but it has. The people's lives, the people's livelihoods, and so many of the people themselves. These were not Islamic fundamentalists, or terrorists, as the western media would have us believe. They were people like you and me. My understanding of Libya, and its 'Great Leader,' is tempered by my horror at witnessing, from abroad, the destruction that our "society" rained down on the people whose daily lives I saw on the streets in Tripoli.

What was the purpose of this war?

What I saw in my brief visit to Libya and what I have found in my journalistic research about Libya and its 'Great Leader' are contradiction after contradiction. This report is just another incomplete picture of an incomplete puzzle—but it seeks to penetrate and expose the ongoing western media propaganda campaigns for what they are: psychological operations against the masses of earth's English-speaking people who have not and do not benefit from the nasty policies and actions implemented to serve a very small and elite group of people.

FROM THE HALLS OF MONTEZUMA, TO THE SHORES OF TRIPOLI

On September 1, 1969 Colonel Muammar Qaddafi and his officers overthrew the pro-western regime that had been ruling Libya. At the time, Libya was home to the largest US Air Base (Wheelus Air Base) in Africa. Agreements between the USA and Libya signed in 1951 and 1954 granted the USAF the use of Wheelus Air Base and its El Watia gunnery range for gunnery and bombing training and for transport and bombing stopovers until 1971. During the Cold War the base was pivotal to expanding US military power under the Strategic Air Command, and an essential base for fighter and reconnaissance missions. The Pentagon also used the base—and the remote Libyan desert—for missile testing: the launch area was located 15 miles east of Tripoli. Considered a 'little America on the shores of the Mediterranean', the base housed some 4600 US military personnel until its evacuation in 1970.

With the discovery of oil in Libya in 1959, a very poor desert country became a very rich little western protectorate. US and European companies had huge stakes in the extremely lucrative petroleum and banking sectors, but Qaddafi soon nationalized these. Thus Libya overnight joined the list of US 'enemy' or 'rogue' states that sought autonomy and self-determination outside the expanding sphere of western Empire. Further cementing western multinational corporate hatred of the new regime, Libya played a leading role in the 1973 oil embargo against the US and maintained cooperative relations with the Soviet Union. Qaddafi also reportedly channeled early oil wealth into national free health care and education.

At one time Qaddafi backed Idi Amin, known as to the world as the most savage African dictator, but long after the rise and fall of Idi Amin in Uganda we find that Qaddafi's ties to other despots—such as Britain's Tony Blair or George H. W. Bush—are far more notable, though far less currently advertised. Thus we can compare and contrast the western propaganda system's treatment of the war in Libya, its characterizations of Colonel Qaddafi, both historical and contemporary, with other regimes, other insurrections and other countries and come to some conclusive evidence of how the capitalist propaganda system works to protect those who assist in predatory imperial expansion (a.k.a. 'allies') versus how it denigrates and maligns those who seek any kind of independent or unique course (a.k.a. 'enemies').[1]

Of course, just as Qaddafi was slammed and maligned in huge disproportion to his actual actions, we find that Idi Amin was not the premier African terrorist he is always billed to be. Idi Amin Dada's crimes paled in comparison and scale to those of the current despots in power in Uganda (Yoweri Museveni) and Rwanda (Paul Kagame). This offers another framework from which to interpret the US government's treatment of Qaddafi.

In 1971 Idi Amin was brought to power by force in Uganda. Trained by Israeli forces in Israel prior to the coup d'etat in Uganda, Amin succeeded only due to the backing of powerful western interests, especially Britain—Uganda was Britain's 'pearl of Africa'—the United States and Israel.[2] Britain's backing included direct involvement of Roland 'Tiny' Rowland and multinational Lonrho (formerly the London Rhodesia Company), and other British-Rhodesian interests, particularly those of John Bredenkamp, a weapons subcontractor for the British MI-6, international weapons dealer and affiliate of the British aerospace firm BAE Systems.[3] Notably, these were some of the same interests that backed Robert Mugabe and the Zimbabwe African National Union (ZANU) guerillas (known as the Zimbabwe African National Liberation Army, or ZANLA) who battled the white supremacist government of Ian Smith in Rhodesia a few years later: ZANU guerrillas were sent to Libya for training during the early years, pre-1978, funded by Qaddafi, but Bredenkamp and Rowland both eventually funded Mugabe's presidential ascension and consolidation of power in the new Zimbabwe from circa 1979 onwards. (After 1990, Tiny Rowland and Lonrho also backed John Garang and the Sudan People's Liberation Army in their terrorist war against Khartoum.)

Mugabe and Qaddafi remained friendly during the 1980s, the decade of brutal atrocities by the ZANU government against the Ndebele people of the Matabelelands. Qaddafi did not condemn Mugabe during the most brutal years of the *Gukurahundi*—Mugabe's name for the genocide against the Ndebele people.[4] In 1992, British financier and gunrunner Tiny Rowland—who also controlled major British newspapers like *The Observer*—angered some of his government cronies by selling off Lonrho's one-third share in British Metropole Hotels for $305.9 million to the Libyan Arab Foreign Investment Company.

Facts like the above are anathema to the western propaganda system. Most western news consumers have swallowed the blue pill of media complacency and disinformation and are therefore easily whipped into hysteria about western bogeyman constructs like Qaddafi or Bin Laden or Saddam Hussein or—the erstwhile 'terrorist' of the Lord's Resistance Army and subject of the KONY2012 hysteria—Joseph Kony. Facts count, and the real facts are hidden behind these facades created through well-planned and coordinated psychological operations, like the one that played out in the media over the invasion of Libya. What the capitalist system seeks to hide are the western mafias and their elite kingpins who are perpetuating the shock doctrines of disaster capitalism. This is what happened in Libya.

Back in Uganda in the early and mid-1970's, Idi Amin pressed his backers to expand and modernize the pro-Amin armed forces, but Israel and Britain had other plans. In the strategic western machinations against the Islamic government of Sudan, Amin was only meant to serve as a counterbalancing force, merely a thorn in the side of Khartoum and Egypt, not a bona fide conqueror. Amin's military fantasies were far more than Israel, Britain or the United States wanted. Thus, when Israel denied Amin's requests for military hardware, in stepped Muammar Qaddafi. On March 3, 1974, at Gulu Airfield in northern Uganda, General Al Haji Idi Amin introduced his senior military officers to his comrade Col. Qaddafi, Chairman of the Revolutionary Command of the Arab Republic of Libya. This was the formal handing over ceremony of Libyan fighter aircraft —mostly Soviet-built MiG-17s and MiG-21s—to the Ugandan air force. Even after Amin's tryst with Qaddafi, some foreign interests, including the Central Intelligence Agency, went to great lengths to conceal their political and economic relationships with the Amin dictatorship, in part due to US corporate interests seeking to destroy the British economic monopolies.[5] The same corporate jockeying for power occurred during the four decades of Qaddafi's rule in Libya.

Uganda's Gulu Airfield has gained even greater currency under the dictatorship of Yoweri Museveni. In 1996 and 1997, the Gulu Airfield in Uganda was used as a major rear base for C-130 transports for the

Pentagon's 1996 invasion of Zaire (Dem. Rep. of Congo). US SOCOM (the Pentagon's Special Operations Command) forces were sighted in the Gulu region, and the Bwindi Impenetrable Forest protected area in western Uganda served as cover for a secret SOCOM training camp.[6] (Such facts as these above are dismissed by Africa experts like Rene Lemarchand[7] and, especially, Gerard Prunier.[8])

Gulu also served as the rear base for the NATO/Israeli invasion of South Sudan, supplying the Sudan People's Liberation Army through their SPLA proxy guerrilla, John Garang, who was trained at the Pentagon's notorious School of the Americas in Fort Benning, Georgia, USA. Through Gulu military base, and with Museveni's Ugandan People's Defense Forces and John Garang's Sudan People's Liberation Army as proxy forces, western powers have prosecuted one of the longest and bloodiest wars in Africa. From roughly 1990 to the present day, war in Sudan has primarily been motivated and maintained through the geopolitical and strategic intervention of Israel, Canada, USA, France and Britain—seeking the overthrow of the Islamic government in Sudan. Western propaganda agents like Smith College Sudan 'expert' Dr. Eric Reeves—an English professor—and former Human Rights Watch and African Rights agent Alex De Waal disappear such inconvenient facts Dr. Eric Reeves does so by hysterically wielding the big, bad G-word: genocide. Always charging the government of President Omar Al-Bashir with war crimes and a 'genocidal counterinsurgency', these experts never tell us who is behind the insurgency that is supposedly being 'countered' and their nonsense takes different forms when they address western enemies like Qaddafi.

In 1972, Idi Amin expelled all Israeli nationals from Uganda. At the time, Israel was the primary backer of the Anyanya rebellion in South Sudan. The Anyanya forces were comprised of animist tribes (Acholi, Bari, Dinka, Lotuko, Madi, Nuer, Zande and other tribes) but South Sudan has always been billed as *Christians* pitted against bloodthirsty Arabs from the north. In 1972 Kampala and Khartoum signed cooperative agreements that further marginalized Israeli influence and compromised Israeli interests in Africa. Why did the West hate Qaddafi? At the Non-Aligned Nations conference in Algiers in 1973, Libya promised compensation to make up for losses incurred by any nation that severed ties with Israel. In October 1973, Syria and Egypt attacked Israel initiating the six-day Yom Kippur war. When General Amin followed Qaddafi's model and nationalized major British interests in 1973, the most powerful corporations—Unilever Corporation, British Petroleum and the three big British banks—were untouched. After Amin expelled all Indian nationals, Britain and Israel began their campaigns against Amin, and the BBC discovered almost overnight that the Amin dictatorship was responsible for "a reign of terror worse than anything in recent African history." [9]

Of course, Israel was furious about Amin's trysts with Libya and Sudan, and they eventually sponsored an insurrection against Amin through the western NATO surrogate state of Tanzania. Yoweri Museveni was a student at the University of Dar es Salaam during the early 1970s, but he joined the military campaign against Amin from Tanzania after Amin attacked Tanzania's western Kagera region in 1978. The Israeli raid to free hostages in Entebbe in 1976 further set the stage for Israel's conflict against Qaddafi-friendly Amin forces in Uganda. Israel and Britain soon installed their new client dictator Yoweri Museveni through massive genocidal bloodletting in northern Uganda and the Lowero Triangle (comprising seven major districts of central Uganda).[10]

As the political winds of the Sahel shifted and re-shifted like so many sand dunes in the Sahara, Colonel Qaddafi supported the western-backed guerrilla insurgencies in both Uganda (National Resistance Army/Movement, 1981-1986) and Rwanda (Rwandan Patriotic Army/Front, 1990-1994). Both of these insurgencies involved invasions that qualify as supreme violations of international law. Yoweri Museveni and his Rwandan Tutsi commanders spearheaded both invasions. The western powers applauded these illegal invasions and protracted insurgencies, because both insurgencies served the interests of western powers—in particular, of Britain, Canada, the USA, and Israel. Of those who fought alongside Museveni in Uganda, especially notable were the exiled Tutsi elites Paul Kagame and Fred Rwigema. In 1986, Museveni promoted his then loyal comrade-in-arms Paul Kagame to be Director of Military Intelligence, and he promoted Fred Rwigema to Deputy Military Commander and Deputy Army Commander-in-Chief, the highest military position after Museveni. Guerillas from both the National Resistance Army and Rwandan Patriotic Army were also trained in Libya. The Rwandan Patriotic Army guerrillas were really battle-hardened National Resistance Army guerrillas fighting under a new name to bring legitimacy to an otherwise illegitimate invasion.[11]

There was no outcry from Washington when Qaddafi served their interests.

Gulu is the heart of the Acholi territory in northern Uganda, the locus of various resistance movements that rose up after 1985 to fight against the new regime of Yoweri Museveni. The NRA consolidated power the way they waged their war: with absolute terrorism and scorched earth campaigns against hundreds of thousands of innocent people. Basing his rule along ethnic lines, Museveni—who hails from the Tutsi-Hima ethic group and region of Uganda—targeted the Acholi people in particular, because the northern Acholis had prospered under the rule of Idi Amin and under both administrations of President Milton Obote (known as Obote I and Obote II). In 1986, a young soldier named Joseph Kony and his now infamous Lord's Resistance Army launched one of the many counter-insurgencies of the 1985-1987 era that sprang up against the fledgling Museveni regime.

Offering a perfect parallel to the emotionally charged and factually oversimplified and openly false western propaganda about Qaddafi and Libya, the KONY2012 video that went viral in March 2012 completely falsified the deeper historical and political realities of the northern Uganda region. The complicated ethnic and political fault lines, the regional geopolitics involving Khartoum, the SPLA, the vast Congo and its wealth, the petrol-mercenary companies (esp., e.g., Sandline International, Branch Energy and Saracen International), the multinational corporate penetration and control, the misery industries (CARE, Save the Children, Medicines Sans Frontieres, etc.) and the war crimes, crimes against humanity and genocide committed by Museveni and Kagame in the NRA war, and the later genocide against the Acholis in Northern Uganda, are all rendered invisible by the KONY2012 propaganda film created by the USAID backed 'non-government organization' Invisible Children. Gulu Airfield provided the main base for Museveni's so-called 'counterinsurgency' operations against the Acholis: this was a full-blown military insurgency and a state-sponsored genocide from 1985 to the present.

The psychological operations and public relations campaigns created by western entities need not deploy facts. Having laid the groundwork over past decades to manufacture the consent of US taxpayers, for example, the western propaganda system only needs to utter false claims that ruthless warlords [sic] like Joseph Kony "capture children and force them to kill and eat their parents" (as stated by Invisible Children founder Jason Russel in March 2012) for such claims to be believed. Similarly, Qaddafi need not do anything more than sit in a chair and burp before he was saddled with the stereotypes that the white power system reserved for its critics and challengers, or accused of genocide on the basis of dead bodies suddenly showing up, no matter that they are the handiwork of the western-backed 'rebels'.

Qaddafi followed the example of other revolutionary figures of the 20th century, like Mao Zedong with his *Little Red Book*, in authoring his own unique and highly idealistic political philosophy and revolutionary handbook. Qaddafi's *Green Book* was published in three volumes between 1975 and 1979 and, as you might expect, it is almost unknown by the western enlightened [sic] world. When the *Green Book* is mentioned, it is generally in ridicule by some arrogant western journalist or corporate propaganda rag or think-thank ideologue.

"While much of the world sees him as an eccentric and brutal demagogue, Qaddafi has tried for decades to portray himself as a statesman-philosopher," wrote Mohammed Bazzi in *The New York Times*, May 27, 2011.[12] "It's an aspiration best embodied in the *Green Book*, his notorious three-part meditation on politics, economics and everything from the evils of mechanized poultry farming to the importance of owning one's car."

The New York Times chose a writer with an Arab name to help assure the reader's confidence in the veracity of the report and, of course, the writer casts the *Green Book* as 'notorious'—the innuendo is that it is vile propaganda—and ridiculous. First, this article is no Orientalist critique by a leading Arab scholar like Edward Said: Mohamad Bazzi teaches journalism at New York University and is an adjunct senior fellow at the Council on Foreign Relations.

Similarly, the capitalist system's choices of examples for ridiculing the *Green Book* are not accidental. Qaddafi was a lunatic, we were forever told, because he mixed up such obviously disjointed issues as chickens and meditation. I mean, who talks about chickens in a revolutionary tract? Only a crazy man, right? Well, as any conscious North American or European chicken consumer has already learned, with horror, mechanized poultry farming *is*, for all practical intents, evil. Most of the people who slam, ridicule and disparage the *Green Book* have either [1] never read it or [2] a vested interest to protect: their paycheck in reward for their silence.

"Because it is muddled, the book is often dismissed as simply a hodgepodge of aphorisms, the ramblings of a mad dictator," Bazzi wrote. "And in fact, the slim 21,000-word treatise does not present a coherent worldview."

Really?

The *Green Book* and the 'Third Universal Theory' it propounds are worth reading. Had it been written by most anyone else who is opposed to the expansion of western empire with all its horrors, it would be more widely appreciated and critically debated. The book addresses the falsification of democracy and the proliferation of organized criminal gangs—like the Republicans and Democrats that call themselves parties of and for the US people. However, most western academics and scholars apparently steer clear of any discussion of the *Green Book* out of pure cowardice.

Green Book (p. 10): "Traditional democracy, prevalent in our world today, confers upon ordinary members of parliament a sanctity and an immunity it denies ordinary citizens." Parliaments [read: the Congress of the United States] "have thus become a means of confiscating and monopolizing the power of the people."

What a dangerous thought. Imagine if the US public were to engage such thoughts on a consistent basis, instead of being consumed with Walt Disney animation films or specious Hollywood gossip or, worse, the media coverage of presidential debates where the subjects under discussion are meant only to be spectacles of ridiculousness between two supposedly unique and oppositional parties.

Green Book (p. 11): "Moreover, the electoral system in the so-called democratic forms of government is a demagogic practice in the literal sense of the word. It is based on propaganda campaigns aimed at winning over the constituents, and involves buying and manipulating votes. This produces closed election campaigns which the poor cannot afford to participate in and thus the rich are always elected."

No wonder the elites ruining the world don't want you to read the *Green Book*. If westerners read the *Green Book* they might be prone to the arising of dangerous thoughts such as these that criticize the system of oppression that now threatens all life on planet Earth.

QADDAFI COMES INTO THE FOLD

Over the past four decades the US and its closest allies, including Israel and Japan, maintained a mostly hostile relationship with Muammar Qaddafi and Libya. This relationship has included economic sanctions, covert attacks, open warfare and other actions of aggression committed by the United States. It also included 'dirty tricks' intelligence operations. The 'international community' repeatedly enforced or renewed sanctions against Libya in the 1980s and 1990s.

Meanwhile, Qaddafi did what Castro has done: he developed the country anyway. Like in Castro's Cuba, there is no doubt that an extremely severe intelligence apparatus, replete with an extremely repressive state security network, was necessary to protect the 'Great Leader' from western assassination plots, coup d'etats, and other foreign covert interventions,[13] or from other contemporary extremist western terrorist constructs like the Phoenix Program, or Phung Oang, as it was called by the Vietnamese.[14]

Qaddafi survived for four decades due to a combination of ambivalent power interests at home and abroad, and a wily shifting of policy and initiatives to self-protect while still pursuing his developmental goals. In some instances, such as the oil sector or investments in post-1994 Rwanda, the regime was ruthlessly opportunistic. Sometimes (other than when it faced an international boycott) the regime itself pursued protective isolationism while at other times it tried to expand peacefully via union with Arab neighbors, Syria, Algeria, Sudan and Egypt. Similarly, after the 15 April 1974 army coup in Niger, Qaddafi developed close relations with Lt. Gen. Seyni Kountche, but the relationship sours after Kountche is lured into the western camp by multinational nuclear interests mining in Agadez and Arlit, Niger. The regime was repressive, but it faced constant attempts at penetration, assassination and reversal by an assortment of western powers. The regime purchased legitimacy, but it did so as a means of bargaining its way out of killing sanctions, and trying to forestall devastation similar to that wreaked on Iraq. The regime meddled in foreign interventions in Africa and abroad, but some see that as supporting liberation movements.[15] The regime invested heavily all around the world but it also invested heavily at home, in domestic infrastructure and in satisfying the Libyan people's needs. How does that measure in comparison with the regimes in power in Israel, Britain, France, the United States or Canada?

If Qaddafi's political actions and policies constituted realpolitik from an African perspective, or perhaps an Arab perspective, the faults of the Libyan regime pale in comparison to the faults of foreign regimes in the countries that persecuted Libya. Which foreign leaders in western countries have developed a high standard of living or social protections for their people as opposed to their preference for domestic repression serving private elites and corporate profit? As usual, the faults and actions of the Qaddafi regime are amplified and distorted beyond all reasonable perspective, while the faults and actions and policies of countries like Britain, Israel, Belgium and the USA are ever downplayed and excused, no matter the orders of magnitude more suffering, destruction or death they are responsible for.

After September 11, 2001, the US issued extensive threats and warnings against Libya to pressure it to accept US demands and collaborate in the US "Global War on Terror" (GWOT). Libya was considered one of the premier 'rogue states' involved in 'terrorism', and Qaddafi was forced to concede some of his country's independence and autonomy. Who were the rogue states declared terrorist havens by the Center for Security Policy—the nerve center of the Pentagon's permanent warfare juggernaut? Libya, Syria, Sudan, Iran, Iraq, Afghanistan, North Korea, Yemen, and, to a lesser extent, Lebanon. Thus in 2004, during heightened western media propaganda about Libyan terrorism and Qaddafi's supporting Al Qaeda—all kinds of disingenuous reports and outright lies—the G. W. Bush administration dropped sanctions against the Qaddafi regime and paved the way for a new era in US-Libyan bilateral trade.

AFTER SANCTIONS REMOVAL, THE DELUGE

US officials were reportedly under pressure from multinational corporations, including big petrol companies BP, ExxonMobil, Halliburton, Chevron, Conoco and Marathon Oil, and defense giants like Raytheon and Northrop Grumman, and other corporations like Dow Chemical and Fluor to drop sanctions. In 2005, these corporations and lobbyists formed a 'trade' association, with $20,000 membership dues, called the US-Libya Business Association (USLBA). Companies like Asea Brown Baveri (former directors include Donald Rumsfeld) and Bechtel Corporation (one of the closest affiliates of the CIA[16]) quickly snatched up contracts. Bechtel's deep penetration in Egypt and Algeria enabled their Egyptian and Algerian subsidiaries to move quickly into Libya after sanctions were dropped in 2007.

USLBA members lobbied the US government to protect and advance their interests in Libya and business executives flocked to Libya and negotiated million or billion dollar deals. Bilateral trade with Libya totaled $2.7 billion in 2010, up from virtually nothing when sanctions were in place prior to 2004. The USLBA also lobbied on behalf of the former outlaw state of Libya and sponsored policy conferences, briefing sessions and events featuring senior US and Libyan officials. Officials traveled to Libya for meetings with Libyan government officials, private business leaders and representatives of American companies working in the country—leading to some of the unbridled development that was evident in 2009.

Through the secretive Libyan Investment Authority, billions of Libya's petrodollars were reportedly invested in US equity and big banks, including JP Morgan Chase, Citigroup and others, and into other private equity like the Carlyle Group, one of America's most seedy arms dealers.[17] The Carlyle Group was founded by Frank Carlucci, former US Secretary of War at the time of the 1986 Reagan bombings of Libya, and current affiliate of the National Endowment for Democracy (described below), and a supporter of the right-wing neo-fascist polices of the extremist Center for Security Policy. Carlucci is also a director (or former director) of Wackenhut, renamed G4S, a private security firm that targeted "opportunities" in post-Qaddafi Libya: in August of 2011, G4S was vying for contracts to protect oil installations and train the new Libyan police.

Bechtel Corporation subsidiary NEXANT has also been involved in the trans-Ugandan pipeline that will connect the oil infrastructure of South Sudan, the far eastern DR Congo and western Uganda (the Semliki Basin), and Rwanda. By transiting Uganda and Kenya and pumping into tankers at the US military port of Mombasa, Kenya, the west can avoid the necessity of working with Khartoum to ship oil out of the Red Sea. However, in 2006, Tamoil East Africa Ltd., the Uganda-based subsidiary of the Libyan African Investment Portfolio (LAIP) won the bid to construct the Eldoret-Kampala pipeline in 2006, and later in 2008, to extend it from Kampala to Kigali. This is serious: the Libyan government's competition and growing investments in East African infrastructure, through the LAIP, clearly alarmed western corporations and the power elites.[18]

The Libya African Investment Portfolio (LAIP) is a subsidiary of the Libyan Investment Authority sovereign investment fund established in 2006. According to some reports, this was a mechanism through which Qaddafi personally poured billions of dollars into Africa. Qaddafi's personal decision-making in the LAIP investments is not clear (to this author). However, LAIP invested heavily in Rwanda under the brutal dictatorship of President Paul Kagame, investments that helped prop up Kagame's criminal regime and whitewash the freshest atrocities, including an ongoing genocide against Hutu people everywhere.[19]

The destruction of Libya resulted in the United Nations and NATO freezing LAIP assets, and as this publication goes to press the assets remain in limbo. Meanwhile, western corporations are jockeying to displace LAIP assets and control.[20]

When the bombing of Libya started in 2011, Kagame stabbed his former backer and subsequent investor in the back and began parroting the line his puppet-masters wanted: Qaddafi must go, Rwanda supports the rebels (sic). Regurgitating his standard "we are the poor victims of genocide" rhetoric, Kagame claimed that the "people of Rwanda" knew only too well why Qaddafi had to be stopped. Kagame squawked that the international community—a.k.a. Washington, NATO allies and Israel—had a "responsibility to protect" the Libyan people from Qaddafi's murderous regime. Of course, it had nothing to do with the Libyan people and everything to do with backing the murderous and illegal rebellion against the sovereign government of Libya, something Kagame's Rwandan Patriotic Army guerrillas certainly did know all too well, since the RPA was also backed by western powers, including Israel, as they stormed Rwanda and slaughtered Hutus and Tutsis left and right from 1990 to 1994.[21]

The CIA has long wanted to eliminate and replace Muammar Qaddafi: his nationalization of western assets, his hostility to a hostile Israel, his support for the Palestinians, and his support for the African National Congress struggle in South Africa offer a few of the more salient reasons. President Reagan bombed Tripoli, killing Qaddafi's infant daughter: the United States bombing of Libya (code-named Operation *El Dorado Canyon*) comprised the joint USAF, Navy, and Marines air-strikes against Libya on April 15, 1986. The US CIA allegedly brought down the Lockerbie Pan Am 103 flight over Scotland in 1988 and blamed this on Qaddafi. When Qaddafi capitulated to international pressure after 2001, the deal included accepting some responsibility for Lockerbie, but this was clearly another opportunistic move by Qaddafi, as viewed by his detractors, or a strategic move necessary for survival, according to Qaddafi's adherents.

Many of the top-level security documents from the Reagan Administration pertaining to Libya remain classified. These include National Security Decision Directives 16 (*Economic and Security Decisions for Libya*), NSDD 205a (*Annex: Acting Against Libyan Support of International Terrorism*), NSDD 224 (*Counter-Terrorist Operations Against Libya*), and NSDD 234 (*Libya Policy*), while even those that have been declassified are partially redacted. The George H.W. Bush NSDD 19 (*US Policy Toward Libya*) also remains classified.

In recent years Qaddafi has played along with the western fiction of Al-Qaeda, though it seems likely that some of the true mercenaries who fought in Libya were 'Al-Qaeda' terrorists trained by the United States to serve US interests in places like Saudi Arabia, Afghanistan, Sudan, Iran, Iraq, Yemen, Somalia and Libya.

Note the double standard in how the western press presents the accusations of Qaddafi using mercenaries, as if it is something unique to Qaddafi and Libya, and not something we westerners ever do. The guerrillas that joined Qaddafi's loyalist forces, including many black Africans from sub-Saharan Africa, are described by Qaddafi's supporters as liberation fighters, and by his detractors as genocidal killers.

NATIONAL FRONT FOR THE SALVATION OF LIBYA

In almost all western media accounts during the early reports of the so-called 'rebellion' in Libya, and well into the farce of an "Arab Spring" uprising, the so-called 'opposition' in Libya included the unspecified, unnamed, unidentified 'rebels' of the National Front for the Salvation of Libya (NFSL). These are not innocent 'pro-democracy' protestors who began with a 'peaceful sit-in' as reported by *The New York Times* and uncritically repeated everywhere else.

Reportage of atrocities in Sudan (Darfur: 2003-2001), Rwanda (1990-1994) and Uganda (1980-1985) was always blamed on the federal governments (Omar Bashir in Khartoum, Juvenal Habyarimana in Kigali, and on Milton Obote in Kampala, respectively) with no context to the foreign backed insurgency and intervention that was then occurring, which in all three cases involved the US, UK and Israel. Similarly, during the annihilation of Qaddafi's Libya, the media provided no context or history to the NFSL 'rebels': they were categorically presented as the good guys, no matter that they appeared out of thin air. No one explained who these people who were cited as sources by *The New York Times* or CNN or Democracy Now were.

The NFSL was part of the National Conference for the Libyan Opposition held in London in 2005, and British resources were used to support the NFSL and other 'opposition' in Libya. The NFSL was actually formed in October 1981 in Sudan under Colonel Jaafar Nimeiri—the US puppet dictator who was openly known to be a Central Intelligence Agency operative, and who ruled Sudan ruthlessly from 1969 to 1985. (In 1966, Nimeiri graduated from the United States Army Command College in Fort Leavenworth, Kansas; Rwandan dictator Paul Kagame attended this military college in 1990.) While Nimeiri armed and trained insurgents that launched attacks against Libya, Qaddafi was supporting the Sudan People's Liberation Army (SPLA) in its early manifestations as a revolutionary guerrilla force challenging the US puppet 'Islamic' dictatorship in Khartoum.

"We tell the agents in Sudan that we are aligned with popular revolution in Southern Sudan for the sake of liberating Sudan inch by inch—just as Lebanon was liberated." Speaking publicly in Arabic on the occasion of the seventh anniversary of the founding of the Libyan Jamahiriya (revolution), Qaddafi continued: "The United States cannot save that mean man [Nimeiri] who is hiding in Khartoum. This is because of us, in the Arab homeland and the revolutionary force [the Dergue] in Ethiopia..."[22]

Libya's policy on Sudan changed after the fall of the Nimeiri dictatorship in 1989, and in 1991 the US began supporting the SPLA against the legitimate sovereign Islamic government of Khartoum. Meanwhile, next door, Libya's alliance with revolutionary Ethiopian forces was dissolved when the 'communist' Dergue government in Ethiopia was overthrown and the US puppet dictator Meles Zenawi was installed.

The National Front for the Salvation of Libya held its national congress in the USA in July 2007. Reports of 'atrocities' and civilian deaths during the war in Libya were channeled into the western press from operations in Washington DC, and the opposition NFSL organized resistance and military attacks from both inside and outside Libya.

Italy and France also backed these opposition groups, as the Italian and French oil companies Total, AGIP and ELF sought to control, protect and expand their penetration into the extractive industries sector in Libya. Examining a PetroConsultants (petroleum industry) map of the petroleum concessions in Africa, dated 1996, we find that Libya, Tunisia, Algeria and Egypt appeared at the time to be held by state-owned oil companies—but foreign interests were deeply involved in joint ventures with Libya's National Oil Company (NOC) for many years.

European, Korean and Japanese penetration of the Libyan oil market had already occurred before the US sanctions were lifted in 2004: US multinationals were losing out. AGIP has been involved in Libya's oil sector for decades in Libya's Elephant Field (and other sites) through its joint ventures between Italian Eni Corporation and Libya's NOC; these operations also involved Korean and British (LASMO) corporations. Eni is Italy's largest multinational oil and gas corporation, involved in 70 countries, and Eni has worked in Libya since 1959. Belgian giant Petrofina also has sizable operations in Libya. Bechtel Corporation was also deeply involved in the Libyan petroleum sector.

France's role behind the Libyan 'revolution' of 2011 has its origins in bilateral intelligence and defense agreements concluded with Israel in the late 1940s, when France became a rear base for Jewish guerrilla operations to help create and consolidate the power of the new state of Israel. The Israeli Mossad and French Service for External Documentation and Counter-Espionage (SDECE) made a pact in 1954 to collaborate on intelligence and defense, a deal that played out on the ground in Francophone Africa over the Cold War years and on into the so-called 'Arab Spring' uprisings in Egypt, Libya, Tunisia and Syria.

"On the one hand, impressive quantities of planes, tanks, cannons and ammunition left French arsenals for Israel," writes French journalist Pierre Paén, in *Carnage: The Secret Wars of the Great Powers in Africa*. "On the other, massive quantities of the Mossad's notes on the activities of the Arab League and the arms traffic between Egypt, Libya and Algeria came into the SDECE."[23]

Chad and Libya fought from 1983 to 1987 in the so-called 'Toyota War' over the uranium rich Aouzou strip: French legionnaires fought disguised as Chadian regulars to prop up their client regime in Chad. In 1982 French president Mitterrand reorganized the SDEGE. The General Directorate for External Security (DGSE)—the SDECE's successor agency—immediately plotted to overthrow Qaddafi. In 1984, Libyan exiles trained in Sudan and infiltrated through Tunisia made two failed attempts to assassinate Qaddafi.

French mercenaries soon enough reared their ugly heads in the new NATO-backed Libyan war—some 17 French and British soldiers-of-fortune were captured by Qaddafi forces in September 2011—but the CIA, Mossad and French DGSE were all along behind certain factions aligned with the 'rag-tag' rebels that rose out of the Libyan desert in Benghazi.

In late February 2011, British Special Forces evacuated hundreds of British nationals from the Libyan desert: the companies they worked for and their reasons for being in Libya were (as usual) never reported. The operations were coordinated with Germany, Italy, and Turkey—and certainly with the US. British Petroleum last year was embroiled in a scandal for influence peddling used to secure a contract for petroleum exploration in Libya. Royal/Dutch Shell also held some 26 high-level meetings in Libya and won [sic] contracts against US rivals like Texas oil corporation Occidental Petroleum (OXY), which had been ejected when Libya's oil fields were nationalized in 1970. OXY was the first US petroleum corporation to resume operations in Libya when sanctions were lifted in 2004. In 2008, OXY reached new 30-year agreements with Libya to redevelop and explore in its "most prolific producing area"—the Sirte Basin. US major ExxonMobil reported "milestone achievements" in the Libyan oil sector in 2009. British mercenaries were doing far more than coordinating evacuations of oil workers however: that was merely a cover story for all kinds of western terrorist operations underway.

NATIONAL ENDOWMENT FOR (NON) DEMOCRACY

In 1983, the Pentagon, USAID, US State Department, and the CIA were all involved in the creation and implementation of 'Project Democracy'—based on National Security Decision Directive 77 (NSDD 77)—and this led to the creation of the quasi-governmental organization National Endowment for Democracy. After that, some of the 'softer' tactics used in covert interventions were shifted away from the CIA and onto the NED, whose involvement with covert operations and foreign interventions are nonetheless well established.

A 'soft' intervention CIA front, the National Endowment for Democracy was deeply involved in subversive operations in Libya, along with the CIA fronted Freedom House (under their Blue Umbrella program and others), prior to the 'rebel uprising' of 2011. These entities backed 'opposition', supported propaganda campaigns and so-called 'pro-democracy' movements, and were known to be involved with backing armed insurgents and interventions.

NED works its overt intelligence sector magic through four organizations under its (own) umbrella: the National Democratic Institute; International Republican Institute, Center for Private

Enterprise, and the AFL-CIO's American Center for International Labor Solidarity. NED is closely aligned with US foreign policy interests and achieves its mission through the revolving doors between US Government and the NED Board of Directors.

Some of these NED directors include: former US Secretaries of State, Henry Kissinger (Nixon) and Madeleine Albright (Clinton), former US Secretary of Defense Frank Carlucci (Reagan), former National Security Council Chair Zbigniew Brzezinski (Carter), former NATO Supreme Allied Command in Europe, General Wesley K. Clark (Clinton), and the former head of the World Bank, Paul Wolfowitz (George W. Bush), who many regard as a key architect and advocate of the US war on Iran.

Freedom House is supportive of NED programs but has been around since its creation by Eleanor Roosevelt and they have been very active against Libya. Freedom House is funded by, amongst others, UNILEVER Corporation, USAID and the US Information Agency (USIA). Freedom House, in alliance with USIA, has provided covert and overt 'Radio Free' disinformation programs all over the world since at least 1952: e.g. Radio Free Europe, Radio Free Asia. The USIA was directly involved with US Army's 4th Psychological Operations Group in planning and coordinating major military operations (e.g. the Gulf War and the UNITAF intervention in Somalia).

Past and present Freedom House trustees include: former CIA director R. James Woosley; former national security adviser (at the time of the 1996 US invasion of Congo-Zaire) Anthony Lake; Harvard professor Samuel Huntington; UNILEVER executive Ned Bandler; intelligence insider and Kagame public relations agent Andrew Young; former Joseph Mobutu confidant and national security insider Jeanne J. Kirkpatrick; former NED director and International Crisis Group trustee Zbigniew Brzezinski; USAID intelligence operative J. Brian Atwood (USAID administrator who oversaw the US-backed genocide against millions of Rwandan (mostly Hutu) and Congolese refugees in Congo-Zaire, 1996-1998) and more.

Freedom House is also very likely affiliated with the phantom US Office of Strategic Information (OSI), formed after September 11, 2001. OSI is said to have been reorganized, all its original functions reassigned to the Office of Global Communications, Information Awareness Office (IAO), and the newly reactivated Counter-Disinformation/ Misinformation Team (Counter-Information Team). However, then-Secretary of War Donald Rumsfeld issued statements affirming that the OSI's operations would continue.

ROGUE STATE PAINTED WITH BLATANT PROPAGANDA

In the ABC NIGHTLINE report "NFSL Leader Speaks from Washington" we found the Washington monument in the background for an interview with an Arab agent being used by the western propaganda system as a credible source—but with zero explanations of who he was or why his claims might require serious scrutiny, at best.

NFSL operative Ibrahim Sahad spoke freely, making any claim he liked, and nothing he said was challenged or counter-balanced. Sahad suggested that the UN Security Council MUST be convened to stop the 'war crimes' and 'mass murder' and 'genocide' being committed by Qaddafi against his own people. Ibrahim Sahad's bias was betrayed by such statements as "The UN Security Council was convened when just one man was killed in Lebanon—so it should be convened to address the most brutal use of live ammunition, heavy arms and mercenaries in Libya."

Here are some of the rallying cries that made media headlines, everywhere the English language was used, in February and March and April of 2011:

- Qaddafi: Stop Killing Your Own People
- Qaddafi has Chemical Weapons and he is
  Ready to Use them
- SAS Ready to seize Col Qaddafi's stores of mustard gas
- EU Prepares for the worst after
  Qaddafi's genocide threats
- Heavy arms used in Libya crackdown
- Qaddafi in crimes against humanity probe
- Qaddafi Brutalizes Foes, Armed or Defenseless

The death tolls in Iraq, Afghanistan and Congo-Zaire—committed by US, NATO and Israeli forces—far surpassed anything that might have occurred in Libya at the time, or later. Meanwhile, most 'news' on Libya was based on false accusations and false assertions—such as the *threat* of nerve gas being used. This is the whipping up of hysteria to encourage public support for yet another massive destabilization campaign against yet another sovereign government and an innocent population—when in actuality the war crimes and crimes against humanity were being committed by the NATO-backed insurgency and, directly, by NATO forces.

However, just prior to the dropping of sanctions in 2004 it was established that Washington, London and Israel were grossly exaggerating claims of Qaddafi's development of nuclear and chemical weapons. The western propaganda about Weapons of Mass Destruction in Libya had the same empty ring as the lies about Weapons of Mass Destruction used to justify the war against Iraq, the lies about the Lord's Resistance Army used to justify the military expansionism in Uganda, the lies about the Taliban used to justify an illegal war in Afghanistan, the lies about the Forces for the Democratic Liberation of Rwanda (FDLR) used to justify Kagame's Pentagon-backed atrocities in the Congo, and the lies about Al-Qaeda, more generally, used to justify the GWOT.

The US has used weapons of mass destruction in Afghanistan and did so since the invasion of 2001: these include phosgene and uranium weapons. A deeper issue might be the loss of certain nuclear weapons, by the west, as claimed by sources in London, which reportedly went missing from US/NATO stocks. These claims asserted that these weapons made their way into the hands of British arms dealer John Bredenkamp, Robert Mugabe's patron and long-time crony and a war lord involved in Congo-Zaire, and that they may have been sold to Libya, Yemen, Iran or North Korea.[24] The nukes were allegedly jettisoned over the Indian Ocean off the coast of Somalia by a US Air Force plane that crashed (en route to the US air base on the island of Diego Garcia after departing the Iraq war theatre in 1991), but this story is in complete media whiteout.

Similarly, western reportage on the alleged [sic] use of Libyan government air forces to attack 'rebel' forces was extremely biased, extremely duplicitous, and extremely hypocritical. First of all, Libya was under attack—an invasion constitutes an act of aggression in contravention of international law—and had every right to defend its government, its territory and its interests. Of course, the 'international community' quickly whipped up the specter of a Qaddafi genocide against his own people, to justify any and all foreign aggression under the new doctrine of "responsibility to protect"—an imperial *faux* doctrine meant to serve the most powerful and ostensibly innocent—even in contravention of international law. In 2009 the air attacks by Israel against Sudan were treated as just and legitimate by the western media. Worse still were the massive Israeli air strikes on Gaza—also in contravention of international law and international humanitarian law. But these are war crimes, crimes against humanity and, in the Palestinian case, they are part of a greater genocidal campaign against the Palestinians. Similarly, Israeli shipments of tanks through the Strait of Hormuz and Somali waters were delivered through the US naval station at Mombasa, Kenya, and traveled overland to Sudan for the war in Darfur: more violations of international law; more war crimes and crimes against humanity by Israel.[25] The western propaganda system covered up the Israeli role, and almost all western military interventions or western economic plots off the coast of Somalia (such as the dumping of nuclear waste or the plunder of Somali fishing stocks) are framed in a rubric of Somali piracy.[26] Blame the victims, just as we did in Libya.

When Muammar Qaddafi met with ABC News correspondent Christiane Amanpour for an interview in Tripoli February 28, 2011, someone should have warned Qaddafi that Amanpour was a US State Department agent pretending to be a journalist. For her interview with Qaddafi, Amanpour presented with the typical western white power arrogance that assumes an air of moral superiority and immunity from criticism, while in confrontation with a nasty rogue mass murderer.

"I asked [Qaddafi] several times about reports that aerial bombardments had been used against protesters," Amanpour said, parroting the western propaganda line, "but Gadhafi said they did not happen and that they had only bombed military and ammunition depots."

"When he can laugh in talking to American and international journalists while he is slaughtering his own people, it only underscores how unfit he is to lead and how disconnected he is from reality," Amanpour quoted Susan Rice, then US Ambassador to the United Nations, as saying.

During the Clinton years, Amanpour was directly linked to pro-Kagame propagandist Philip Gourevitch and Madeleine Albright's undersecretary of state Jamie Rubin, and together Gourevitch and Amanpour produced some of the most blatant lies on 'genocide in Rwanda'. Gourevitch and Amanpour covered up the Pentagon's role in supporting the Rwandan Patriotic Front/Army and Uganda People's Defense Forces invasion of Rwanda (1990-1994). Amanpour later married Jamie Rubin, and she followed Gourevitch's lead in reporting blatant and racist propaganda about a "home grown rebellion in [Congo] Zaire" for CNN from the Congo-Zaire border in 1996. Meanwhile, the Pentagon's C-130's were shipping troops into Congo-Zaire through Entebbe, Uganda and millions of innocent Hutu people were being targeted and hundreds of thousands of innocent Hutu people being killed in the Kagame/RPA war crimes and genocide against Hutus which ensued. US Special Forces were on the ground shelling refugee camps and slaughtering people.[27] Christiane Amanpour and the rest of the western press covered it up. They are still covering up the atrocities in Congo, Rwanda, Burundi, Sudan, Uganda, Ethiopia, Somalia, and on, and on.

DID QADDAFI SIDE WITH THE EMPIRE?

"[T]he fundamental problem and issue before the people in

the region is that the US rulers seek imperial control and imposition of semi-colonial country-selling regimes," reported Ralph Schoenman. "The more autocratic and brutal, the better from the point of the US imperialism that is unrelenting history. Every time the population is given the opportunity to shape its own destiny, to seek its national independence, to seek its own control over its own resources, to seeks its own sovereignty and determination of its own future, that is incompatible with the US imperialism."[28]

The *Green Book* says that workers should be involved and self-employed, and that the land must belong to those who work it and similarly, the house must belong to those who live in it. And power shall be exercised by the people directly, without intermediaries, without politicians, through popular congresses and committees, where the whole population decides the fundamental issues of the district, city and country. These are fighting words to our predatory system of international capitalism.

When Qaddafi bowed to Western demands in 2004 it was most likely in part due to the incredible alignment of forces against Libya. Qaddafi and the Libyan government—like the legitimate or illegitimate governments of other countries—apparently agreed to a lot of imperialist dictates, circa 2003, to try to avoid having a war launched against his country and to allow the people to still enjoy some decent standard of living and peaceful lives. In the end it didn't matter what Qaddafi did to try to please the greater forces of evil in the world—the leaders in Washington, Tel Aviv, Brussels, London, Paris, Ottawa.

Perhaps Qaddafi played along with the West's moral righteousness about the "Global War on Terror" knowing that he didn't have much choice. His opening to western interests made no difference, as too many forces have desired his destruction for far too long. When he fell, he fell hard. There was no international criminal court for Qaddafi, no, no, no. Secretary of State Hillary Clinton—what did Harvard scholar and genocide propagandist Samantha Power call Hillary Clinton? A wicked woman?[29]—decided it was time for Qaddafi's murder, she called for Qaddafi's capture or assassination.[30] When Qaddafi was duly murdered, Clinton publicly gloated.[31]

This was no 'popular revolution' sweeping Libya, though there were significant popular elements to the revolts we saw there.

THE PENTAGON INVASION

The US used any and all propaganda necessary to whip up American fervor over Qaddafi and justify intelligence (CIA, Mossad,

MI-6, DGSE) and defense (Pentagon, NATO) operations. US and British warships sat off the coast of Libya—and they didn't sit there idly. The imposition of a 'no-fly' zone meant that US/NATO planes could do as they like, undertaking bombing and fighter sorties against Libya.

US troops landed early in Libya, and they joined the 'opposition' and 'rebel' forces in 'rebel' controlled territories. The US, France and Britain openly set up bases in Libya, while Israel worked behind the scenes. Reports openly announced that British and US special forces had entered Libyan port cities of Benghazi and Tobruk on February 23 and 24, and yet the media continued to hammer the North American public with meaningless tripe about anti-Qaddafi rebels.

By the time that the Libyan insurgency reached the fever pitch necessary to hit the headlines of *The New York Times*, US covert operatives had already been on the ground for weeks, and probably much longer than that, whether they entered by sea (SEALS) or by way of Niger or Mali. The US had openly published information about its covert operations in Niger: see, for example, the travelology reports, more psyops tripe, by former US Special Forces now 'journalist' Robert Kaplan in "America's African Rifles", a Pentagon massaged and approved propaganda feature (April 2005) in the pro-war *Atlantic Monthly*. The Pentagon had been launching military operations all over the Sahel under the Pan-Sahel Initiative (in west and Central Sahara) and the Golden Spear Initiative (in East Africa and the Horn). On 10 January 2004, for example, some 500 US troops landed in the unheard-of backwater of Mauritania—just south of Algeria and Libya.[32] In 2009, AFRICOM launched US Special Forces 'training' operations in Chad, Niger and Nigeria, sending in hundreds more additional troops likely to have been involved in penetrating Libya from the south; these deployments occurred under SOCOM—the Pentagon's Special Operations Command.

Ethiopia, one of six or seven East African countries involved in a Pentagon program titled "Golden Spear", has also been a major theatre for mass murder by US forces.[33] The government of President Meles Zenawi in Ethiopia has been prosecuting genocide against the Anuak, Oromo and Ogaden peoples, but western countries turn a blind eye because the United States, Britain, Canada, Israel and others are backing Zenawi and Ethiopia provides major bases for western military covert operations against Djibouti, Somalia, Yemen, Sudan and Syria.[34]

Unmanned aerospace vehicles (UAVs), Predators and other drones have been operating over the entire North African region. Any opportunity to attack, destabilize, or invade has been exploited by the Pentagon. The US media prepared the ground for the English-news consuming masses to see the Pentagon invasion as a 'humanitarian' mission in Libya. There is nothing humanitarian about anything the Pentagon does, and there has never been.

IT'S NOT ONLY THE OIL, STUPID

Using state-of-the-art satellite remote sensing, the western powers certainly mapped the mineral deposits that lie beneath the sands of the Libyan desert long before the invasion began. For example, Canada's Barrick Gold has for years had concessions in Niger and Mali—this is the corporation intimately affiliated with former US President George Herbert Walker Bush, former US Senator Howard Baker, William Jefferson Clinton's former lawyer Vernon Jordan, and former Canadian Prime Minister Brian Mulroney—and Libya has a huge landmass with massive untapped mineral potential that goes way beyond the known petroleum deposits.

Another strategic geopolitical concern of the western powers is the protection and control of the massive nuclear (uranium) resources both inside Libya and nearby. France and Canada had already signed memorandums (circa 2007-2008) with Libya to explore and exploit uranium in Libya. France's entire nuclear weapons complex (and their massive nuclear power industry) revolve around uranium extracted from Agadez and Arlit in northern Niger and it was built, over the past 50 years, out of the blood, sweat and tears of the Toureg and Toubou people. Japanese companies have been extracting uranium out of Niger through the Overseas Uranium Resources Development Corporation (OURD), in cooperation with US, Israeli, German and French corporations and the innocent people of the Sahara now share something horrible in common with the innocent people of Japan and so many people of the Midwest US states: radiation poisoning, birth defects, leukemia and immune-deficiencies. Qaddafi's support for the nomadic Tuareg rebellions in the Sahara over the forty years of Qaddafi's tenure also brought him into the sights of the capitalist bombers.

In 2008, France and former colony Algeria signed defense and civil nuclear power accords, including cooperation in research, training, technology transfer and the exploration and production of uranium, all of interest to French nuclear giant Areva Corporation. Canadian and Australian corporations are also mining in Libya's other southern neighbor, Burkina Faso. And yet, unlike Libya, where the people had seen some benefits from the extraction of wealth from their land, thanks to Muammar Qaddafi, Niger remains the second poorest country in the world and Burkina Faso is close behind.

Russia and Ukraine had also signed memorandums with Libya

regarding uranium exploration and development. However, China intends to quadruple its uranium consumption and China's largest nuclear power corporation, the China National Nuclear Corp, has signed an agreement with China-Africa Development Fund to jointly develop uranium resources in Africa. Western nuclear corporations aim to monopolize Libya's uranium sector and exclude China and Russia from the exploration and development—so they can build the nuke plants themselves and sell uranium to their Asian competitors.

How, then, do we view the western imperialist war against the country of Libya, given that all these multinational corporations had already begun to expand, and many—like Bechtel and Asea Brown Baveri—already had contracts? Beyond the simple arguments about the GWOT—where Qaddafi is the bad guy and Barack Obama and Tony Blair and Benjamin Netanyahu are the good guys—is the simple fact that corporations are fighting corporations for profits and land and control of monetary systems and water systems. Predatory capitalism destroys countries in order to create markets.

The profits to be made on reconstruction—replete with all the media's bell-and-whistle proclamations about democracy and human rights and good governance, and, oh, our deep humanitarian concerns for the people of Libya—far exceed those that were being made by the multinationals already inside Libya prior to the 2011 invasion. In any case, it is loudly proclaimed that the sophisticated weapons of the Pentagon and its allies never hit civilians, or civilian infrastructure. We never hit churches or mosques or hospitals—only the terrorists like Qaddafi and Bashir would do such horrible things. Blah, blah, blah.

While trillions of dollars have literally gone up in smoke in the western wars, thus serving the permanent warfare economies of NATO countries, and Israel, the aftermath markets are also of interest to the capitalist elites. The misery industry, the World Bank, IMF, Overseas Private Investment Corporation and other multinational lending institutions insure the profitability of post-warfare corporate reconstruction.

One of the largest profit margins to be made in post-warfare Libya was made by the criminal western landmines apparatus. Corporations that behave more like mafias—outside of any public oversight and never scrutinized by governments or the mass media—have reaped millions of dollars (at least) in USAID and DFID and other government contracts to 'clean-up' the landmines and other unexploded ordinance (UXO) now littered like rocks over the Libyan desert.

"I have worked in DR Congo and Gaza," said Alexandra Arango, a highly paid consultant with the Mines Advisory Group (MAG), "and

I would say the contamination in Sirte is the worst I have ever seen." MAG is a so-called 'non-government' and 'non-profit' organization (NGO) operating in Libya (Alex DeWaal, mentioned above, was Chair of the Mines Advisory Group from 1993-1998).

"Children are particularly attracted to 23mm bullets as they are in abundance and easy to pick up," said Arango, who works as a Community Liaison Manager for MAG. "Most children play with them for a while until they decide to throw rocks at them or tap them onto a surface and they explode, injuring their hand and causing shrapnel injuries on their chest or face."

Since 1989, the Mines Advisory Group has worked in over 35 countries and in 1997 was awarded the Nobel Peace Prize as part of the International Campaign to Ban Landmines. Also part of that campaign, and a Nobel Peace Prize recipient in 1997, was the NGO Norwegian People's Aid, widely known—if you work in places where they operate, like Sudan and Ethiopia—as Norwegian People's Army, due to their propensity to ship weapons under the cover of so-called humanitarian AID.[35]

THE POLITICAL ECONOMY OF GENOCIDE

Libya is a country of approximately six million people, having a huge geographical area but low population density. Claims that Qaddafi uplifted his people over the course of his 40-year dictatorship demand scrutiny indeed. Supporters claimed that poverty was low and enemies claimed that poverty was high throughout the country. However, in Tripoli in September 2009 there were the obvious signs of capitalism: overcrowding, traffic, poverty, pollution and the widespread destruction of the environment. There was also an element of fear visible in people's faces. Prior to the western military onslaught of 2011, meaning, thanks to Muammar Qaddafi, Libya was ranked very high according to the United Nations Human Development Index on education, health care, low infant mortality, low malnutrition, and general poverty.

Now all these questions about Libya's development under Qaddafi have been rendered somewhat moot due to the vast destruction, torture, massacres and—for example—radioactive weaponry that the United States and Israel and France and the rest of our European military allies have rained down on Libya.

It is completely hypocritical for citizens of the United States to speak of the outrage of 'poverty' abroad when that poverty is so often the result of US militarization, unjust trade, and plundering entities like the World Bank and International Monetary Fund. Further, some of the worst poverty in the world can be found in US cities like Gary, Indiana and on Native American reservations like Pine Ridge. Hillary Clinton's complaints about Muammar Qaddafi are really just a projection of her shadow—a long, dark shadow steeped in bloodshed and deception— and another example of the hypocrisy on Libya. And Hillary Clinton should be tried for war crimes for calling for (and then gloating over) Muammar Qaddafi's brutal murder.

Qaddafi funded Pan-African organizations and individuals, some of whom have very noble missions and serve to challenge the downtrodden, while he also funded armed factions involved in unjust wars or destabilizations. On the one hand, Qaddafi supported one state in Palestine with equal rights for everyone, and he spoke forcefully about the unjust war against the Palestinians by Israel.

On the other, Qaddafi funded Jean Pierre Bemba and the euphemistically-named *Movement for the Liberation of Congo* (MLC), the 'rebellion' [sic] that was also backed by Yoweri Museveni and allied with Rwandan 'rebel' forces (*Congolese Rally for Democracy*) backed by Paul Kagame, and these forces were responsible for a very definite genocide in the Democratic Republic of Congo (Congo-Zaire). Bemba is on trial at the International Criminal Court (ICC) for war crimes committed in the Central African Republic. In DRC, Bemba's forces looted and raped and plundered goods, artifacts and minerals that were sold in Kampala or Kigali.[36] The ICC is, of course, part of the farce of western rigged international justice: imagine issuing international indictments only against black Africans, as if black Africans have a monopoly on warlordism, dictatorship or mass atrocities.[37]

The very same human rights mafia that criminalized the Qaddafi regime and protected the illegal invaders committing the most egregious atrocities in Libya have never named the most obvious genocides in Congo and Uganda. The stellar performers are Human Rights Watch, watching (and demonizing) our enemies and watching out only for those friendly to us that challenge our enemies, and Amnesty International, but this means amnesty (immunity) for those that serve our corporate and military agenda, and punishment for those who don't.

Human Rights Watch reported that international arms dealer Victor Bout illegally shipped weapons into Congo-Zaire, picking them up in Libya and delivering them to Rwandan Hutu forces. However, Human Rights Watch is deeply compromised when it comes to reporting and not reporting the facts—or selectively reporting them—on Central Africa as elsewhere. If Qaddafi did supply or facilitate the provision of arms to Rwandan Hutu insurgents in Congo-Zaire, it may be one of the more reasonable actions he took. It might also have been just another example of Qaddafi's wiliness, where he privately supported a 'rebellion' against western interests while publicly supporting western client dictators (Kagame, Museveni, etc.). The Pentagon and its propaganda minions forever malign the Forces for the Democratic Liberation of Rwanda (FDLR) precisely because they fought against the illegal invasion of Rwanda by Paul Kagame and Yoweri Museveni and their Pentagon backers. Meanwhile, it is Rwanda, Uganda and their foreign multinational corporate allies that are responsible for the preponderance of killing in Central Africa, not the FDLR. Meanwhile, the FDLR was destroyed long ago and yet in June 2012 we still found Hillary Clinton and Hollywood actorvist Ben Affleck shedding crocodile tears for the people of the Congo, covering up for Kagame, and blaming everything on the FDLR. Of course, the Clinton's and Ben Affleck both have clear economic and political connections with the regime in Kigali.[38] According to Amnesty International, another selective human rights organ serving western interests, Qaddafi also reportedly armed Sudanese in Darfur—long before the Darfur conflict 'began' in 2003—to fight against western backed interventions in Chad and Sudan.

In 2009, as a result of the African Union (AU) rotation process for determining its chair, Muammar Qaddafi became chairman of the AU, another elite organization designed to serve western exploitation—or run by a cabal of thieves, at the very least, who all have the goods on each other, and so none will ever challenge the way things are—while the people, the masses of Africa, have everywhere suffered. At the same time, Qaddafi sought to use his chairmanship of the African Union to advance his plan for a United States of Africa operating with one currency and one passport. These are fighting words to the western capitalist elite.

The AU had signed on with Washington in May 2000 for the devastating neo-liberal trade and tariffs agreement known euphemistically as the Africa Growth and Opportunity Act (AGOA). The AU special report on genocide in Rwanda was a complete whitewash serving US and UK interests and protecting dictators Paul Kagame and Yoweri Museveni. African leaders have also slammed the AU for its inaction and silence regarding various developments on the continent.

Former African Union chairmen have included some of Africa's most criminal dictators, such as Dennis Sassou-Nguesso, who has reigned with absolute military brutality in the Republic of Congo for some 20 years (with a gap from 1992-1997). Gabon's present ruler Albert-Bernard Bongo is the son-in-law of Dennis Sassou-Nguesso, and both have been sustained with millions of Elf petrol dollars. Sassou-Nguesso's elite Cobra militia was also trained by French advisers and, like Colonel Joseph Mobutu, Sassou-Nguesso relied on Israeli security and intelligence for his personal protection and for state-sanctioned terrorism. Why is Sassou Nguesso not a household name like Gaddafi?

The AU's alliance with NATO began long ago, and it saw expanded joint military operations in Sudan, where the AU served as NATO's 'African face' for US/UK and Israeli military interventions in the war for Darfur. For example, forces fighting for the NATO interests, commanded and commandeered under an AU banner, came from Paul Kagame's Rwanda Defense Forces (formerly called Rwandan Patriotic Front/Army) responsible for genocide, war crimes and crimes against humanity in Uganda, Rwanda, Congo-Zaire and, subsequently, Darfur. Rather than condemning western military expansion and different forms of AFRICOM or CIA-backed terrorism, for example, the AU backs the western war of annihilation in Somalia, involving Ugandan troops trained by US Special forces, and the Pentagon's expansion in Ethiopia and support for dictator Meles Zenawi there. Ethiopia is the site of ongoing genocide(s) and no one has reported the atrocities in the blood drenched oil-rich Ogaden basin. What does the AU say? What do those who complain about Qaddafi committing genocide against his own people say?

Nothing. They are silent. Or they accuse the victims of committing atrocities that the west has a moral responsibility to go in and stop.

On February 22, 2011, the Libyan deputy ambassador to the United Nations called on Muammar Qaddafi to step down and face trial over "war crimes and genocide". The charge was widely repeated in other news venues. "European diplomats are meeting around the clock to minimize risks for their nationals after a speech by Libya's Muammar Qaddafi yesterday (22 February) was interpreted as code to start genocide."

"Qaddafi's Genocide!" declared one CNN news pundit. A Stop Qaddafi Genocide! page was created on Facebook.

Such claims made by the Libyan 'opposition' and reported in the western press that Qaddafi was already committing genocide or about to commence doing so against his own people represented the height of arrogance and hypocrisy.

If there were acts of genocide being committed in Libya, they were never being committed by Qaddafi or his loyalists. Reports indicated that anti-government forces—meaning the western media's precious 'rebels'—were targeting black Africans because black Africans were equated with pro-Qaddafi mercenaries.

Those being unjustly targeted included black Africans from

Sudan, Chad, or Egypt, many of whom were laborers who had been working in the service industry and lower menial jobs in Libya. However, this report seeks to remind people that there is a political economy of genocide, just as there is a political economy of human rights. Thus it is imperative that any sincere and comprehensive discussion or application of the term 'genocide' be informed by an agreement or understanding of what we do and don't mean by such terminology. In fact, it is best never to use the genocide terminology at all: so debased has its meaning become that people like Dr. Eric Reeves amount to Holocaust deniers for so candidly brandishing the genocide term to serve Pentagon interests.

The disinformation frenzy and hysteria had no bounds. A web site dedicated to English language disinformation about Cuba had this headline: "Human Rights in Cuba: Is Castro Supporting Qaddafi's Genocide?" "Are Cuban pilots flying Qaddafi's military jets, which are being deployed to attack peaceful Libyan protesters?" the article began. Interestingly, Fidel Castro was the first international leader to publicly assert that Washington was about to invade Libya: Castro was right.

If one were to apply a hypothetical Universal Moral Index, what might the standing be of the USA and its allies, including Japan, Europe, Israel, South Africa, Canada and Australia, whose wars have far dwarfed the 'atrocities' that were attributed to Qaddafi in Libya, many of which never happened? While we had no credible reporting about who was killing, who the opposition was, how many were really dead, etc., out of Libya, we had, and still have, credible report after credible report establishing that the US and its allies have perpetrated massacres, tortures, and other atrocities, including crimes against humanity and war crimes, in the millions of people, in Congo-Zaire, Rwanda, Uganda, Afghanistan, Iraq and Sudan—for a short list.

The claims of genocide here, akin to the one-sided charges against former Rwandan president Juvenal Habyarimana, or against Sudan's Omar al-Bashir, offer further examples of the politics of genocide delineated in great detail by this writer and others.[39] Reports in western media—provided, again, by the NFSL and other western intelligence entities and flak organizations—were filled with harsh condemnatory language and characterizations not seen in reporting produced about western military campaigns. For example, in many western reports we saw, such as the one titled "Gruesome Footage Proves Libya Using Heavy Arms", there were claims that *"newspapers obtained shocking footage of corpses with bodies blasted off and several torsos in Libyan hospitals."*

So there were several torsos. That is not quite genocide. Where are the images? If such images of death and destruction had appeared it would have been in sharp contrast to the complete whiteout on dead bodies produced in the Pentagon's other theaters of war, in the eastern Congo-Zaire or Somalia, or in Afghanistan. Meanwhile, some videos purporting to be 'violence in Libya' disappeared from the web after their authenticity was blown.

Images of dead bodies can be produced and published but these are easily stripped of context. How do western audiences and propaganda consumers know that these were authentic and not recycled images of protests from Yemen or Bahrain dumped into the western press (with their willing acknowledgment), as was alleged, or recycled by the BBC, as was done later in Syria?[40] Al-Jazeera showed its true western colors by not reporting much of anything that had any grounding in real and honest facts, and certainly nothing critical of western manipulation or involvement. By producing absolute nonsense or, worse, planted stories from intelligence ops, Al-Jazeera consistently fanned the flames of war and covered up the truth.

We saw the tactic of collecting dead bodies and skeletons used in Rwanda by the Pentagon's agents of the Rwandan Patriotic Front, and in Darfur and South Sudan, where journalist Nicholas Kristof produced some photos of dead shriveled bodies from some desert somewhere and claimed these photos were from a classified African Union archive.[41] The atrocities were committed, we were told, by President Omar al-Bashir and the government of Sudan. We saw the same propaganda tactic on Libya

However, there was never any mention of US military involvement or mercenaries (Pacific Architects and Engineers, Dyncorp, others) on the ground in Sudan. Dead men tell no tales, or dead women: these dead bodies were as likely dead from US or Israeli-backed 'rebels'—the Justice and Equality Movement or Sudan Liberation Army backed by the US, NATO, Israel and our puppet dictator in Uganda.

The double-standards and outright lies are quickly recognized, if one knows there are deeper truths, by examining propaganda produced by the International Crisis Group, or such propaganda tracts as Smith College English teacher Eric Reeves' *A Long Day's Dying: Critical Moments in the Darfur Genocide*—where there is not one reference to Ugandan dictator Yoweri Museveni and his backing of the Sudan People's Liberation Army (SPLA) in South Sudan (a US military covert operation) and the Sudan Liberation Army (SLA) in Darfur, in all of the 386 pages. Further, Dr. Eric Reeves invented facts that served the propaganda system. Reeves regularly and hysterically screamed about the 'genocidal counter-insurgency' by the Bashir government, and he inflated the death tolls to the point that the whole world was believing his numbers, until even *The New York Times* was forced to publish some damage control.[42]

"In March 2009, Jordan and Egypt were informed by the US of new Iranian plans to ship a cargo of 'lethal military equipment' to Syria with onward transfer to Sudan and then to Hamas," reported Reeves in a January 2011 flak piece in the *Guardian* newspaper. "Host nations were requested to require that the flights land for inspection or deny them overflight rights. ***It is not known whether any deliveries went ahead*** (emphasis added). In April Egypt's interior minister, General Habib al-Adly, was described in US cables as being behind the dismantling of a Hezbollah cell in Sinai as well as 'steps to disrupt the flow of Iranian-supplied arms from Sudan through Egypt to Gaza.'"

There was never any verification or validation of these invented accusations, and notice that Dr. Reeves managed to tie all the supposed terrorists up in one massive terrorist plot: Syria, Hamas, Hezbollah, Sudan government, Iran...well, almost all of them.

Professor Reeves didn't forget to malign Libya elsewhere, however. Reeves called Barack Obama's decision to intervene in Libya "profoundly inconsistent" when considered next to the Obama administration's approach with Sudan. The mad doctor Reeves was not concerned about the immoral and illegal war in Libya, one that soon led to additional massive US war crimes and Israeli-backed crimes against humanity and the piles and piles of skeletons an top of those already produced across sub-Saharan Africa. No, no, no. Dr. Reeves was complaining that the Obama administration has failed because it has not ordered air strikes and tanks and radioactive weaponry deployed against President Omar al-Bashir in Sudan. Dr. Reeves' feelings were hurt that his own private war was not getting the attention that he—having helped to whip up the specter of genocide, practically out of thin air—felt it deserved. This is a perfect example of the illegal international warfare being advanced by western liberals on the grounds of humanitarian necessity and the doctrine of "Responsibility to Protect."

Another phantom intelligence operative involved in advancing the western images of 'humanitarianism' and just guerrilla wars is the French Israeli operative Bernard-Henri Lévy. Described as a "Jewish public intellectual, philosopher and journalist in France", Levy was directly supporting the illegal invasion of Libya.

The agents of capitalist propaganda, like Smith College English professor Eric Reeves, and *New York Times* hack Nicholas Kristof, and French Israeli operative Bernard-Henri Levy have also routinely made comparisons between Libya and Rwanda, or Syria and Rwanda, and now Iran and Rwanda. For example, testifying before the US Congress on 29 November 2011, General Romeo Dallaire, one of the key (criminal) agents of 'genocide' in Rwanda, stated: "[But] what's going on in Iran now is the genocide of the Baha'is. They're literally wiping out other religions in order to purify. Well, that's a cause that can be amplified and we can use that. Not only the nuclear argument, but also the fundamental human rights argument of ethnic cleansing and genocide."

Western mercenaries that have been deeply involved, and remain so, in some of the world's bloodiest conflicts, in *coups d'etat*, in massacres and other atrocities are never challenged for the most blatant crimes. These include British mercenary Tony Buckingham—whose mercenary past is legendary. Founder of Heritage Oil & Gas, a petroleum company he linked to mercenary firms Branch Energy and Sandline International, Buckingham was also a partner in the infamous Executive Outcomes, with former British Special Air Services (SAS) soldier-of-misfortune Tim Spicer—the recipient of massive Pentagon contracts in Iraq.

Similarly, there was no public outcry about the use of mercenaries to shore up a dictator when Central African Republic dictator Ange Felix Patasse called in Libyan troops and commanders to protect his private diamond republic. No one said a word when Ethiopian troops joined the Pentagon's efforts to overthrow Col. Joseph Mobutu and reorganize capitalist interests in Congo-Zaire (1996).

What, in reality, is the position of United Nations troops from Pakistan, Guatemala, India, Belgium, Canada or Bangladesh deployed in Congo or Sudan or Haiti? These are *mercenaries,* paid to carry a gun and use it if necessary in support of protecting capitalist interests. In Congo, the United Nations mercenaries—the so-called 'peacekeeping' forces of MONUC and MONUSCO—have supported multiple genocides throughout their tenure from 2001 onward to the present, and they are supporting war crimes, depopulation and plunder in the Congo as this report goes to press, and the death toll exceeds ten million since the initial US invasion (1996).

In short, almost everything in the western press on the crises in Libya was deeply slanted by some faction, or interest, or it was—and remains—tainted by western arrogance, or by anti-imperialist ideology (of 'solidarity' with Qaddafi), even in the case of what is perceived to be the 'alternative' media. There was very little accurate reporting of any kind.

Muammar Qaddafi was often portrayed as a champion for people of color—providing funding, hope and solidarity where none other existed—and this correspondent is aware that this [white] correspondent's writing herein is deficient in presenting all the positive aspects of his collaboration with people of color.

"The lies of the media cannot hide the fact that Qaddafi has supported the struggles of peoples for liberation in Nicaragua, Cuba, Angola, Mozambique, South Africa and many other countries, specifically concretely helping the people who fought for liberation," wrote Antonio Cesar Oliviera, in "Who Is Muammar Qaddafi?"[43] "In practice, Qaddafi has always been a benefactor of mankind," Oliviera continued, "but for the mercenary [western] media, a benefactor is one who creates wars in search of profits for the arms industry or to dominate the world, as were the wars created by the US in Korea, Vietnam, Iraq, Palestine, Afghanistan, El Salvador, Nicaragua and many other countries."

Qaddafi's alliance with Islam and his support for truly revolutionary movements must be understood for what the capitalist system saw them as: slaps in the face of power and threats to that power. This was one of the biggest reasons that Washington and London et al considered Qaddafi, throughout his tenure as leader of the Libyan Revolution, the devil incarnate. However, there remains so much left to be understood about Qaddafi's deeper relations with the west, his influence in Africa and the world, his relations with pan-African organizations or individuals, and questions about who he funded and when and why. Honest historians have some work to do to properly situate Muammar Qaddafi in the locus of world events.

It is equally important to compare and contrast the historical representations of Muammar Qaddafi with those of other African leaders who thrived under the tutelage of the western corporate apparatus during the same years Qaddafi was in power. Qaddafi is a household name all over the world, and for all the wrong reasons. Meanwhile, how many readers can situate the very real dictators responsible for some of the world's worst human rights crimes during the same decades? Daniel Arap Moi? General Gnassingbe Eyadema? Paul Biya? General Ibrahim Babangida? General Olusegun Obasanjo? Lt. Jerry John Rawlings? Omar Bongo?[44]

I see little moral currency or legitimacy by those who criticize Qaddafi. Thus all serious criticisms are reserved for those agents of repression involved in the unjust and illegitimate invasions and wars in Iraq, Afghanistan, Rwanda, Congo-Zaire, Uganda, Somalia… and now Libya and Syria. We know who the white-skinned power brokers are who have created war and destruction in these places, and they are never brought to justice, or hardly even mentioned, no matter the piles of corpses they have produced. There are no western war criminals like John Bredenkamp or Madeleine Albright or Maurice Tempelsman or Marc Rich on trial, or under indictment, or even being investigated, by the International Criminal Court, or any court, anywhere, no matter their extensive and well-documented involvement in bonafide terrorism.

Qaddafi has opposed the unjust International Criminal Court, and so do I, for precisely these reasons.

People wishing to support the legitimate grievances and actions for freedom and truth in Libya should challenge the western terrorist apparatus out of Washington, Tel Aviv, Paris, Brussels, London and Toronto. A truly just 'international community' would hold war crimes hearings and indict the western agents of oppression and propaganda—not only the military and intelligence operatives most responsible, but also their elite ministers of propaganda like Dr. Eric Reeves and CNN reporters.

Until the western news consuming public wakes up to the propaganda it is eating, and how sick it is making us, we will suffer from the mental illness unleashed by these psychological operations spun by the Pentagon, the think tanks and the corporate press. Hysteria about genocide by Bashir in Sudan, hysteria about genocide by Qaddafi in Libya, hysteria about Islamic jihad, hysteria about Ugandan warlord Joseph Kony, all part of the psychological operations that whitewash the true histories of western intervention in advancement of the new old 'humanitarian' warfare doctrine of the 'Responsibility to Protect'.

Perhaps nothing was so pitiful and demeaning to the people of the free world as the murder of Muammar Qaddafi. No international law, no international court, no trial, to rights, no justice, only the grim spectacle of Secretary of State Hillary Clinton, tired and withered and overweight, sadistically gloating and giggling over the inhuman and immoral death of Muammar Qaddafi. I see this as one of the saddest moments in the history of the United States—though one that merely underscores, yet again, the inhumanity of our leaders. Perhaps there is nothing more dishonorable and cruel than laughing as she did, having called for the death of a man, and seeing him brought to such an inglorious end.

ENDNOTES

1   See the discussion about worthy versus unworthy victims and enemy versus client states in Noam Chomsky and Edward S. Herman, *Manufacturing Consent,* Pantheon, 1988; and Noam Chomsky and Edward S. Herman, *The Washington Connection and Third World Fascism: The Political Economy of Human Rights: Vol. 1,* South End Press, 1979.

2   With caution to the reader to properly understand the historiography and contextualization by the Indian-Ugandan Mahmood Mamdani, a professor at Columbia University and Makerere University in Kampala, whose relationship to Museveni and Kagame has impacted his post 1982 scholarship, the author provides the following source material for this claim: Mahmood Mamdani, *Im-*

perialism and Fascism in Uganda, Heinemann Educational Books Ltd, 1983.

3   See, e.g., "Zimbabwe: Arms and the Men," *Africa Confidential*, Vol. 49, No. 16, 1 August, 2008.

4   The literal translation of 'Gukurahundi' is 'the rain that washes away the chaff'. See: Keith Harmon Snow, *The Great Betrayal: Mugabe's Gang and Genocide in Zimbabwe*, www.allthingspass.com, 2002; see also source material such as: Catholic Commission for Justice and Peace, *Breaking the Silence, Building True Peace: A Report on the Disturbances in Matabeleland and the Midlands, 1980-1988,* Legal Resources Foundation, 1997.

5   With caution to the reader, see: Mahmood Mamdani, *Imperialism and Fascism in Uganda*, Heinemann Educational Books Ltd, 1983.

6   Personal interviews with eyewitnesses, and Keith Harmon Snow, "Merchants of Death: Exposing Corporate Financed Holocaust in Central Africa," Global Research, 2008. See also: Wayne Madsen, *Genocide and Covert Operations in Africa, 1993-1999*, Mellon Press, 1999.

7   Rene Lemarchand, *The Dynamics of Violence in Central Africa*, University of Pennsylvania Press, 2009.

8   Gerard Prunier, *Africa's World War*, Oxford University Press, 2009.

9   With caution to the reader, see: Mahmood Mamdani, *Imperialism and Fascism in Uganda*, Heinemann Educational Books Ltd, 1983: p. 66.

10   See, e.g.: A. Milton Obote, *Notes on Concealment of Genocide in Uganda,* April 1990. There is widespread agreement amongst the Ugandan community that Museveni's National Resistance Army used tactics whereby they committed atrocities disguised as the government forces, or blamed their own massacres on Obote government forces, to justify their own terrorism in response. These military tactics are widely used by the US, Britain, Israel, and their surrogate proxy warriors commanded by Museveni and Kagame. The tactics were developed by Maj. Frank Kitson under the Mau Mau insurgency in Kenya, and are known as "pseudo operations". See: Frank Kitson, Low Intensity Operations: Subversion, Insurgency & Peacekeeping, Faber & Faber, 1971.

11   See: Keith Harmon Snow, "Pentagon Produces Satellite Photos of 1994 Rwanda Genocide, www.ConsciousBeingAlliance.com, April 6, 2012. See also, e.g.,: Robin Philpot, Ça ne s'est pas passé comme ça à Kigali, Les Intouchables, (That's Not What Happened in Kigali), published in English by the (Phil) Taylor Report: Rwanda 1994: Colonialism Dies Hard, 2004, <http://www.taylor-report.com/Rwanda_1994/>

12   Mohamed Bazzi, "What did Qaddafi's Green Book Really Say?" *New York Times*, May 27, 2011.

13   See: William Blum, *Killing Hope: US Military and CIA Interventions Since World War II*, Common Courage Press, 2004.

14   Douglas Valentine, *The Phoenix Program*, iUniverse, 2000.

15   This author is not one of these.

16   Laton McCartney, *Friends in High Places: The Bechtel Story: The Most Secret Corporation and How It Engineered the World,* Ballantine Books, 1989.

17   Marcus Baram, "Libya's Billions Invested in US Private Equity, Big Banks," Huff Post, March 1, 2011.

15   See, e.g., "Rwanda Freezes Gaddafi Assets," *East African Business Week*, April 11, 2011; and "Uganda, Rwanda Stop Tamoil Pipeline Contract," AllAfrica.com, August 20, 2011.

19   See: Keith Harmon Snow, "Pentagon Produces Satellite Photos of 1994 Rwanda

Genocide," www.ConsciousBeingAlliance.com, April 6, 2012; Keith Harmon Snow, "Apocalypse in Central Africa:The Pentagon, Genocide and the War on Terror," www.ConsciousBeingAlliance.com, July 20, 2010; and Keith Harmon Snow, "Brutal Regimes: Apocalypse in Central Africa: Ongoing repression, war crimes, and US involvement," Z Magazine, July 2010.

20   See, e.g.: "Libya: Gaddafi Ghost Still Haunts Investments in East Africa," All-Africa.com, February 18, 2012; and Mark Tran, "Libya Undecided on Future of African Investments," *The Guardian,* January 27, 2012.

21   See: Wayne Madsen, *Genocide and Covert Operations in Africa, 1993-1999,* Mellen Press, 1999; Pierre Paen, *Carnages: Les guerres secrets des grandes puissances en Afrique,* Fayard, 2010; Charles Onana, *Ces Tuers Tutsi: Au Coeur de la tragedie congolaise*, Duboiris, 2009; Keith Harmon Snow, "The Rwanda Hit List: Revisionism, Denial, and the Genocide Conspiracy," ConsciousBeingAlliance.com, March 12, 2010; Jean Marie Vianney Ndagijimana, *How Paul Kagame Sacrificed the Tutsis,* Edition La Pagaie, 2012.

22   "The Involvement of Ethiopia and Libya," *Horn of Africa*, Vol. 8, No. 1, 1985, p. 56-57.

23   Pierre Paén, *Carnages: Les guerres secrets des grandes puissances en Afrique,* Fayard, 2010, with partial translations in English by Mick Collins.

24   See: Keith Harmon Snow, "Darfurism, Uganda and the US War in Africa: The Specter of Continental Genocide," Global Research, November 11, 2007; and Alexander Cockburn, "Lost Nuclear Warheads from a B-52 Now in Iran?" Counterpunch, July 30, 2005.

25   Keith Harmon Snow, "The Winter of Bashir's Discontent: AFRICOM's Covert War in Sudan," ConsciousBeingAlliance.com, March 4, 2009.

26   See, e.g.: "Somali Pirates Seize 33 Tanks," BBC, September 26, 2008; and Jeffrey Gettleman, "Hijacked Arms Ship Limps into Port," *New York Times*, February 12, 2009.

27   Private interview with eye-witnesses.

28   Ralph Schoenman, "US Imperialism Against Democratic ME," PressTV, February 23, 2011.

29   "Obama advisor resigns; called Clinton 'monster'," Associated Press, March 7, 2008.

30   See, e.g.: Associated Press, "Hillary Clinton Says Libya's Muammar Gaddafi Must be Killed or Captured," *Herald Sun*, October 19, 2011; and Shirin Sadeghi, "Hillary Clinton Wants Gaddafi Killed," Huffington Post, October 19, 2011.

31   "We came, we saw, he died: What Hillary Clinton told news reporter moments after hearing of Gaddafi's death," Mail Online, October 21, 2011.

32   See: Jeremy Keenan, *The Dark Sahara: America's War on Terror in Africa*, Pluto Press, 2009.

33   Keith Harmon Snow, "Ethnic Cleansing on Ethiopia: Tip of the Golden Spear?" AllThingsPass.com and World War III Report, November 2004.

34   On genocide in Ethiopia, see e.g.: Keith Harmon Snow and Maxine Marcus, *Livelihoods and Vulnerabilities Study, Gambella Region of Ethiopia,* UNICEF, February 5, 2006.

35   Amongst development and 'humanitarian' sector professionals in the field, the Norwegian People's Aid is known as Norwegian People's Army, precisely because of their covert military operations. However, the European Sudanese Public Affairs Council and *Executive Intelligence Review* have both accused Norwegian People's Aid of running weapons in South Sudan. The Sri

Lankan Ministry of Defense also claimed that NPA was arming the Liberation Tigers of Tamil Eelam (LTTE). See also: Walter Jayawardhana, "Norwegian NGO used by LTTE, also delivered arms to insurgency in Sudan," Ministry of Defense and Urban Development, Sri Lanka, http://www.defence.lk/new.asp?fname=20080728_02, July 28, 2008.

36   See: Keith Harmon Snow, "A People's History of Congo's Jean Pierre Bemba," Toward Freedom, September 18, 2007.

37   See: Keith Harmon Snow, "White Collar War Crimes, Black African Fall Guys," *Black Star News*, December 4, 2008.

38   Keith Harmon Snow, "Ben Affleck, Rwanda and Corporate Sustained Catastrophe," Dissident Voice, January 23, 2009.

39   Edward S. Herman and David Peterson, *The Politics of Genocide,* Monthly Review Press, April 2010.

40   "Slaughter Slant: Houla Massacre prompts media blame game," RT TV, May 29, 2012; and Keith Harmon Snow, www.ConsciousBeingAlliance.com.

41   Reproduced in his *New York Times* piece of February 23, 2005, *"The Secret Genocide Archive".*

42   Marc Lacey, "The Mournful Math of Darfur: The Dead Don't Add Up," *New York Times,* May 18, 2005.

43   Pravda, January 3, 2011.

44   See, e.g.: Keith Harmon Snow, "The Crimes of Bongo: Apartheid & Terror in Africa's Gardens of Eden," Black Agenda Report, July 21, 2009.

POSTSCRIPT

MUAMMAR QADDAFI'S SPEECH TO THE UN GENERAL ASSEMBLY*

September 23, 2009

In the name of the African Union, I would like to greet the members of the General Assembly of the United Nations. I hope that this meeting will be the most historic in the history of the world. In the name of the General Assembly in its sixty-fourth session, presided over by Libya of the African Union, of one thousand traditional African kingdoms, and in my own name, I would like to take this opportunity, as President of the African Union, to congratulate our son, Mr. Obama, because he is attending the General Assembly. and we welcome him as his country is hosting this meeting.

This session is taking place in the midst of so many challenges facing us. The whole world should come together and unite its efforts to defeat the challenges that are our principal common enemy: those of climate change, and international crises such as the capitalist economic decline, the food and water crises, desertification, terrorism, immigration, piracy, manmade and natural epidemics, and nuclear proliferation. Perhaps influenza H1-N1 was a virus created in a laboratory that got out of control, originally being meant as a military weapon. Such challenges also include hypocrisy, poverty, fear, materialism, and immorality.

As is known, the United Nations was founded by three or four countries against Germany at the time. The United Nations was formed by the nations that joined together against Germany in the Second

* Transcribed by Vernon Huffman, Bike4Peace

World War. Those countries formed a body called the Security Council, made their own countries permanent members, and granted them the power of veto.

We were not present at that time. The United Nations was shaped in line with those three countries, who wanted us to step into shoes originally designed against Germany. That was the real purpose of the United Nations when it was founded over sixty years ago. That happened in the absence of some 165 countries at a ratio of one to eight. That is, for every one that was present, eight were absent. They created the Charter, of which I have a copy.

If one reads the Charter of the United Nations, one finds that the Preamble of the Charter differs from its articles. How did it come into existence? All those who attended at the San Francisco conference in 1945 participated in creating the Preamble, but they left the Articles and the internal rules and procedures of the so-called Security Council to experts, specialists from interested countries, which were those countries that had established the Security Council and united against Germany.

The Preamble is very appealing and no one objects to it, but all the provisions that follow it completely contradict the Preamble. We reject such provisions and will never uphold them. They ended with the Second World War.

The Preamble says that all nations, small or large, are equal. Are we equal when it comes to the permanent seats? No, we're not equal. The Preamble states in writing that all nations are equal, whether they are small or large. Do we have the right of veto? Are we equal? The Preamble says that we have equal rights whether we are large or small. That is what is stated and what we agreed in the Preamble. So the veto contradicts the Charter. The permanent seats contradict the Charter. We neither accept these nor recognize the veto.

The Preamble of the Charter states that armed force shall not be used save in the common interests. That is the Preamble that we agreed to and signed when we joined the United Nations, because we wanted the Charter to reflect that. It says that armed force shall only be used in the common interests of all nations. But what has happened since then? Sixty-five wars have broken out since the establishment of the United Nations and the Security Council. Sixty-five since their creation, with millions more victims than in the Second World War.

Are those wars and the aggression and force that were used in those sixty-five wars in the common interests of us all? No. They were in the interests of one or three or four countries, but not of all nations. We will talk about whether those wars were in the interests of one country or of all nations. That flagrantly contradicts the Charter of the United

Nations that we signed. Unless actions are in accord with the Charter to which we've all agreed, we will reject them and will not be afraid to speak diplomatically to anyone.

Now we are talking about the future of the United Nations. There should be no hypocrisy or diplomacy, because it concerns the important vital issue, the future of the world. It was hypocrisy that has brought about sixty-five wars since the establishment of the United Nations.

The Preamble also states that if armed force is used, it must be a United Nations force. Thus military intervention by the United Nations with the joint agreement of the United Nations, not by one or two or three countries using armed force. The entire United Nations will decide to go to war to maintain international peace and security. Since the establishment of the United Nations in 1945, if there is an act of aggression by one country against another, the entire United Nations should deter and stop that act.

If a country, Libya for instance, were to exhibit aggression against France, then the entire organization would respond because France is a sovereign state, a member of the United Nations and we all share the collective responsibility to protect the sovereignty of all nations. However sixty-five aggressive wars have taken place without any United Nations action to prevent them. Eight other massive, fierce wars whose victims number some two million have been waged by member states that enjoy veto powers. Those countries, who would have us believe that they support the sovereignty and independence of peoples, actually used aggressive force against peoples. While we would like to believe that these countries want to work for peace and the security of the world to protect peoples, they have instead resorted to aggressive wars and hostile behavior. Enjoying the veto they granted themselves as permanent members of the Security Council, they have initiated wars and claimed millions of victims.

The principle of noninterference in the internal affairs of states is enshrined in the Charter of the United Nations No country therefore has the right to interfere in the affairs of any government, be it democratic or dictatorial, socialist or capitalist, reactionary or progressive. This is the responsibility of each society. It is an internal matter for the people of the country concerned.

The Senators of Rome once appointed their leader, Julius Cesar, a dictator, because it was good for Rome at that time. No one can say of Rome at that time that it gave Cesar the veto. The veto is not mentioned in the Charter.

We joined the United Nations because we thought we were equals, only to find that one country can object to all the decisions we make. Who gave the permanent members their status in the Security Council? Four of them granted this status to themselves. The only country that we elected in this chamber to the Security Council is China. This was done democratically, but the other seats were imposed upon us undemocratically, through a dictatorial procedure carried out against our will and we should not accept it.

The Security Council reform we need is not an increase in the number of members, which would only make things worse. To use a common expression, if you add more water, you get more mud. It would add insult to injury. It would make things worse simply by adding more large countries to those that already enjoy membership of the Council. It would merely perpetuate the proliferation of superpowers. We therefore reject the addition of any more permanent seats.

The solution is not to have more permanent seats, which would be very dangerous. Adding more superpowers would crush the peoples of small, vulnerable, and third world countries, which are coming together in what has been called the Group of One Hundred. One hundred small countries banding together in a form that one member has called a forum of small states. These countries would be crushed by superpowers were additional large countries to be granted membership in the Security Council. This door must be closed. We reject it strongly and categorically.

Adding more seats to the Security Council would increase poverty, injustice, and tension at the world level, as well as create competition between certain countries such as Italy, Germany, Indonesia, India, Pakistan, the Philippines, Japan, Brazil, Nigeria, Argentina, Algeria, Libya, Egypt, the Democratic Republic of Congo, South Africa, Tanzania, Turkey, Iran, Ukraine, and Greece. All these countries would seek a seat on the Security Council, making its membership almost as large as that of the General Assembly and resulting in an impractical competition. What solution can there be?

The solution is for the General Assembly to adopt a binding resolution under the leadership of Mr. Treki[1] based on the majority will of the Assembly members and taking into account the consideration of no other body. The solution is to close Security Council membership to the admission of further states. This item is on the agenda of the General Assembly during the present session presided over by Mr. Treki. Membership through unions and the transference of mandates should supersede other proposals.

We should focus on the achievement of democracy based on the equality of member states. There should be equality among member states and the powers and mandates of the Security Council should be transferred to the General Assembly. Membership should be for unions, not for states. Increasing the number of member states will give the right to all countries for a seat in the importance of the spirit of the Preamble of the Charter.

No country could deny a seat on the Council for Italy for instance. If a seat was given to Germany, for the sake of argument, Italy might say that Germany was an aggressive country and was defeated in the Second World War. If we gave India a seat, Pakistan would say that it, too, was a nuclear country and deserves a seat. And those two countries are at war. It would be a dangerous situation. If we gave a seat to Japan, then we should give one to Indonesia, the largest Muslim country, and Turkey, and Iran. Ukraine would make the same claim. What could we say to Argentina or Brazil? Libya deserves a seat for its efforts in support of security by discarding its weapons of mass destruction, and South Africa, Tanzania, Ukraine demand the same. All these countries are important. The doors to Security Council membership should be closed.

This approach is also the trick that has been exposed. If we want to reform the United Nations, bringing in more superpowers is not the way. The solution is to foster democracy at the level of the General Congress of the World—the General Assembly—to which the powers of the Security Council should be transferred. The Security Council will become merely an instrument for implementing decisions taken by the General Assembly, which would be the Parliament, the legislative assembly of the world. This assembly is our democratic forum and the Security Council should be responsible to it. We should not accept the current situation.

These are the legislative members of the United Nations and their resolutions should be binding. It is said that the General Assembly should do whatever the Security Council recommends. On the contrary, the Security Council should do whatever the General Assembly decides. This is the United Nations, the assembly that includes 192 countries, not the Security Council, which includes only 15 of the member states.

How can we have any global security if the whole world is controlled by only five countries? We are 192 nations and we are like Speakers' Corner in London's Hyde Park. We just speak and nobody implements our decisions. We're a mere decoration, without any real substance. We are Speakers' Corner, no more, no less. We just make speeches and then disappear. This is who you are right now.

Once the Security Council becomes only an executive body for resolutions adopted by the General Assembly, there will be no competition for membership in the Council. Once the Security Council becomes a tool to implement General Assembly resolutions, there will be no need for any competition. The Security Council should quite simply represent all nations in accordance with the imposed rules submitted to the General Assembly.

There will be permanent seats on the Security Council for all unions and groups of countries. The 27 countries of the European Union should have a permanent seat on the Security Council. The countries of the African Union should have a permanent seat on the Security Council. The Latin American and ASEAN countries should have permanent seats. The Russian Federation and the United States of America are already permanent members of the Security Council. The Southern African Development Community, SADC, once it's fully established, should have a permanent seat. The 22 countries of the Arab League should have a permanent seat. The 57 countries of the Islamic Conference should have a permanent seat. The 118 countries of the Nonaligned Movement should have a permanent seat.

Then there is the G-100. Perhaps the small countries should also have a permanent seat. Countries not included in the unions that I have mentioned could perhaps be assigned a permanent seat to be occupied by them in rotation every six or twelve months. I'm thinking of countries like Japan and Australia that are outside of organizations as ASEAN or like the Russian Federation that is not a member of the European, Latin American, or African Unions. This would be a solution for them, if the General Assembly votes in favor of it.

The issue is a vitally important one. As has already been mentioned, the General Assembly is the Congress and Parliament of the world, the leader of the world. We are the nations and anyone outside this General Assembly will not be recognized. The President of the Assembly, Mr. Ali Abdussalam Treki and Secretary General Ban Ki Moon will produce a legal draft to set up the necessary committees to submit this proposal for a vote.

From now on the Security Council will be made up of unions of nations. In this way we will have justice and democracy. We will no longer have the Security Council consisting of countries which have been chosen because they have nuclear weapons, large economies, or advanced technology. That is terrorism. We cannot allow the Security Council to be run by superpowers. That is terrorism in itself. If we want a world that is united, safe, and peaceful, this is what we should do. If we want to remain in a world at war, that is up to you. We will continue to have conflict and to fight until doomsday or the end of the world.

All Security Council members should have the right to exercise the veto or else we should eliminate the whole concept of the veto with this new formation of the Council. This will be a real Security Council. According to the new proposal submitted to the General Assembly, it will be an executive council under the control of the General Assembly, which will have the real power to make the rules. In this way all countries will be on an equal footing at the Security Council, just as they are in the

General Assembly. In the General Assembly, we are all treated equally when it comes to membership and voting. It should be the same in the Security Council.

Currently one country has a veto; another country does not have a veto. One country has a permanent seat; another country does not have a permanent seat. We should not accept this, nor should we accept any resolution adopted by the Security Council in its current composition. We were under trusteeship. We were colonized, and now we are independent. We are here today to decide the future of the world in a democratic way that will maintain the peace and security of all nations, large and small, as equals.

Otherwise, it is terrorism. For terrorism is not just Al Qaeda, but can also take other forms. We should be guided by the majority of the votes of the General Assembly alone. If the General Assembly makes a decision by voting, then its wishes should be obeyed and its decision should be enforced. No one is above the General Assembly. Anyone who says he is above the Assembly should leave the United Nations and be on his own.

Democracy is not just for the rich or west half, or those who practice terrorism. All nations should be, and should be seen to be, on equal footing. At present the Security Council is security feudalism, political feudalism, for those with permanent seats, protected by them and used against us. It should be called not the Security Council, but the Terror Council.

In our political life, if they need to use the Security Council against us, they turn to the Security Council. If they have no need to use it against us, they ignore the Security Council. If they have an interest to promote, an axe to grind, they respect and glorify the Charter of the United Nations. They turn to Chapter Seven of the Charter and use it against poor nations. If, however, they wish to violate the Charter, they will ignore it, just as if it did not exist at all.

If the veto of the permanent members of the Security Council is given to those who have the power, this is injustice and terrorism and should not be tolerated by us. We should not live in the shadow of this injustice and terror. Superpowers have complicated global interests and they use the veto to protect those interests. For example, in the Security Council, they use the power of the United Nations to protect their interests and to terrorize and intimidate the third world, causing it to live under the shadow of terror.

From the beginning, since it was established in 1945, the Security Council has failed to provide security. On the contrary, it has provided terror and sanctions. It is only used against us. For this reason, we will no longer be committed to implementing Security Council

Resolutions after this speech, which marks the fortieth anniversary. Sixty-five wars have broken out, either fighting among small countries or wars of aggression waged against us by superpowers.

The Security Council, in clear violation of the Charter of the United Nations, failed to take action to stop these wars or acts of aggression against small nations or peoples. The General Assembly will vote on a number of historic proposals. Either we act as one, or we will fragment. If each nation were to have its own version of the General Assembly, the Security Council and the various instruments, and each would have to have an equal footing, the powers that currently fill the permanent seats would be confined to use of their own sovereign bodies, whether they be three or four of them, and would have to exercise their rights against themselves. This is of no concern to us.

If they want to keep their permanent seats, that's fine. Permanent seats will be of no concern to us. We shall never submit to their controls or their exercise of the veto that was given to them. We are not so foolish as to give up the right of veto to the superpowers to use so they can treat us as second class citizens and outcaste nations. It is not we who decided that those countries are the superpowers and the correct nations with the power to act on behalf of 192 countries.

You should be fully aware that we are ignoring the Security Council resolutions because those resolutions are used solely against us and not against the superpowers, which have the permanent seats and the right of veto. Those powers never use any resolutions against themselves. They are, however, used against us. Such use has turned the United Nations into a travesty of itself. It has generated wars that have violated the sovereignty of independent states. It has led to war crimes, genocides. All of this is in violation of the Charter of the United Nations.

Since no one pays attention to the Security Council of the United Nations, each country in the community has established its own security council. The Security Council here has become isolated. The African Union has established its own Peace and Security Council. The European Union has established a security council. The ASEAN countries have already established their own security council. Soon, Latin America will have its own security council, as will the 120 nonaligned nations. This means that we've already lost our confidence in the United Nations Security Council, which has not provided us with security and that's why we've arranged the new regional security councils.

We are not committed to obeying the rules or the resolutions of the United Nations Security Council in its present form, because it is undemocratic, dictatorial, and unjust. No one can force us to join the security councils or obey or comply with the orders given by the Security Council in its present composition. Furthermore, there is no respect for the United Nations and no regard for the General Assembly, which is actually the true United Nations. But if its resolutions are not binding, the decisions of the International Court of Justice, the international judicial body, aim only at small countries and third world nations. Powerful countries escape the notice of the court, or if judicial decisions are taken against these powerful countries, they are not enforced.

The International Atomic Energy Agency, IAEA, is an important agency within the United Nations. Powerful countries, however, are not accountable to it or under its jurisdiction. We have discovered the IAEA is only used against us. We are told that it's an international organization, but if that's the case, then all the countries in the world should be under its jurisdiction. If it is not truly international, then right after this speech, we should no longer accept it and should close it down.

Mr. Treki, in his capacity as president of the General Assembly, should talk to the Director General of the IAEA, Mr. El Baradei, and should ask him if he's prepared to verify nuclear energy storage in all countries and inspect all suspected increases. If he says yes, then we accept the agency's jurisdiction, but if he says that he cannot go into certain countries that have nuclear power and he does not have any jurisdiction over them, then we should close the agency down and not submit to its jurisdiction.

For your information, I called Mr. El Baradei when we had the problem with the Libyan nuclear bomb. I called Mr. El Baradei and asked him if the agreements by the superpowers to reduce nuclear supplies were subject to agency control and under inspection, and whether he was aware of any increases in their activity. He told me that he was not in a position to ask the superpowers to be inspected. So is the agency only inspecting us? If so, it does not qualify as an international organization since it is selective, just like the Security Council, and International Court of Justice. This is not equitable, nor is the United Nations. We totally reject the situation.

Regarding Africa, Mr. President, whether the United Nations is reformed or not, and even before a vote is taken on any proposals of a historic nature, Africa should be given a permanent seat on the Security Council now, having already waited too long. Leaving aside the United Nations reform, we could certainly say that Africa was colonized, isolated, and persecuted, and its rights usurped. Its people were enslaved and treated like animals and its territory was colonized and placed under trusteeship. The countries of the African Union deserve a permanent seat. This is a debt from the past that has to be paid and has nothing to do with United Nations reform.

It's a priority matter and is high on the agenda of the General Assembly. No one can say that the African Union does not deserve a permanent seat. Who can argue with that proposal? I challenge anyone to make a case against it. Where is the proof that an African Union on the African Continent does not deserve a permanent seat? No one can possibly deny this.

Another matter that should be voted on in the General Assembly is that of compensation for countries that were colonized, so as to prevent the colonization of a continent, the usurpation of its rights and the pillaging of its wealth from happening again. Why do Africans go to Europe? Why are the Asians going to Europe? Why are Latin Americans going to Europe? It is because Europe colonized those nations and stole the material and human resources of Africa, Asia, and Latin America, the oil, the minerals, the uranium, the gold, the diamonds, the fruit, the vegetables, the livestock, and the people, and used them.

Now new generations of Africans, Asians, and Latin Americans are seeking to reclaim that stolen wealth, as they have the right to do. At the Libyan border, I recently stopped a thousand African migrants headed for Europe. I asked them why they were going there. They told me it was to take back their stolen wealth, that they would not be leaving otherwise. You can restore the wealth that was taken from us. If you decide to restore all this wealth, there will be no more immigration from the Philippines, Latin America, Mauritius, and India.

Let us have the wealth that was stolen from us. Africa deserves $777 Trillion in compensation from countries that colonized it. Africans will demand that amount. If you do not give it to them, they will go to where you have taken those trillions of dollars. They have the right to do so. They have to follow that money and bring it back again.

Why is there no Libyan immigration to Italy, even though Libya is so close by? Italy owed compensation to the Libyan people. It accepted the fact and signed an agreement with Libya, which was adopted by both the Italian and the Libyan parliaments. Italy admitted that its colonization of Libya was wrong and should never be repeated and promised not to attack the Libyan people by land, air, or sea. Italy also agreed to provide Libya with $250 Billion in compensation over the next twenty years and to build a hospital for Libyans maimed as a result of mines planted in Libyan territory during the Second World War. Italy apologized and promised that it would never again occupy the territory of another country. Italy, which was a kingdom during the fascist regime, has made rich contributions to civilization, should be commended for this achievement, together with Prime Minister

Berlusconi and his predecessors who made their own contributions in that regard.

Why is this third world demanding compensation? So there will be no more colonization. So that larger, powerful countries will not colonize, knowing that they will have to pay compensation. Colonization should be punished. The countries that harmed other people during the colonial era should pay compensation for the damage and suffering inflicted under their colonial rule.

There's another point that I'd like to make. However, before I say it, and start addressing a sensitive issue, I should like to make an aside. We Africans are happy and proud indeed. The son of Africa is now President of the United States of America. That is an historic event. Now, in a country where blacks once could not mingle with whites in cafes or restaurants or sit next to them on a bus, the American people have elected as their President a young black man, Mr. Obama, of Kenyan heritage. That is a wonderful thing and we are proud. It marks the beginning of a change.

However, as far as I am concerned, Obama is a temporary relief for the next four or eight years. I'm afraid that we may then go back to square one. No guarantee how America will be dealt with after Obama. We would be content if Obama could remain President of the United States forever. The statement that he just made shows that he's completely different from any American President that we have seen.

American presidents used to threaten us with all manner of weapons, saying that they would send us desert storm, grapes of wrath, rolling thunder, poisonous roses for Libyan children. That was their approach. American presidents used to threaten us with operations such as Rolling Thunder, sent to Vietnam; Desert Storm, sent to Iraq; Musketeer, sent to Egypt in 1956, even though America opposed it; and the poisonous roses visited upon Libyan children by Reagan.

Can you imagine? One would've thought the presidents of a large country with a permanent seat on the Security Council and the right of veto would have protected us and sent us peace. What did we get instead? Laser guided bombs, carried to us on an F-111 aircraft. This was their approach. We will lead the world, whether you like it or not, and we will punish anyone who opposes us.

What our son, Obama, said today is completely different. He made a serious appeal for nuclear disarmament, which we applaud. He also said that America alone could not solve the problems facing us, and that the entire world should come together to do so. He said that we must do more than we are doing now, which is making speeches. We agree with that and applaud it. He said that we have to come to the

United Nations to talk against one another. It is true that when we come here we should communicate with one another on an equal footing.

He said that democracy should not be imposed from outside. Until recently, American presidents have said that democracy should be imposed upon Iraq and other countries, but he said that this was an internal affair. He spoke truly when he said that democracy cannot be imposed from outside.

So we have to be cautious. Before I make these sensitive remarks, I note that the whole world has so many polarities. Should we have a world with so many polarities? Can we not have nations on an equal footing? Let's have an answer. Does anyone have an answer as to whether it's better to have a world with so many polarities? Why can we not have equal standing? Should we have patriarchs? Should we have popes? Should we have gods? Why should we have a world of so many polarities? We reject such a world and call for a world where big and small are equal.

The other sensitive point is the headquarters of the United Nations. Can I have your attention, please?

All of you came across the Atlantic Ocean, the Pacific Ocean, across the Asian continent or the African continent to reach this place. Why? Is this Jerusalem; is this the Vatican? Is this Mecca? All of you are tired; you have jet lag and have sleepless nights. You're very tired, very low physically. Somebody arrived just now, flying twenty hours and we wanted to make a speech and talk about this. All of you are asleep. All of you are tired. It is clear that all of you are lacking energy because of having to make such a long journey. Why did we do that?

Some of our countries are in night time and people are asleep. Now you should be asleep because your biological mind is accustomed to being asleep at this time. I wake up at 4:00 New York time, before dawn, because in Libya it's 11:00 in the morning. When I wake at 11:00 it's supposed to be daytime. At 4:00 I am awake. All I think about is if this was decided in 1945, should we still retain it? Why can we not think about a place that's in the middle, that is comfortable.

Another important point is that America, our host country, bears the expenses and looks after the headquarters, diplomatic missions, looks after the peace and security of the heads of state who come here. They are very strict. They spend a lot of money, New York and all of America being very tight.

I want to relieve America of this hardship. We should thank America. We should say to them, "thank you for all the trouble that you've taken upon yourself." We say thank you to America. We want to help reassure America and New York, and keep them calm.

They should not have the responsibility of looking after security. Perhaps some day terrorists could cause a bomb explosion. This place is targeted by Al Qaida, this very building. Why was it not hit on Sept 11th? It was beyond their power. The next target would be this place. I'm not saying this in an offhand manner. We have tens of members of Al Qaida detained in Libyan prisons. Their confessions are very scary. That makes America live under tension. One never knows what will happen. Perhaps America or this place will be targeted again by a rocket. Perhaps tens of heads of state will die. What we want is to relieve America from this worry. We should take the place to where it is not targeted.

Now after 50 years, the United Nations headquarters should be taken to another part of the hemisphere. After 50 years in the western hemisphere, for the next 50 years it should be in the eastern hemisphere or in the middle hemisphere by rotation. Now at 64 years, we have an extra 14 years over the 50 that headquarters should be moved to somewhere else.

This is not an insult to America, it's a service to America. We should thank America. This was possible in 1945 but we should not accept it now, of course. This should be put to a vote of the General Assembly. Only the General Assembly because Section 23 of the headquarters agreement says that the United Nations headquarters can be moved to another location only by a resolution of the General Assembly. If 51% of the Assembly approves relocation of the headquarters then it can be moved.

America has the right to make its security tight, because it's targeted by terrorists, by Al Qaida. America has the right to take all security measures. We're not blaming America for that, however, we do not tolerate these measures. We do not come to New York to be subjected to all these measures.

One president told me that he was told that his co-pilot could not come to America because there were restrictions. He asked how he could cross the Atlantic without a co-pilot. Why? He does not have to come here. Another president complained that his honor guard could not come because there was some misunderstanding about his name when it came to granting a visa. Another president said his own doctor could not get a visa and could not come to America.

Security measures are very strict. If a country has any problem with America, they will set up restrictions on the movement of the delegations, as if one is in Guantanamo. Is this a member state in the United Nations or is it a prisoner in the Guantanamo camp that can't be allowed free movement? This is what is submitted to the General Assembly for a vote, moving the headquarters.

If 51% agree, then we come to the second vote. To the middle of the globe or the eastern part. If we say that we must move the Headquarters to the middle hemisphere, why don't we move it to Sirte or Vienna? One could come even without a visa. Once you come as a president, Libya is a secure country. We are not going to restrict you to a hundred or five hundred meters. Libya has no hostile actions against anybody and I think the same holds true for Vienna.

If the vote says we shall move headquarters to the eastern part then it will be Delhi or Beijing, the capital of China or the capital of India. It's logical, my brothers. I do not think there will be any objection to that and you will thank me for this proposal and for eliminating the suffering and trouble of flying 14 or 15 or 20 hours to come here.

No one can blame America or say that America will reduce its contributions to the United Nations. No one should have that bad a thought. America I'm sure is committed to its international obligations. America will not be angry. It will thank you for alleviating its hardship, for taking on all the hardship and all the restrictions, even though this place is targeted by terrorists.

We come now to the issues that will be considered by the General Assembly. We are about to put the United Nations on trial. The old organization will be finished and a new one will emerge. This is not a normal gathering. Even Son Obama said that this is not a normal gathering. It is an historic meeting.

The wars that took place after the establishment of the United Nations, why did they occur? Where was the Security Council? Where was the Charter? Where was the United Nations? There should be investigations and judicial intervention. Why have there been massacres? We can start with the Korean War, because it took place after the establishment of the United Nations. How did a war break out and cause millions of victims? Nuclear weapons could have been used in that war. Those who are responsible for causing the war should be tried and should pay compensation and damages.

Then we come to the Suez Canal war of 1956. That file should be opened wide. Three countries with permanent seats on the Security Council and with the right of veto in the Council attacked a member state of this General Assembly. A country that was a sovereign state, Egypt, was attacked, its army was destroyed, thousands of Egyptians were killed, and many Egyptian towns and entities were destroyed, all because Egypt wanted to nationalize the Suez Canal. How could such a thing have happened during the era of the United Nations and the Charter? How is it possible to guarantee that such a thing will not be repeated unless we make amends for past wrongs? Those were dangerous events. The Korean War and Suez Canal files should be reopened. Next we come to the Vietnam War. There were three million victims in that war. During 12 days, more bombs were dropped than during four years in the Second World War. It was a fearsome war and it took place after the establishment of the United Nations and after we had decided that there would be no more wars.

The future of humankind is at stake. We cannot stay silent. How can we feel safe? How can we be complacent? This is the future of the world, and we who are in the General Assembly of the United Nations must make sure that wars are not the face of the future.

Then Panama was attacked, even though it was an independent member state of the General Assembly. Four thousand people were killed and the President of that country was taken prisoner and put in prison. Noriega should be released. We should open that file. How can we entitle a country that is a United Nations member to wage war against another country, capture its President, treat him as a criminal, and put him in prison? Who would accept that? It could be repeated. We should not stay quiet. We should have an investigation. Any one of us member states could face the same situation, especially if such aggression is by a member state with a permanent seat on the Security Council and with responsibility to maintain peace and security worldwide.

Then there was the war in Grenada. The country was invaded even though it was a member state. It was attacked by 15 war ships. 7,000 troops, dozens of military aircraft. It's the smallest country in the world. This occurred after the establishment of the United Nations and the Security Council and its veto, and the President of Grenada, Mr. Morris Bishop, was assassinated. How could that have happened with impunity? It's a tragedy. How can we guarantee that the United Nations is good or not and that a certain country is good or not? Can we be safe or happy about the future or not? Can we trust the Security Council or not? Can we trust the United Nations or not?

We must look into and investigate the bombing of Somalia. Somalia is a United Nations member state. It's an independent country under the rule of law. We want an investigation. Why did that happen? Who allowed it to happen? Who gave the green light for that country to be attacked?

Then there's the former Yugoslavia. No country was as peaceful as Yugoslavia, reconstructed step by step and piece by piece after being destroyed by Hitler. We destroyed it, as if we were doing the same job as Hitler. Tito built that peaceful country step by step, brick by brick, and them we arrived and broke it part for an imperialist state and personal interests. How can we be complacent about that? Why can we not be satisfied? If a peaceful country like Yugoslavia faced such a travesty, the General Assembly should have an investigation and should decide who should be tried before the International Criminal Court.

Then we have the war in Iraq, the mother of all evils. The United Nations should investigate that. The General Assembly, presided over by Mr. Treki, should investigate that. The invasion of Iraq was a violation of the United Nations Charter. It was done without any justification by the superpowers who have permanent seats on the Security Council. Iraq is an independent country and a member state of the General Assembly. How could those countries attack Iraq? As provided for in the Charter, the United Nations should have intervened and stopped the attack.

We spoke in the General Assembly and urged it to use the Charter to stop that attack. We were against the invasion of Kuwait and the Arab countries fought Iraq alongside foreign countries in the name of the United Nations Charter. In the first instance, the Charter was respected. But the second time, when we wanted to use the Charter to stop the War in Iraq, no one used it and that document was ignored. Why did that occur? Mr. Treki and the General Assembly should investigate to determine whether there was any reason at all to invade Iraq. Because the reasons for that attack remain mysterious and ambiguous and we might face the same destiny.

Why was Iraq invaded? The invasion itself was a serious violation of the United Nations Charter and it was wrong. It was also a total massacre or genocide. One and a half million Iraqis were killed. We want to bring the Iraqi file before the International Criminal Court and we want those who committed mass murder against the Iraqi people to be tried.

It was easy for Charles Taylor to be tried, or Bashir to be tried, or for Noriega to be tried. It's all easy for them. But what about those who've committed mass murder against the Iraqis? They cannot be tried. They cannot go before the ICC? If the Court is unable to accommodate us, then we should not accept it. Either it is meant for all of us, large or small, or we should not accept it. We should reject it.

Anyone who commits a war crime can be tried, for we are not livestock or animals like those that are slaughtered to eat. We have the right to live and we are ready to fight to defend ourselves. We have the right to live in dignity, under the sun and on Earth. They have already tested us and we have withstood the test.

There are other things as well. Why is it that Iraqi prisoners of war could be sentenced to death? When Iraq was invaded and the President of Iraq was taken, he was a prisoner of war. He should not have been tried. He should not have been hanged. When the war was over, he should have been released. We want to know why a prisoner of war should have been tried. Who sentenced the President of Iraq to death? Is there an answer to that question? We know the identity of the judge who tried him. But as to who tied the noose around the President's neck on the day of sacrifice and hanged him, those people wore masks.

How could this have happened in the civilized world? These were prisoners of war of a civilized country under international law. How could government ministers and a Head of State be sentenced to death and hanged? Were those who tried them lawyers or members of a judicial system?

Do you know what people are saying? They're saying that the faces behind the masks were those of the President of the United States and the Prime Minister of the United Kingdom and it was they who put the President of Iraq to death. Why did the executioners not unmask their faces? Why do we not know their ranks? Why do we not know whether they were officers, judges, soldiers, or doctors? How does it come about that the President of a Member State when the United Nations was sentenced to death and killed? We don't know the identity of the executioners.

The United Nations is duty bound to answer these questions. Who carried out the death sentence? They must have legal status and official responsibilities. We should know their identities and we should know about the presence of a physician and the nature of all the legal proceedings. That would be true for an ordinary citizen, let alone for the President of a State Member of the United Nations, who was put to death in this manner.

My third point on Iraq relates to Abu Ghraib. This was a disgrace to humankind. I know the United States authorities have investigated this scandal, but the United Nations must not ignore it either. The General Assembly should investigate this matter. Prisoners of war held in Abu Ghraib prison were tortured. Dogs were set on them. Men were raped. This is unprecedented in the history of war. It was sodomy and it was an unprecedented sin, never before committed by past aggressors or invaders. Prisoners of war are soldiers, but these were raped in prison by a State, a permanent member of the Security Council. This goes against civilization and humankind. We must not keep silent. We must know the facts. Even today, a quarter of a million Iraqi prisoners, men and women alike, remain in Abu Ghraib. They are being maltreated, persecuted, and raped. There must be an investigation.

Turning to the War in Afghanistan, this too must be investigated. Why are we against the Taliban? Why are we against Afghanistan? Who are the Taliban? If the Taliban want a religious state, that's fine. Think of the Vatican. Does the Vatican pose a threat to us? No, it's a religious and very peaceful state. If the Taliban want to create an Islamic emirate, who says that this makes them an enemy? Is anyone claiming that bin Laden is of the Taliban or that he is Afghan? Is bin Laden of the Taliban? No, he is not of the Taliban and he is not an Afghan. Were the terrorists who hit New York of the Taliban? Were they from Afghanistan? They were neither Taliban nor Afghani. Then what was the reason for the wars in Iraq and Afghanistan?

If I truly wanted to deceive my American and British friends, I would encourage them to send more troops, and I would encourage them to persist in this bloodbath. But they will never succeed in Iraq or Afghanistan. Look what happened to them in Iraq, which is a desert. It's even worse in mountainous Afghanistan. If I wanted to deceive them, I would tell them to continue the wars in Iraq and Afghanistan. But no, I want to save the citizens of the United States and the United Kingdom and other countries who are fighting in Iraq and Afghanistan. So I tell them, leave Afghanistan to the Afghans, leave Iraq to the Iraqis. If they want to fight each other, they are free to do so. America had its Civil War and no one interfered in it. There were civil wars in Spain, China, and countries all over the world. No place on Earth has been free of civil wars. Let there be a civil war in Iraq. If the Iraqis want to have a civil war and fight each other, that's fine.

Who says that if the Taliban form a government, they would possess intercontinental missiles or the kind of airplanes that hit New York? Did those airplanes take off from Afghanistan or Iraq? No, they took off from American airports. So why is Afghanistan being struck? The terrorists were not Afghans or Taliban or Iraqis. Why are we silent? We must never be war devils. Anyone who does not speak the truth is a silent devil. We are committed to international peace and security. We do not wish to scorn or ridicule humankind. We want to save humanity.

As President of the General Assembly, Mr. Treki, you should open an investigation of the assassinations files, in addition to the war files. Who killed Patrice Lumumba and why? We merely want to record it in the annals of African history. We want to know how an African leader, a liberator, came to be assassinated. Who killed him? We want our sons to be able to read the history of how Patrice Lumumba, the hero of Congo's liberation struggle, was assassinated. We want to know the facts, even fifty years on. That is one file that should be reopened.

And who killed Secretary-General Dag Hammerskjold? Who fired on his airplane in 1961 and why?

And then there's the assassination of United States President

Kennedy in '63. We want to know who killed him and why. It was someone called Lee Harvey Oswald, who was then killed by one Jack Ruby. But why did he kill him? Jack Ruby, an Israeli, killed Oswald, who killed Kennedy. Why did this Israeli kill Kennedy's killer? And Jack Ruby, the killer of the killer of Kennedy, died under mysterious circumstances before he could be tried. We must open the files. The whole world knows that Kennedy wanted to investigate the Israeli Dimona nuclear reactor. This involves international peace and security and weapons of mass destruction. That is why we should open this file.

Then there's the assassination of Martin Luther King, the black reverend and human rights activist. His assassination was appalling, and we should know why he was killed and who killed him.

Then there was Khalil al-Wazir or Abu Jihad, a Palestinian who was attacked. He was living peacefully in Tunisia, a member state, and that country's sovereignty was not respected. We cannot keep silent. Even though submarines and ships were detected along the coast of Tunisia, where he was killed, no one was accused or tried. Abu Iyad was also killed and we should know how he was killed. He was killed in ambiguous circumstances. In Operation Spring of Youth, Khamal Nassir, a poet, Khamal Adwan, and Abu Youssef al-Najjar, three Palestinians, were killed in Lebanon, a country that is a free, sovereign state, a member of the General Assembly. They were attacked and killed while sleeping peacefully. We should know who killed them, and he should be tried, so that those crimes against humanity are not repeated.

We've already talked about the size of the force used in the invasion of Grenada—7,000 troops, 15 battleships, and dozens of bombers. President Bishop was killed, even though Grenada was a Member State. Those are crimes and we cannot keep silent. Otherwise we will look like sacrificial beasts. We are not animals. Year after year, we are attacked. We defend ourselves, our sons, our children, and we are not afraid. We have the right to live, and the Earth is not destined for violence but for us all. We can never live on the Earth in such humiliation. So those are the wars.

The last file is out of Damascus. At the Sabra and Shatila Massacre, three thousand people were killed. That area was under the protection of the occupying Israeli army and was the site of a huge and calamitous massacre in which three thousand Palestinian men, women, and children were killed. How can we keep quiet? Lebanon is a sovereign state, a member of the General Assembly. It was occupied. Sabra and Shatila were under Israeli control and then the massacre took place.

Then there was the 2008 massacre in Gaza. Over a thousand women and 2,200 children were the victims killed in the massacre in

Gaza in 2008. Sixty United Nations facilities and another thirty belonging to non-governmental organizations were damaged. Fifty clinics were destroyed. Forty doctors and nurses were killed while carrying out humanitarian activities. This took place in Gaza in December 2008.

The perpetrators are still alive, and they should be tried by the International Criminal Court. Should we try only the underdogs, the weak and the poor of the third world countries, and not important and protected figures? Under international law, they should all face trial for the consequences of the crimes that they have committed. Otherwise the role of the ICC would never be recognized. If the decisions of the ICC are not respected or implemented, if the General Assembly and the Security Council mean nothing, and if the International Atomic Energy Agency serves only certain countries and national organizations, then what is the United Nations? It would mean that the United Nations is nothing significant. There is no United Nations.

Then while piracy may be a phenomenon of the high seas, a form of terrorism, we may talk about the piracy in Somalia. Somalis are not pirates. We are the pirates. We went there and usurped their economic zones, their fishing and their wealth. Libya, India, Japan, America, any country in the world. We are all pirates. We've all entered the territorial waters, economic zones of Somalia, and stole. The Somalis are protecting their own fish, their sustenance. They have become pirates because they are defending their children's food. Now we seek to address that matter in the wrong way. Should we send warships to Somalia? We should send warships to the pirates who have attacked and seized the economic zones and wealth of the Somalis and the food of their children.

I met the pirates and I told them that I would negotiate an agreement between them and the international community that respects the 200 mile exclusive economic zone under the Law of the Sea, that protects all marine resources belonging to the Somali people, that stops all countries from disposing of toxic waste on the Somali coast. In return, the Somalis would no longer attack any ships. We will propose and draft such a treaty and submit it to the General Assembly. That is the solution. The solution does not lie in sending more military ships to fight the Somalis. That is not a solution.

We are addressing the phenomena of piracy and terrorism in the wrong way. Today there is Swine Flu. Perhaps tomorrow there will be Fish Flu, because sometimes we produce viruses by controlling them. It is a commercial business. Capitalist companies produce viruses so that they can generate and sell vaccinations. This is a very shameful lack of ethics. Vaccinations should not be sold. In *The Green Book*, I maintain that medicines should not be sold or subject to commercialization. Medicines should be free of charge and vaccinations given free to children. But capitalist companies produce the viruses and vaccinations and want to make a profit. Why are they not free of charge? We should give them free of charge, not sell them. The entire world should strive to protect our people, create and manufacture vaccinations, and then give them for free to children and women, and not profit by them. All those items are for the agenda of the General Assembly, which has only to exercise that duty.

The Ottawa Convention on Land Mines forbids the production of land mines. That is wrong. Land mines are defensive weapons. If I place them along the border of my country and someone wants to invade me, they may be killed. That's alright, because they're invading me. The Convention should be reconsidered. I'm not taking that defensive weapon to another country. The enemy is coming to me and on the al-Qadaffi website I call for that treaty to be modified or annulled. This treaty should be modified or annulled. I want to use anti-personnel mines to defend my home against invasion. Eliminate weapons of mass destruction, not land mines, which are defensive weapons.

With regard to the Palestinian situation, the two state solution is impossible. It is not practical. Currently these two states completely overlap. Partition is doomed to failure. These two states are not neighbors. They are coextensive, in terms of both population and geography. A buffer zone cannot be created between the two states because there are half a million Israeli settlers in the West Bank and a million Arab Palestinians in the territory known as Israel.

The solution therefore is a democratic state without religious fanaticism or ethnicity. The generation of Sharon and Arafat is over. We need a new generation, in which everyone can live in peace. Look at the Palestinian and Israeli youth. They both want peace and democracy. And they want to live under one state. This conflict poisons the world.

The White Book actually has the solution. I hold it here. The solution is Isratine. Arabs should have no animosity or hostility toward Israel. We are cousins of the same race. We want to live in peace and refugees should go back.

You are the ones who brought the holocaust upon the Jews. You, not we, are the ones who burned them. We gave them refuge. We gave them safe haven during the Roman era, and the Arab reign of Jerusalem, and during the reign of Hitler. You are the ones who poisoned them. You are the ones who annihilated them. We provided them with protection. You expelled them. Let us see the truth. We are not hostile. We are not enemies of the Jews. One day the Jews will need the Arabs. At that point Arabs will be the ones to give them protection, to save them, as we have done in the past. Look at what everybody else did to the Jews. Hitler is an example. You are the ones who hate the Jews, not us.

In brief, Kashmir should be an independent state, neither Indian nor Pakistani. We must end that conflict. Kashmir should be a buffer state between India and Pakistan.

With regard to Darfur, I truly hope that the assistance provided by the international organizations can be used for development projects, for agriculture, for industry, and for irrigation. You are the ones who made it a crisis. You built the altar. You wanted to sacrifice Darfur, so you could interfere in its internal affairs.

You've turned the Hariri problem into a United Nations problem. You are selling Hariri's corpse. You just want to settle scores with Syria. Lebanon is an independent state. It has law courts, judiciary, and police. At this stage, it is no longer the perpetrators that are being sought. The real wish is to settle scores with Syria, not insure justice for Hariri. The cases of Khalil al-Wazir, Lumumba, Kennedy, and Hammerskjold should also be turned over to the United Nations, if the Hariri case merits such attention.

The General Assembly is now under the Presidency of Libya. This is our right. Libya hopes that you will assist in making the transition from a world full with crises and tension to a world in which humanity, peace, and tolerance prevail. I will personally follow up on this issue with the General Assembly and President Treki and the Secretary General. It is not our habit to compromise when it comes to the destiny of humanity and the struggles of the third world and the hundred small nations. We should live in peace always!

ENDNOTES

1   On June 10th, 2009, the General Assembly elected by acclamation Ali Abdussalam Treki, a three-time Permanent Representative of Libya to the United Nations and former Foreign Minister, as President of its sixty-fourth session. < http://www.un.org/News/Press/docs//2009/ga10831.doc.htm>

CHRONOLOGY OF THE NATO-LED ASSAULT ON THE GREAT SOCIALIST PEOPLE'S LIBYAN ARAB JAMAHIRIYA

A CRIME AGAINST HUMANITY AND A CRIME AGAINST PEACE

Mike Raffauf

1942: WWII Allies oust Italians from control of Libya. Libya is divided among French, who control Fezzan region (southwestern), and British, who control Cyrenaica (eastern) and Tripolitania (northwestern). Libya is now 97% Muslim, mostly Sunni, and 97% Arab and Berber.

2011: On the eve of war Libya has a population of 6.5 million. Approximately 85% are Arab and Arabic is spoken by 95% of the population. Approximately 10% are Berber who are also Muslim. However, there is a large number of Africans in Libya, more than 1 million, some illegal and some legal - workers invited there by Qaddafi. Libya is vulnerable as a strategically placed country with weak defenses, a small population, but huge oil reserves.

1951: Libya becomes independent under King Idris al-Sanusi, a member of the Senussi Muslim order based in Cyrenaica. He fought against Italy and Germany in WWII and afterward continued his close ties to the US and UK. His heirs, considered to be royalty, supported the war against Libya in 2011.

1959: The discovery of significant oil reserves begins Libya's transition from one of poorest to one of richest African countries by 2010. Libya is now the holder of Africa's largest oil reserves and second in production.

1969: King deposed in military coup led by Colonel Muammar Qadaffi who pursues pan-Arab agenda and introduces socialism by nationalizing most economic activity, including the oil industry as international oil companies are ousted.

1970: Qadaffi closes British and American air bases in Tobruk and Tripoli and nationalizes foreign owned property.

1973: Qadaffi declares a "cultural revolution" which establishes administrative districts and leads to government control of schools, universities, hospitals and workplaces.

1977: Qadaffi declares a "peoples' revolution" and changes name of country to Great Socialist People's Libyan Arab Jamahiriya.

1979: US Embassy in Tripoli closed after civil protests that lead to fire at US Embassy.

1981: US shoots down two Libyan aircraft which challenged US military aircraft over the Gulf of Sirte which Libya had claimed as territorial waters.

1986: President Reagan orders bombing of Libyan military facilities and residential areas of Tripoli and Benghazi, killing over 100 people, striking Qadaffi's home, killing a Qadaffi adopted daughter. The bombings were "retaliation" to alleged Libyan involvement in bombing of Berlin disco frequented by US military personnel.

1992: UN imposes sanctions on Libya to force Libya to hand over Libyan citizens suspected of involvement in the blowing up of PanAm airliner over Lockerbie Scotland in December 1988.

1999: Libya hands over Lockerbie suspects in Netherlands and UN sanctions lifted.

2000: Mobs in western Libya (Benghazi) kill dozens of African immigrants. Killings followed increased tensions between local anti-Qadaffi forces, who later would lead and identify themselves as rebel forces in 2011, and African laborers brought in by Qadaffi.

2001: Abdelbaset Ali Mohamed al-Megrahi found guilty in Netherlands by special Scottish court in Pan-Am Lockerbie bombing case and sentenced to life in prison.

2002: Libya and US announce that they have held talks to mend relations because of hostility caused by US accusations of Libya sponsored terrorism including Lockerbie bombing.

2002: May 6, 2002, then-Undersecretary of State John R. Bolton gives a speech entitled "Beyond the Axis of Evil". In it he added three more nations to be grouped with the already mentioned rogue states: Libya, Syria, and Cuba.

2003: US State Department shows that Libya has the highest literacy rate in North Africa as over 82% of the population can read and write.

2003: Limited covert US efforts to effect regime change in Libya exposed.

2003: Libya signs UN deal to accept responsibility for Lockerbie and compensate victims in the amount of $2.7 billion. In exchange, UN sanctions are lifted. US and France abstain from vote in 13 member UN Security Council but US does not lifts its arms embargo

2003: In December, Libya also pledges not to develop weapons of mass destruction and missile technology. In exchange, the International arms embargo is lifted.

2004: Libya has the 10th largest oil reserves of any country in the world and largest in Africa and has the 17th highest petroleum production and second largest in Africa.

2004: September: Libya agrees to pay $35 million to compensate victims of 1986 Berlin nightclub bombing. US ends economic sanctions.

2005: Feb. 1: Libya auction of oil and gas exploration licenses for the first time in 20 years marks return of US, as well as international, oil companies. Among American companies were Occidental, Chevron, Amerada Hess.

2006: US restores full diplomatic ties with Libya as Condi Rice personally visits Libya

2007: After over five years of preparation the US Africa Command (AFRICOM) is formally established in order to have a unified military operation for Africa. It is responsible for US military operations and military relations with 53 African nations. The military objectives identified were international terrorism, the increasing importance of African oil and the expansion and improvement of Sino-African relations.

2007: May: Tony Blair visits Libya and helps secure a BP exploration and production agreement which calls for BP to commit its largest single exploration of $900 million.

2007: In July, 2007 Sarkozy publicly announces the release of Bulgarian nurses detained in Libya for many years. In exchange, Sarkozy entered into an agreement with Qadaffi on health care, security and immigration. Among the benefits to Libya and French companies were a $230 million dollar sale of antitank missiles and a pledge of three civil nuclear power stations for Libya. The deal was immediately criticized in France and by other European nations, especially Germany and England. Later, Sarkozy would deny the deal and referred to it as only "negotiations." Documents released in March 2012 revealed that in 2007, as part of same deal, Qadaffi agreed to finance Sarkozy's French election with a $50 million contribution.

December 10-15, 2007: At Sarkozy's invitation Qadaffi visits France. France's Secretary of Human Rights and Foreign Affairs Minister refused to meet with Qadaffi because of alleged Human Rights issues.

March, 2008: Qadaffi announces Wealth Distribution Program where oil revenues would be distributed directly to the people on a monthly basis.

August 14, 2008: US and Libya sign comprehensive Claims Settlement Agreement. The Agreement establishes fund for terrorism victims in the amount of $1.8 billion and terminates and precludes any legal actions.

2009: Libya has the highest Human Development Index (HDI) in Africa and the highest Gross Domestic Production (GDP) in Africa.

January, 2009: Qadaffi proposes one state solution for Israel and Palestine with Palestinian refugees since 1948 being granted a right of return. Qadaffi had consistently opposed negotiation or reconciliation with Israel promoting armed struggle as the only viable solution to ending Israel's occupation.

May, 2009: Italy and Libya launch controversial joint naval patrols, intercepting and forcibly returning immigrating Libyans trying to cross the Mediterranean to Italy as Europe is upset that many Africans use easy entry into Libya as launching point for immigration to Europe

2009: Qadaffi elected chairman of African Union, calls for "United States of Africa."

August, 2009: Lockerbie bomber, Abdelbaset al-Megrahi, who continues to maintain his innocence, is freed from jail in Scotland on compassionate grounds and returns to a controversial 'hero's welcome' in Libya. The decision is wildly unpopular in Britain and is defended by the government. Professor Robert Black of the University of Edinburgh, one of Scotland's top legal experts and who devised the non-jury trial called the conviction "the most disgraceful miscarriage of justice in Scotland for 100 years." Black said he felt "a measure of personal responsibility" for persuading Libya to allow al-Megrahi to stand trial under Scot law. He emphatically said that al-Megrahi was an "innocent man" and was "the victim" of political pressure in the case.

January, 2010: January: Russia agrees to sell Libya $1.8 billion in arms, fighter jets, tanks and missile system.

July, 2010: US politicians push for inquiry into claims that BP lobbied for Lockerbie bomber's release, just as BP announces drilling off Libyan coast.

September, 2010: September: A report generated by the London Office of the consulting firm KPMG begins to circulate exposing that billions of Libyan funds managed by European banks were invested poorly and resulted in huge loses to Libya and high fees by the banks. After international sanctions were lifted over $64 billion in Libyan oil money was made available beginning in 2006 for investment. During the height of the civil war *Forbes Magazine* revealed on May 31, 2011 that Goldman Sachs had lost 98% of $1.3 billion invested from Libya through its investment fund.

October, 2010: Euro Union and Libya sign agreement designed to slow illegal immigration. Libya cooperation seen as crucial to stem flow of illegal African immigration to Europe.

October, 2010: WikiLeaks publishes US diplomatic cables involving Libya relations. Ambassador Gene Cretz, a career diplomat, was exposed as filing personal reports detailing Qaddafi's health and personal habits. The leaks disclosed: that former jihadist fighters who trained in Afghanistan, Lebanon and West Bank in the 1980s had recently returned to Eastern Libya, Benghazi and Derna, to propagate their religious beliefs; that the US, France, England and Italy as "accomplices" of Qaddafi who collaborated with him (up until they supported the civil uprising in 2011), armed him and supported him as US and European corporations reaped vast profits from Libya's oil wealth; that the US was concerned about US corporations not cashing in on "billions of dollars in opportunities" in Libya and feared that Qaddafi nationalize the oil or use the threat to extract more favorable contracts.

December 29, 2010: US Ambassador Cretz becomes "first casualty" of Wikileaks and reportedly "quits" his post. However, he resumes as Ambassador on September 20, 2011, after the war.

2011: On the eve of war Libya has a population of 6.5 million. Approximately 85% are Arab and Arabic is spoken by 95% of the population. Approximately 10% are Berber who are also Muslim. However, there is a large number of non-Libyan Africans in Libya, more than 1 million, some illegal and some legal - workers invited there by Qaddafi. Libya is vulnerable as a strategically placed country with weak defenses, a small population, but huge oil reserves.

February 11, 2011: Since demonstrations and strikes erupted against the Mubarak regime on January 25, the Egyptian military has arrested, tortured and "disappeared" thousands, according to reports from the *Guardian* newspaper and human rights organizations.

February 15, 2011: Approximately 200 people waving Royalist flags demonstrate, then riot, in front of police headquarters in Benghazi, a city with strong Berber presence, following the arrest of human-rights activist Fethi Terbil, a critic of Qadaffi regime. Terbil incited people to arrive at the Abu Salim prison under the pretext that the prison was burning. Terbil instigated the crowd to storm the prison. The crowd was armed with petrol bombs and threw stones. Marchers hurled Molotov cocktails in a downtown square in Benghazi, damaging cars, blocking roads, and hurling rocks. Counter demonstrators marched against Terbil and met his crowd in the same downtown square. Police separated the two opposing groups with tear gas, water cannons, and rubber bullets. No deaths were reported. There were no victims on this day. Mass media such as Al Jazeera switch rapidly from mass demonstrations in Cairo and Bahrain to the violence in Benghazi, leaving the impression that huge mass demonstrations had been occurring in Benghazi. No images of comparable mass demonstrations in Benghazi are ever presented. Later the same day, Terbil was released from government custody and admitted that his charges against the government were unsubstantiated.

February 16, 2011: A group of lawyers staged a demonstration in front of the North Benghazi Court calling for legal and political reforms. Government forces did not challenge this demonstration. Sleeper cells of Al Qaeda extremists returned from Iraq, Afghanistan, and Guantanamo declared themselves. In Benghazi, internal security police forces were attacked at two police stations and set ablaze. Weapons were stormed. 6 people were killed. At the same time, coordinated attacks took place all across the country. Abrag Air Base, 25 kilometers from al Bayda, and soldiers' barracks in the center of the city were among those sites attacked. Soldiers and police were ordered not to open fire on the "demonstrators". Instead, soldiers were detained, killed, and one was hanged according to tell-tale Al Qaeda methods, and then put on public display. Weapons depots were also attacked, catching government guards off guard. Weapons, including tanks and anti-aircraft weapons, were confiscated by the demonstrators.

February 17, 2011: Benghazi main police station was targeted. Attackers attempted to enter soldiers' barracks and 14 people from both sides were killed as soldiers defended themselves and their barracks against the attacks.

February 18, 2011: TNT bombs and molotov cocktails and heavy vehicles confiscated from the Libyan and foreign companies were were used by the attackers to demolish the walls of soldiers' barracks. After three days of violent protest, active resistance to the government began in Benghazi. Security forces had reportedly killed fourteen protesters the previous day, and a funeral procession for one of those killed passed the Katiba compound, where clashes erupted. Demonstrators used violence against security forces, who retaliated, killing twenty four protesters. Two of the Libyan policemen who had participated in the clash were caught and hanged by protesters. Protesters around the city and in nearby Bayda and Derna attacked and overwhelmed government forces, and some police and army units defected and joined the protesters. Security forces were overwhelmed and forced to withdraw. Saif Qadaffi later reiterates that government soldiers acted in self defense as they were attacked by mobs.

February 19, 2011: Machine guns confiscated from military camps were used. Another funeral procession passed the Katiba (loyalist) compound, and was reportedly fired on by snipers, which was met with retaliatory attacks by opposition forces. Fifty African workers, falsely called mercenaries by the opposition, were killed by anti-Qadaffi protesters in Bayda, with some being locked up in a police station which was then burned down, while fifteen were lynched in front of the Bayda courthouse. At least 236 others were captured alive. Meanwhile, opposition forces commandeered bulldozers and tried to breach the walls of the Katiba compound where Qadaffi loyalists were housed, but were met with withering fire. Protesters also used stones and crude bombs made of tin cans stuffed with gunpowder. As the fighting continued, a mob attacked an army base on the outskirts of Benghazi and disarmed the soldiers. Among the equipment confiscated were three small tanks, which were rammed into the compound.

February 20, 2011: The first suicide attack occurred on this date. Attackers used tanks, bombs and light rifles for the first time and succeeded in storming the soldiers' barracks in Benghazi. Violent clashes also broke out in Misrata between government forces and demonstrators. Demonstrators used tanks for the first time against government forces. A third funeral procession passed the compound, and under the cover of the funeral, a man sacrificed himself by blowing up his car loaded with propane tanks with makeshift explosives and destroying the compound's gates. Opposition fighters resumed their assault, bolstered by reinforcements from Bayda and Derna. During the final assault, forty two people were killed. Libyan Interior Minister Abdul Fatah Younis showed up with a special forces squad to relieve the compound, but Younis defected to the opposition and announced safe passage for loyalists out of the city. Rebels stormed most of the police stations across the country from the East to the West. They also stormed most of the army barracks across the country where soldiers had a no-fire order. Therefore demonstrators (rebels) were able to confiscate 250 tanks, 73 armored vehicles, 112 artillery, 176 anti-aircraft machine guns, 254 rocket launchers, 222 light machine guns, 3,628 rifles, a large quantity of ammunition, according to government military sources, giving the rebels more firepower than, perhaps, many of Libya's neighboring countries.

February 22, 2011: Qadaffi makes his defiant speech declaring that he is willing to "die a martyr" for Libya's independence. The next day US President Obama responds; 'the suffering and bloodshed is outrageous and it is unacceptable." No such statement had been issued in relation to events in Tunisia, Egypt and Bahrain, where significantly greater violence against significantly greater and more prolonged peaceful demonstrations was taking place.

21 February 2011: Both the FIDH (Federation Internationale des Ligues des Doits de l'Homme and has ties to the U.S. National Endowment for Democracy) and the Libyan League for Human Rights (associated with FIDH) launched a communiqué calling for the international community to "mobilize" over Libya. They called on the International Criminal Court to become involved because, they claimed, 400 - 600 people had been killed by the Libyan Government since February 15, 2011. The joint letter also falsely claimed that 80% of Libyan soldiers were comprised of foreign mercenaries. (In 2010, the NED spent $183,900 for its three Libyan NGOs registered in London. The NED also directly funds FIDH.) Libyan deputy Permanent Representative to the UN Ibrahim Dabbashi called "on the UN to impose a no-fly zone on all Tripoli to cut off all supplies of arms and mercenaries to the regime."

February 22, 2011: The Libyan deputy ambassador to the United Nations called on Muammar Qaddafi to step down and face trial over "war crimes and genocide."

23 February 2011: French President Nicolas Sarkozy pushed for the European Union (EU) to pass sanctions against Qaddafi (freezing Qaddafi family funds abroad) and demand he stop attacks against civilians

February 23, 2011: The general news media report extensively on a range of themes to underscore their perception of the precarious state of the Qadaffi regime—former justice minister Mustafa Abdul Jalil alleged that Qaddafi personally ordered the 1988 Lockerbie bombing, resignations and defections of close allies, the loss of Benghazi, the second largest city in Libya, reported to be "alive with celebration" and other cities including Tobruk, Misrata, Bayda, Zawiya, Zuwara, Sabratha and Sorman falling with some reports that the government retained control of just a few pockets, amid mounting international isolation and pressure.

February 23, 2011: Tribal allegiance cited in Libya uprising. Although most Libyans live in largest cities there are approximately 140 identifiable clans and tribes in Libya that sometimes show more allegiance to family than country.

February 24, 2011: Qadaffi forces in Zawiya reportedly fired on a mosque where protesters were holding a sit in, and were fired on with automatic weapons and an anti aircraft gun. Thousands of anti-government protestors rallied in Martyr's Square. The same day, government forces, including tanks, launched a counterattack on Misrata airbase, engaging in battles with local residents and defecting military units, and managed to retake part of it.

February 25, 2011: Sliman Bouchuiguir, Secretary General of the Libyan League for Human Rights, testified before the United Nations Human Rights Council that thousands of Libyans had been killed by the Government. Bouchuiguir called for action from the Security Council. US imposes sanctions, freezing Libyan assets that had been placed with foreign banks for investment. NPR headlined the story as "Gadhafi's Frozen Assets: 32 Billion and Counting", though the article itself conceded that the assets belonged to "Moammar Gadhafi, his family or perhaps the government of Libya", and later, "the U.S. government won't say how much is in the Gadhafi clan's personal accounts, as opposed to Libyan government accounts" The Libya Investment Authority, the country's sovereign wealth fund, is estimated to control around $70 billion

February 25, 2011: Sarkozy says Qaddafi "must go".

February 27, 2011: The formation of the NTC was announced in the city of Benghazi on 27 February 2011 with the purpose to act as the "political face of the revolution". On 5 March 2011, the council issued a statement in which it declared itself to be the "only legitimate body representing the people of Libya and the Libyan state. On March 10, it was recognized by France as the legitimate government of Libya, and on July 20 by the US. <http://en.wikipedia.org/wiki/National_Transitional_Council> Former US State Department legal advisor John Bellinger noted that the US recognition of the TNC "is especially unusual under international law because the TNC does not control all of Libyan territory, nor can it claim to represent all of the Libyan people ... International lawyers have viewed recognition by states of an insurgent group, when there is still a functioning government, as an illegal interference in a country's internal affairs."

February 28, 2011: British Prime Minister David Cameron proposed the idea of a no-fly zone to prevent Qaddafi from "airlifting mercenaries" and "using his military aeroplanes and armoured helicopters against civilians."

February 28, 2011: By the end of February, Qaddafi's government had lost control of a significant part of Libya, including the major cities of Misrata and Benghazi, and the important harbors at Ra's Lanuf and Brega.

March 1, 2011: United Nations Human Rights Council cancels consideration of its Universal Periodic Review of the Libyan Arab Jamahiriya originally scheduled for March 18, 2011 in which Libya's human rights record was praised.

March 1, 2011: The US Senate unanimously passes non-binding Senate resolution S.RES.85 urging the United Nations Security Council to impose a Libyan no-fly zone and encouraging Qaddafi to step down. The US had naval forces positioned off the coast of Libya, as well as forces already in the region, including the aircraft carrier USS *Enterprise*.
March 2, 2011: UN suspends Libya from Human Rights Council over violence against protesters. UN vote against Qaddafi regime is first time any country has been suspended from 47-member body since it was formed.

March 3, 2011: Bernard-Henry Levy, French intellectual, goes to Benghazi to meet with rebel leaders. He proclaims that Qadaffi is not capable of waging an offensive war. He called for the scrambling of communications, destruction of airports, and bombardment of Qadaffi's personal bunker. On March 6 he returns to France to meet with Sarkozy and on March 11 Sarkozy declares the Libyan NTC as the legitimate representative of the Libyan people.

March 3, 2011: An ICC press release states International Criminal Court Prosecutor, Luis Moreno-Ocampo will open an investigation in Libya. <http://www.icc-cpi.int/NR/exeres/3EEE2E2A-2618-4D66-8ECB-C95BECCC300C.htm>

March 3, 2011: House Foreign Affairs Committee Member Howard Berman delivers an opening statement praising the role of United Nations Watch and Hillel Neuer inside the U.N. Human Rights Council calling Neuer "one of the strongest and most informed critics of the Human Rights Council."

March 6, 2011: Rebel advance along the coastline was stopped by government forces in Bin Jawad. Government troops ambushed the rebel column and dozens of rebels were killed or wounded. The rebels were forced into a chaotic retreat, leaving some of their troops behind, and a rescue force was repulsed by artillery fire. At the same time, loyalist airstrikes hit a rebel held airbase in Ra's Lanuf, killing at least two and injuring forty. At the same time, Qaddafi's forces attempted an attack on Misrata and managed to get as far as the center of the city before their attack was halted by rebel forces, and they retreated to the city's outskirts.

March 6, 2011: A British SAS unit is held by rebel forces it had approached in Benghazi in an attempt to open up diplomatic channels to opponents of Muammar Qaddafi.

March 6, 2011: Aid Agencies launch regional Flash Appeal as foreign African workers continue to flee Libya out of fear of rebels as Qaddafi had welcomed them with jobs. By that time it was estimated that 147,000 Africans had fled, many being housed in makeshift camps along the borders. Other reports estimate that nearly 500,000 Africans, working in Libya at Qadaffi's invitation, had fled.

March 10, 2011: France became the first country in the world to recognize the National Interim Council (later the NTC) as Libya's only legitimate government. The same day, government forces retook Zawiya and Ra's Lanuf, supported by tanks, artillery, warplanes, and warships. Witnesses claimed that dozens of rebels were killed.

March 12, 2011: Nine of the twenty-two members of the Arab League "called on the United Nations Security Council to impose a no-fly zone over Libya in a bid to protect civilians from air attack"; the others were not in attendances The Arab League calls for no-fly zone.

March 15, 2011: Ajdabiya, the last rebel held city before Benghazi, had been subjected to airstrikes for three days. Government forces launched a rolling artillery barrage coupled with airstrikes and naval shelling against the city, after which they attacked and broke through rebel defenses through a flanking maneuver. Most rebels had by then retreated from the city. After encircling the city, tanks were sent into the city center, and battled the remnants of rebel forces. Meanwhile, two Free Libyan Air Force jets attacked loyalist warships; apparently they were allowed by NATO to violate the no-fly zone. After a few hours, the city was under government control, but armored forces pulled back to the outskirts to avoid surprise attacks, although the shelling continued.

March 17, 2011: US Ambassador to the United Nations Susan Rice, together with Samantha Power and US Secretary of State Hillary Clinton, persuaded US President Barrack Obama to support intervention in Libya.

March 17, 2011: The United Nations Security Council, pressured mainly by England and France, passes a resolution, in order to "protect the civilian population" to impose a no fly zone in Libyan airspace; enforce the arms embargo already in place; and to freeze Libyan assets. As a result of the UN resolution, on March, 18, Qaddafi's government declared an immediate ceasefire, but a few hours later, *Al Jazeera* reported that government forces were still battling rebels.

March 18, 2011: U.S. President Obama responds to his support for the UN no-fly zone: "Left unchecked, we have every reason to believe that Qaddafi would commit atrocities against his people. Many thousands could die." The next day

284

US President Obama announces "a limited military action in Libya in support of an international effort to protect Libyan citizens."

March 19, 2011: The US begins Operation Odyssey Dawn to enforce the UN Security Council imposed "no fly" zone, only giving the operation over to NATO Operation Unified Protector after March 31. The American destroyer *USS Barry* launches a Tomahawk cruise missile against Libyan defenses. An American B 2 Spirit bomber lands at Whiteman Air Force Base after a bombing mission over Libya. Three US B 2 Spirit stealth bombers flew non-stop from the US to drop forty bombs on a major Libyan airfield, while other US aircraft searched for Libyan ground forces to attack. Twenty five coalition naval vessels, including three US submarines, began operating in the area.US and British ships and submarines fired at least 114 Tomahawk cruise missiles at twenty Libyan integrated air and ground defense systems. NATO ships and aircraft began enforcing a blockade of Libya, patrolling the approaches to Libyan territorial waters.

March 19, 2011: Nineteen French Air Force aircraft enter Libyan airspace to begin reconnaissance missions, and fly over Benghazi to prevent any attacks on the rebel controlled city. Italian Air Force planes reportedly also begin surveillance operations over Libya. In the evening, a French jet destroyed a government vehicle. Shortly afterward, a French airstrike destroyed four tanks southwest of Benghazi.

March 20, 2011: Several Storm Shadow missiles were launched against Libyan targets by British jets] Nineteen U.S. jets also conducted strikes against Libyan government forces. A loyalist convoy south of Benghazi was targeted. At least seventy vehicles were destroyed, and loyalist ground troops sustained multiple casualties. Strikes also took place on the Bab al Azizia compound in Tripoli from late March 20 to early March 21.

March 20, 2011: Arab League condemns broad Western bombing campaign in Libya. Secretary-General Amr Moussa said the Arab League's approval of a no-fly zone on March 12 was based on a desire to prevent Qadaffi's air force from attacking civilians and not designed to endorse the intense bombing and missile attacks—including on Tripoli and on Libyan ground forces.

March 20, 2011: Airstrikes were being carried out on loyalist armored and supply columns, rebel forces began a renewed offensive from Benghazi towards Tripoli. They advanced 240 kilometres (150 mi) along the coast of the Gulf of Sidra. The first objective was Ajdabiya, which the rebels reached on 21 March after taking Zuteinia along the way. Rebel forces attempted to attack Ajdabiya and relieve rebels inside the city, but were repulsed by government troops using tanks and multiple rocket launchers. That night, US airstrikes hit loyalist positions reportedly shelling the city.

March 21, 2011: Libyan government's SA 2, SA 3, and SA 5 air defense systems had been completely neutralized, while further strikes took place on targets in

Tripoli, and according to the Libyan government, in Sabha and Sirte.

March 21, 2011: Libyan rebels in Benghazi say they have created a new national oil company to replace the corporation controlled "designated the Central Bank of Benghazi as a monetary authority competent in monetary policies in Libya and the appointment of a governor to the Central Bank of Libya, with a temporary headquarters in Benghazi." (*Bloomberg*)

March 22, 2011: Loyalist shelling of rebel positions and Coalition airstrikes against loyalist forces continued. Hussein El Warfali, the commander of a Libyan Army Brigade stationed near Tripoli, was reportedly killed during the strikes. Rebel in Ajdabiya claimed that three government tanks were destroyed. On 24 March, government troops still held the main east and west gate areas and most of the city, except the city center, and managed to hold off advancing rebels with the help of mortar and artillery fire. Some rebel reinforcements managed to slip inside the city, and the situation became fluid, with large parts of Ajdabiya changing sides. During the night, British jets attacked government armor. By the following day, Qaddafi forces controlled the western and central parts of the city, while rebels controlled the eastern part.

March 23, 2011: Libyan Air Force had been largely destroyed by NATO, with most of its aircraft destroyed or rendered inoperable. The Libyan government's integrated air defense system was also degraded to a point where Coalition aircraft could operate over Libya with almost total impunity. On that same day, Coalition aircraft flew at least two sorties against government forces in Misrata. Later in the day, it was announced that all government forces and equipment, with the exception of individual snipers, had retreated from the city or were destroyed. In the early morning hours, four Canadian CF 18 jets supported by two CC 150 Polaris tankers bombed a government ammunition depot in Misrata, marking the first time Canadian jets bombed Libya since the campaign began.

March 23, 2011: NATO began enforcing a naval blockade of Libya, with warships and aircraft patrolling the approaches to Libyan territorial waters. The ships and aircraft conducted their operations in international waters, and did not enter Libya's territorial waters. Ships used surveillance to verify the actions of shipping in the region. NATO forces worked to interdict ships and aircraft carrying weapons or mercenaries, while working with the International Maritime Organization to ensure that legitimate private and commercial shipping to Libya continued.

March 23, 2011: NTC forms executive board, chaired by Mahmoud Jibril, former Qadaffi economic adviser and minister, who had since aligned himself with Arab and French interests. Jibril remained in power until October 31, 2011. Jibril was educated in Cairo, Egypt and the United States, receiving his doctorate in political science from the University of Pittsburgh in 1985.

March 24, 2011: Libyan Soko G 2 Galeb that allegedly violated the no fly zone was shot down by a French Dassault Rafale as it attempted to land near Misrata. Another five Galebs in the area were destroyed on the ground by a French airstrike the following day. The same day, a British submarine fired multiple Tomahawk Land Attack cruise missiles at Libyan air defenses.

March 24, 2011: US Secretary of State Hillary Clinton announces that the command and control of the no-fly zone will be transferred to NATO.

March 25, 2011: NATO announced that it would be taking over the command of the no fly zone operations, after several days of heated debate over who should control operations in Libya. The US had continuously reiterated that it wished to hand over command to an international organization. Airstrikes continued during the day. Two Royal Norwegian Air Force F 16s destroyed a number of Libyan government tanks. French Air Force jets destroyed a government artillery battery outside Ajdabiya, and British and French jets carried out a joint mission outside Ajdabiya, destroying seven government tanks. On that day, the Libyan Health Ministry reported that 114 people had been killed and 445 wounded since the bombing campaign started. A Vatican official in Tripoli reported on March 31 that Coalition airstrikes had killed at least 40 civilians in Tripoli.

March 26, 2011: Norwegian F 16s bombed an airfield in Libya during the night. Canadian CF 18s bombed government electronic warfare sites near Misrata. French aircraft destroyed at least seven loyalist aircraft, including two military helicopters. British jets destroyed five armored vehicles with Brimstone missiles, and Royal Danish Air Force F 16s destroyed numerous loyalist self propelled rocket launchers and tanks.

March 26, 2011: Rebels were in full control after loyalist forces withdrew from the city. During their retreat, government forces left behind large amounts of weapons and munitions, as well as intact armor and artillery. Loyalist forces also left their dead behind. Rebels seized military equipment abandoned by loyalist forces. Throughout the offensive, fighting also took place in Misrata. Despite continuous strikes on loyalist vehicles by aircraft and Tomahawk cruise missiles, Qaddafi forces regained control of much of the city, using tanks, artillery, mortars, and snipers. The attacks caused civilian casualties, including among children, and a hospital being used by rebels to treat their injured was overrun and used as a sniper position. Regime warships took the city's port.

March 27, 2011: NATO Danish aircraft destroyed government artillery south of Tripoli, while NATO Canadian jets destroyed ammunition bunkers south of Misrata. French jets knocked out a command center south of Tripoli, and conducted joint patrols with Qatari aircraft.

March 27, 2011, Qatar, base of Al Jazzera, and the Libyan opposition signed an oil export deal, which would see the National Transitional Council exporting oil to Qatar from rebel held areas in exchange for money to finance the rebel cause. Qatar also supplied petroleum products to the rebels.

March 28, 2011: NATO Coalition forces fought their first naval engagement when the USS Barry, supported by a P 3 Orion patrol aircraft and A 10 Thunderbolt attack aircraft, engaged the Libyan Coast Guard vessel Vittoria and two smaller craft, after the vessels began firing indiscriminately at merchant vessels in the port of Misrata. The Vittoria was disabled and forced to beach, another vessel was sunk, and the third abandoned.

March 28, 2011: Russia says attacks on forces loyal to Libyan leader Muammar Qaddafi amounted to intervention in a civil war and were not backed by the UN resolution authorising no-fly zones.

March 28, 2011: Qatar becomes the first Arab country to recognize rebels NTC as Libya's legitimate government.

March 28, 2011: The Libyan National Council, the Benghazi-based group that speaks for the rebel forces fighting the Qaddafi regime, appoints Khalifa Hifter, a long-time CIA collaborator, to head its military operations.

March 29, 2011: Government forces launched a counteroffensive, forcing the rebels into a retreat from Bin Jawad toward Ra's Lanuf. The same day, loyalist forces led by the Khamis Brigade captured the western and northwestern parts of Misrata. On 30 March, the rebels said that they were pulling out of Ra's Lanuf due to heavy tank and artillery fire from loyalist forces. Following a government counter offensive, Qaddafi forces took control of Brega.

March 31, 2011: NATO took command of Coalition air operations in Libya from U.S. Subsequent operations were carried out as part of Operation Unified Protector. Daily Coalition strikes continued to target Libyan government ground forces, air defenses, artillery, rocket launchers, command and control centers, radars, military bases, bunkers, ammunition storage sites, logistical targets, and missile storage sites. These strikes took place all over the country, many of them in Tripoli, where the Bab al Azizia compound was also targeted. The strikes caused numerous material losses and casualties among government forces.

April 1, 2011: Rebels attempted a counter attack to retake Brega. For eight days, loyalists and rebels battled for Brega. In the end, Qaddafi's forces repelled numerous rebel attacks on the city and managed to force the rebels out of Brega by April 7, despite continued NATO strikes. During the battles, a NATO airstrike accidentally hit rebel forces, destroying 3 tanks, damaging 5, and killing 27 rebels. NATO claimed that it did not know the rebels were using tanks. Rebel forces retreated, fleeing in several different directions. The rebels regrouped in Ajdabiya. Following the rebel retreat, government troops consolidated their control over Brega and prepared to advance on Ajdabiya.

April 6, 2011: An apparent NATO attack against the Sarir oil field, killing three guards and injuring other employees, and causing damage to a pipeline connecting the field to a Mediterranean port. The Libyan government claimed that

NATO aircraft carried out the attack. Both the rebels and the information manager at the Arabian Gulf Oil Company denied the Libyan government's claims, and attributed the attack to loyalist forces.

April 9, 2011: Rebel forces attacked Brega, but only managed to reach the University before being forced back by intense shelling by Qaddafi's forces. The Libyan government claimed that its forces had shot down 2 rebel helicopters (violating the no-fly zone) near the eastern oil facilities in Brega. The rebels confirmed that they had sent 2 helicopters into combat, and journalists claimed to have seen at least one helicopter apparently fighting for the rebels in action. Qaddafi's forces managed to retain control of the western part of the city.

April 10, 2011: Qaddafi's forces managed to push closer the city center, although they continued to be hit by NATO air attacks. The following day, rebels managed to completely push Qaddafi's forces out of the city, but fighting continued west of Ajdabiya. The front line then stagnated outside of the city, down the road to Brega.

April 11, 2011: Rebel leaders reject a plan presented by the African Union for a ceasefire and an end to the conflict. Qaddafi has accepted roadmap to peace, says Zuma. African Union negotiators appeal to Nato to halt air raids as they head for Benghazi.

April 15, 2011: Migrant workers trapped in Misrata began protesting their conditions, demanding repatriation from the city, which led to several instances of rebels opening fire on them, killing some.

April 19, 2011: UK announced that it was sending military advisors to Libya to help the rebels improve their organization and communications, but not to train or arm them which would have been a violation of UN resolutions. The British government also supplied the rebels with telecommunications equipment and body armor.

April 20, 2011: US announced a $25 million aid package to the Libyan rebels, which consisted of fuel trucks and fuel containers, ambulances, medical equipment, protective vests, binoculars, food, and non secure radios. The first aid shipment arrived in Benghazi on May 10. In addition, Italy and France were reported to be sending military advisors to aid Libyan rebels. Qatar supplied MILAN anti tank missiles, pickup trucks, and uniforms to the rebels. The Libyan government claimed that Qatar also sent 20 military trainers to Benghazi to train over 700 rebel fighters. In addition, Qatar assisted a rebel satellite television operation in broadcasting from Doha.

April 21, 2011: A convoy of 9 loyalist vehicles attacked the rebel held al Boster oil facility in the eastern Libyan desert, southwest of Tobruk, deep inside rebel held territory. The facility was damaged during the attack. Rebel spokesman

Ahmed Bani said that the attack was carried out to disrupt oil sales by rebels.

April 22, 2011:   Rebels managed to drive Qaddafi's forces from several locations near the Misrata city center with NATO air support.   The Deputy Foreign Minister of Libya subsequently pledged that the Libyan Army would withdraw from Misrata.

April 23, 2011:   US carried out its first UAV strike, when two RQ 1 Predator drones destroyed a Multiple rocket launcher near Misrata.

April 23, 2011: Qaddafi's forces withdrew from Misrata, but continued to shell the city.

April 26, 2011, a Qaddafi force attempted to retake Misrata, but was stopped by a NATO airstrike. Qaddafi's troops launched an artillery bombardment against rebel held areas in the Jabal al Gharbi district in the Nafusa Mountains, leaving 110 rebels and civilians dead.

April 26, 2011: British Defense Minister Liam Fox and US Defense Secretary Robert Gates, had told reporters at the Pentagon that NATO planes were not targeting Qaddafi specifically but would continue to attack his command centers. Within the United Nations Security Council, Russia and China voiced concerns that NATO has gone beyond the UN resolution's authorization to take "all necessary measures" to protect civilians. Russia expressed "increasing concern" regarding reports of civilian casualties, and doubted claims that the attacks did not deliberately target Qaddafi and his family. Following the attacks, angry mobs of Qaddafi loyalists burned and vandalized the British and Italian embassies, a US consulate, and a UN office, prompting the UN to pull its staff out of Tripoli. The strike came shortly after Qaddafi called for a mutual cease fire and negotiations with NATO. A NATO official said before Saturday's strike that the alliance would keep up pressure until the U.N. Security Council mandate on Libya was fulfilled. The NATO official noted that Qaddafi's forces had attacked Misrata hours before his speech. Opposition leaders called the cease fire offers publicity stunts. "We don't believe that there is a solution that includes him or any member of his family. So it is well past any discussions. The only solution is for him to depart," said rebel spokesperson Jalal al Galal.

April 28, 2011: Qaddafi's forces recaptured the Wazzin border crossing with Tunisia after a swift advance during which they pushed the rebels into Tunisia. Fighting continued on the edge of the Tunisian border town of Dehiba, which included a failed rebel counterattack. Loyalist forces captured Al Jawf with minimal resistance, and the rebels quickly retreated.

April 30, 2011: NATO airstrike hits the home of Saif al Arab Qaddafi, Qaddafi's youngest son. Libyan officials reported that Saif and three of Muammar Qaddafi's grandchildren were killed in the strike. Qaddafi was apparently there, but "escaped".

May 4, 2011: NATO Secretary General Anders Fogh Rasmussen claimed that the Libyan government's military capabilities had been significantly degraded since the operation started, stating that "every week, every day we make new progress, hit important targets. But I'm not able to quantify the degree to which we have degraded Muammar Qaddafi's military capabilities, but definitely it is much weaker now than when our operation started". NATO claimed that it was enforcing the UN no fly zone on rebels as well as on government forces. However, an unidentified rebel pilot and an air traffic controller claimed that NATO agreed to let them attack government targets after approving a request by the rebel military council.

May 1, 2011: NATO carried out 60 airstrikes throughout Libya, targeting ammunition storage sites, military vehicles, a communications facility, and an anti aircraft gun. Rebels claimed that a NATO airstrike destroyed 45 military vehicles in an attack on a loyalist convoy leaving Jalu. The following day, government tanks tried to enter the city from the al Ghiran suburb. Six people were killed and several dozen wounded. Misrata was still subjected to continuous rocket fire from government forces, with a spokesperson claiming that the shelling had not stopped for 36 hours. Government forces halted their shelling of Misrata at about midday following NATO strikes, but the port remained closed, having been bombarded earlier in the day.

May 3, 2011: Loyalist forces shelled Misrata. The attack reportedly stopped briefly when a NATO plane flew overhead, but resumed shortly afterward. NATO aircraft conducted 62 airstrikes against loyalist targets near Misrata, Ra's Lanuf, Sirte, Brega, and Zintan.

May 6, 2011: NATO conducted 57 airstrikes against loyalist military targets throughout Libya, while opposition forces gained full control of Kufra and Abu Rawaya after Qaddafi forces stationed there surrendered. Loyalists attacked the town of Jalu, but were repulsed by rebel resistance and a Coalition airstrike.

May 7, 2011: Qaddafi forces continued shelling the port of Misrata, hitting a large fuel tank. Government forces also used small crop dusters to bomb four fuel tanks. The attacks started a fire, which spread to four more fuel tanks. Loyalist artillery and mortar fire also hit Tunisia after renewed clashes broke out at the Wazzin border crossing. Clashes also took place in Zintan and Yefren, and in the area between. The area between Zintan and Yefren was being secured, but Yefren was still under siege.

May 8, 2011: Heavy fighting took place near Misrata Airport, and the city came under renewed attack by Qaddafi forces. Meanwhile, NATO strikes hit numerous government targets in the vicinity of Misrata, Zintan, Ajdabiya, Houn, and Brega.

May 8, 2011: NATO claimed to have carried out its first interception when it escorted a Free Libyan Air Force MiG 23 back to base, while the unidentified pilot claimed that he had been allowed to take off (in clear violation of the no-fly zone) and destroyed a fuel truck and two other vehicles.

May 8, 2011: It was reported that US Central Intelligence Agency (CIA) inserted small groups of clandestine operatives into Libya to gather intelligence on loyalist military targets and troop positions for airstrikes. The agents also met with rebels to fill in gaps in understanding their leaders and allegiances. US officials denied, however, that they were assisting rebels. In addition, dozens of British MI6 operatives and special forces soldiers were inserted into Libya to direct RAF airstrikes and gather intelligence on the whereabouts of Libyan government tank columns, artillery positions, and missile installations. Stratfor claimed that other states may have also sent intelligence and special forces operatives to Libya. Stratfor reported that foreign operatives also met with rebels to prepare them for upcoming events, create channels of communications and logistics, and create a post war political framework. In addition, the US Air Force utilized U 2 spy planes, JSTARS aircraft, and a high altitude Global Hawk drone to monitor government forces. Satellites were also used for surveillance operations against Libya.

May 9, 2011: The shelling of Misrata by Qaddafi forces continued to choke off supplies to the city, while fighting continued near Misrata Airport. Meanwhile, Coalition strikes hit two targets in Tripoli.

May 10, 2011: Rebels from Misrata and Zlitan joined up and engaged in close combat that rendered loyalist long range rockets useless. The rebels managed to drive loyalist forces on the west side of Misrata out of rocket range, and to push loyalist troops from Misrata Airport, burning their tanks as they retreated. Rebels also claimed to have made gains near Jalu, and the area between Ajdabiya and Brega in fierce fighting. The same day, a NATO strike hit a government command center in Tripoli. Rebels subsequently began an advance towards Zliten.

May 11, 2011: On 11 May, NATO aircraft fired four rockets at Qaddafi's compound in Tripoli, killing at least two people. Strikes also hit government military targets throughout the country.

May 12, 2011: NATO carried out 52 strikes against loyalist targets. Loyalist forces fired at least three rockets into Ajdabiya. Loyalist forces also launched an attack on Misrata port, using a number of small boats, but were forced to abandon their attack after NATO warships intervened. Regime forces onshore covered their retreat with artillery and anti aircraft fire directed at the warships. The warships HMCS Charlottetown and HMS Liverpool responded with machine gun fire.

May 13, 2011: NATO carried out 44 airstrikes. According to the Libyan government, a strike in the vicinity of Brega killed 11 Islamic clerics and wounded 45 civilians while dozens of imams and officials from around Libya had gathered there to pray for peace. In Tripoli, shortages of food and fuel were worsening, along with increasing NATO attacks. According to an activist, a wave of anti government protests took place in several Tripoli neighborhoods throughout the week. Italian Foreign Minister Franco Frattini said that Qaddafi was probably wounded in a NATO airstrike, and had left Tripoli. The Libyan government dismissed the claim as "nonsense", and state television broadcast a brief audio recording of what it said was Qaddafi, taunting NATO as a cowardly crusader, and claiming to be in a place where NATO could not reach him.

May 14, 2011: Human Rights Watch accuses NATO of underplaying civilian deaths in Libya, says there were 72 of same.

May 15, 2011: NATO conducted 48 airstrikes against loyalist targets. British jets and missiles hit two intelligence facilities. NATO also hacked into Libyan Army frequencies, and broadcast claims of atrocities and appeals to stop fighting, telling them to either "build a peaceful Libya for the benefit of your family and a better future for your country" or face continued airstrikes.

May 16, 2011: NATO conducted 46 airstrikes on loyalist targets. Among the targets hit was a training base used by the bodyguards of members of Qaddafi's inner circle, which was hit by British jets. At least four Grad rockets fired from Libya landed in Tunisian territory.

May 17, 2011: NATO carried out 53 strikes.

May 18, 2011: Throughout the following days, NATO continued to carry out dozens of airstrikes on government military capabilities, a large percentage of the targets being in Tripoli. Meanwhile, government forces continued artillery attacks on rebel areas.

May 19, 2011: British jets carried out a massive strike against the Libyan Navy, hitting naval facilities in the harbors Tripoli, Khoms, and Sirte. Eight warships were sunk or severely damaged. A dockyard for launching rigid hull inflatable speedboats was also hit, and the attacks caused damage to naval infrastructure. Increased rebel activity was reported between Brega and Ajdabiya, with new recruits and ammunition arriving in large numbers at the front lines.

May 20, 2011: Another 60 strikes were carried out. In Brega, a rebel unit with artillery support launched an attack against Qaddafi troops at Brega University, an area in which rebels had trouble engaging in before due to the extensive use of artillery by loyalists. The university was attacked from multiple angles, but government troops managed to retain their positions at the university by the end of the day.

May 21, 2011: NATO naval forces intercepted a fuel tanker destined for Libya, carrying fuel alleged to be for government use. In addition, the harbor of Tripoli was again one of the targets bombed in NATO attacks. Also on the same day a ship loaded with food and medical supplies docked in Misrata and unloaded its cargo, while two ships loaded with humanitarian aid departed from Benghazi and docked in Zarzis, Tunisia, where their aid was unloaded to be taken by truck to the Nafusa Mountains region. A French military spokesman announced that the French Navy amphibious assault ship Le Tonnerre had departed Toulon the previous week, and was sailing towards the Libyan coast with a load of twelve Tiger helicopters. Later, the British military said that it was also deploying four Apache helicopters.

May 25, 2011: Rebels clashed with what they called "Sudanese mercenaries" near the Sudanese border, a claim not disproved until weeks later. The NATO-Rebel propaganda war thus escalated as national and international support for war was waning.

May 26, 2011: NATO warplanes bombed more than twenty targets in Tripoli. All of the strikes were conducted within less than half an hour. It was widely described as the heaviest attack on the city since the campaign began. According to Libyan government spokesman Moussa Ibrahim, the strikes targeted buildings used by volunteer units of the Libyan Army. NATO claimed that a vehicle storage facility near the Bab al Azizia compound was hit. At least three people were killed and dozens injured. NATO strikes continued to target Qaddafi's forces with an increasing frequency, attacking dozens of targets all around the country daily, many of them in Tripoli. The Bab al Azizia compound continued to be targeted. Qaddafi forces continued their artillery and rocket attacks, and laid a minefield in the Misrata area.

May 26, 2011: African Union demands an outright end to NATO air strikes on Libya, accusing the West of sidelining African nations in efforts to end a conflict on their home turf.

May 29, 2011: Government soldiers and eight officers defected from the government and left Libya. The eight officers included five generals, two colonels, and a major. One of the defectors, General Melud Massoud Halasa, said that Qaddafi's forces were weakening daily, and were only twenty percent as effective as they were before the war began. Halasa estimated that only ten generals remained loyal to Qaddafi. On the same day, an anti government protest broke out in Tripoli, when about 1,000 people gathered for the funeral of two opposition members killed in a clash with security forces. The demonstration was broken up by loyalist militia, who used live ammunition to disperse it, killing two people. The protest was the largest that took place in Tripoli in nearly three months. NATO jets launched a series of airstrikes against targets around the country. According to an anonymous Libyan government official, an educational institute in eastern Tripoli where military officials and civilians studied engineering, computers, and communications was among the targets hit.

June 2, 2011: French philosopher and interventionist Bernard-Henry Levy announces that the NTC is ready to recognize Israel, something Qadaffi had consistently refused to do.

June 3, 2011: U.S. media, typified by New York Times, continues drumbeat for war emphasizing accusations of atrocities and war crimes by Qadaffi regime that are later mostly exposed as false and downplaying civilian deaths caused by NATO and the rebels that are later mostly verified.

June 7, 2011: NATO forces dropped over 60 bombs and missiles in and on Tripoli, In the heaviest onslaught of the war, killing at least dozens and spreading terror within the Capitol. However, some media did acknowledge on that day that NATO launched at least forty airstrikes against government targets in Tripoli. The Bab al Azizia compound was heavily bombed, with a government soldier claiming that it was subjected to eight separate airstrikes. Babal-Azizia was the sight of daily civilian pro Qadaffi rallies. That day the NATO bombing had a paralyzing effect on Tripoli, a city of some 2.5 million. If you were in the central part of the city that day you would have experienced a major bombing attack.

-8am until 10am: Approximately 13 bombs are dropped inside the city. Following earlier patterns, most civilians, including school children, believe that bombing for the day is over and resume daily activities. One of the first bombs causes a large ominous dust plume covering one half square mile of Tripoli. Suddenly at 1pm while everyone in Tripoli has assumed daily bombing has ended 'hell' does break lose:

14. -1:00pm Another NATO bomb drops
15 -1:13pm Another bomb
16 -1:14pm Another bomb
17 -1:15pm Another bomb
18 -1:27pm Sounds more like Missile strike
19- 1:45pm Bomb
20 -1:47pm Bomb
21 - 1:47pm Missile
22 - 1:48pm Bomb
23 - 1:48pm Bomb
24 - 1:49pm Bomb
25 - 1:50pm Bomb
26 - 1:51pm Bomb
27 - 1:53pm Bomb
28 - 1:54pm Bomb
29 - 1:59pm Bomb
30 - 1:59pm Bomb hits very close by as ground shakes and building rattles
31 - 1:59pm Bomb hits very close
32 - 2:02pm Bomb hits so close a flash of light can be seen
33 - 2:06pm Bomb sounds like it hits harbor target
34 - 2:07pm Bomb hits very close
35 - 2:09pm Bomb hits close
36 - 2:12pm Bomb hits close by
37 - 2:22pm Missile hits very close
38 - 3:03pm Bomb
39 - 3:15pm Bomb
40. 3:21pm Bomb

41 - 6:00pm Bomb
42 - 6:00pm Bomb
43 - 6:00pm Bomb
44 - 6:07pm Bomb
45 - 6:07pm Bomb
46 - 6:23pm Bomb
47 - 6:23pm Bomb
48 - 6:23pm Bomb
49 - 6:26pm Bomb
50 - 6:28pm Bomb
51 - 6:31pm Bomb
52 - 6:37pm Bomb
53 - 6:46pm Bomb
54 - 6:46pm Bomb
55 - 6:50pm Bomb
56 - 7:39pm Bomb
57 - 7:44pm Bomb
58 - 7:53pm Bomb
59 - 10:10pm Bomb
60 - 10:10pm Bomb
61 - 10:10pm Bomb then stopped counting

June 7, 2011: Rebel forces in the Nafusa Mountains advanced somewhat closer to Tripoli, taking the strategically important town of Yafran, which strengthened their control of the mountains area. This left the rebels less than 160 kilometers (99 mi) from Tripoli.

June 8, 2011: Qaddafi forces again advanced on Misrata, with renewed shelling killing 10 rebels and injuring 24. In Tripoli, NATO attacks briefly ceased during the day, but resumed in the evening.] NATO airstrikes continued on Tripoli.

June 9, 2011: Clashes between rebel and government forces broke out in Zliten, with regime forces shelling the city, while NATO aircraft attacked government forces in the area. NATO airstrikes hit Tripoli the same day, hitting the Bab al Azizia compound and nearby military barracks. Libyan state television also reported that airstrikes hit targets in the Ain Zara neighborhood.

June 9, 2011: Turkey donated $100 million to the National Transitional Council for humanitarian assistance.

June 11, 2011: Rebel forces fought their way into Zawiya, and continued advancing from the west. London based National Transitional Council spokesman Guma el Gamaty announced that the rebels had captured a large part of the western side of the city. NATO airstrikes also hit mobile radar units in Metiga, weapons depots in Jufra, Waddan, and Hun, and targets in Tripoli. Government commander Khweldi Al Hmeldi was allegedly wounded. Government forces set up checkpoints to the west of Zawiya, and closed the coastal road. Government soldiers continued shelling Misrata, and clashes continued around Zliten.

June 12, 2011: Libyan government spokesman Moussa Ibrahim announced that the rebels were defeated in Zawiya. Reporters taken to Zawiya saw secure streets and Qaddafi's national flag in the central square. Government forces also continued to shell Misrata, and attack rebel forces massed in Dafniya with tanks, artillery, and incendiary rockets. Clashes also took place in Misrata and Zliten. In an attack on Brega, four rebels were killed and dozens injured. NATO aircraft bombed the Bab al Azizia compound and a military airport.

June 13, 2011: NATO conducted 62 airstrikes against targets in Tripoli and four other cities. NATO helicopters attacked two Libyan Navy boats off the coast of Misrata, and military equipment and vehicles concealed beneath trees in Zliten.

June 14, 2011: NATO jets bombed the Bab al Azizia compound and two other targets in Tripoli. NATO aircraft also dropped propaganda leaflets urging government soldiers to abandon Zliten. Throughout the following days, NATO jets and helicopters continued to target the Bab al Azizia compound and military targets across Libya.

June 15, 2011: US Defense Secretary Gates announces that NATO alliance is in danger of breaking, indicating that the United States would not continue to play a dominate role in the NATO alliance because of national economic concerns as well as national political concerns.

June 15, 2011: US President Obama continues to argue that he does not need Congressional approval for the Libya intervention as the intervention does not amount to "full-blown hostilities" because there are no American troops on the ground. He further argued that the nature, scope , and duration of 'air power to defend civilians' did not make this a war not subject to the War Powers Act.

June 17, 2011: Rebels and US reject Qadaffi proposal to end war and hold elections in three months.

June 18, 2011: NATO airstrike mistakenly hit a rebel column, and expressed regret for any casualties that may have resulted.

June 19, 2011: Nine civilians were killed in a NATO airstrike on Tripoli. Reporters were taken to the location of the strike and saw bodies being pulled out of the rubble of a destroyed building. NATO acknowledged being responsible for the airstrike and the civilian deaths. NATO claimed that it was targeting a missile site, but that a bomb apparently missed its target due to a weapon systems failure and hit a civilian target instead. Finally, it is documented that this NATO airstrike hit a residence in one of Tripoli's larger districts (Soul al-Juma), killing 5 and wounding 8. Human Rights Watch finally issues report on May 14, 2012 underscoring NATO's numerous attacks on civilians during the war: "NATO has not provided sufficient information on the intended targets in individual cases to demonstrate that the strikes identified in this report were legally justified." Human Rights Watch also documented 7 other instances of civilian deaths caused by NATO during the Libyan War.

June 19, 2011: Rebel oil chief Ali Tarhouni said that rebels were running out of money and blamed Western countries for not living up to their promises of financial aid.

June 20, 2011: NATO strikes hit a walled farm in Sorman killing 13 civilians, four men, four women and five children. Human Rights Watch finally issues report on May 14, 2012 underscoring NATO's numerous attacks on civilians during the war, including this incident: However, "NATO was unwilling to confirm any civilian casualties," according to HRW. Human Rights Watch also documented 7 other instances of civilian deaths caused by NATO during the Libyan War.

June 20, 2011: Qaddafi government officials claimed that NATO killed 19 civilians in the town of Sorman, 70 km (43 mi) west of Tripoli. This came only a day after NATO admitted to accidentally killing civilians in a separate airstrike in Tripoli. NATO stated that the target in Sorman was a military command and control node.

June 22, 2011: NATO continued its airstrikes on Qaddafi forces, conducting 44 strikes the following day. Meanwhile, fighting in and near Zliten continued, while Qaddafi forces continued to bombard rebel held areas.

June 24, 2011: Amnesty International releases report that disproved much of the propaganda dished out by the NATO-Rebel Alliance including their claims of mass rapes and other abuses allegedly perpetuated by forces loyal to Qadaffi. First, the rebels had repeatedly charged that Qadaffi used mercenary troops from Cental and West Africa, but AI found no evidence for this. "Moist were sub-Saharan migrants working in Libya without documents." AI found that the rebels had, in fact, lynched or executed some of these African workers. Second, AI found that there was no proof of mass killings of civilians by the Qadaffi regime, which was the basis for the initial NATO military intervention. The AI findings confirmed a report by the authoritative International Crisis Group that there was no question of genocide. "[M]uch Western media coverage has from the outset presented a very one-sided view of the logic of events, portraying the protest movement as entirely peaceful and repeatedly suggesting the regime's security forces were unaccountably massacring unarmed demonstrators who presented no security challenge." Third, AI found no evidence of mass rapes. This part was confirmed by Human Rights Watch head who dismissed the charge of mass rapes: "We have not been able to find evidence."

June 26, 2011: NATO increased its airstrikes in western Libya during the week, striking more than 50 military targets. Tripoli and Gharyan were repeatedly hit, along with a network of tunnels storing military equipment about 50 kilometres (31 mi) southeast of Tripoli.

June 27, 2011: The International Criminal Court issues an arrest warrant for Qaddafi, accusing him of crimes against humanity. The arrest warrant is issued prior to any ICC investigation having taken place, and despite Amnesty International repudiation of a range of rebel claims in its report of June 24.

June 28, 2011: In what AP terms a victory for President Barack Obama, a Senate panel votes to approve US participation in the military campaign against Libya begun on March 19, 2011.

June 29, 2011: France acknowledges that it had airdropped arms supplies to rebels in the Nafusa Mountains in early June that would have been a violation of the UN arms embargo. The French military claimed to have supplied only light arms and ammunition to help Libyan civilians defend themselves from attacks by government forces. However, a report in *Le Figaro* claimed that rocket launchers and anti tank missiles were among the weapons dropped. Meanwhile, the British government offered the rebels 5,000 sets of body armor, 6,650 uniforms, 5,000 high visibility vests, and communications equipment for the National Transitional Council's police force.

July 1, 2011: Qaddafi government reveals that it has distributed 1.2 million weapons to supporters, including women, in Tripoli. This underscores Qaddafi's philosophy of gender equality espoused by Qaddafi as he established a military academy for women, did not force women to be veiled and allowed them to travel freely.

July 5, 2011: Qadaffi troops report that they have captured a shipment of Qatari weapons that were headed to the rebels by boat; the shipment would have violated UN weapons ban. Qatar eventually admits that it supplied the rebels with arms and ground soldiers - all in violation of the UN resolutions.

July 6, 2011: Opposition forces in strongholds in the Misrata and the Nafusa Mountains attacked Qaddafi forces in separate coordinated attacks. The Misrata offensive sought to repel Gaddaffi forces in Zliten, a town located on the route to the Libyan capital. Rebel fighters came with technicals armed with anti armor weapons and overwhelmed a military base in the village of al Qawalish.

July 13, 2011: Human Rights Watch documented rebel mistreatment of civilians in town of al-Awaniya, Rayayinah, al-Qawalish and Zawit al-Bagul:—most disturbingly the vandalisation of three medical clinics [and] local small hospitals, including the theft of some medical equipments.

July 14, 2011: Rebels claimed to have retaken al Qawalish. Rebel forces also launched an attack on Brega, with the Libyan government claiming that NATO supported the attack by striking government targets from the sea and air. NATO confirmed that it had hit five targets in the vicinity of Brega, as well as targets in the vicinities of Gharyan, Sirte, Tripoli, Waddan and Zliten.

July 16, 2011: Libya's Berbers are described as key to uprising. Berbers cited as unhappy Qaddafi tried to make them Libyans and called them Arabs and "ruthlessly denied the existence of Libyan Berbers." Berbers represent approximately 10% of Libyan population and many believe, although Muslim (Ibadi), they are culturally and ethnically distinct from the majority Arab Libyans.

July 18, 2011: Rebels claimed to have taken all of Brega after Qaddafi's forces withdrew to Ra's Lanuf. This is seen as a major victory since it gives the rebels access to 2 million barrels of crude oil, as well as complete control over eastern Libya's oil network.

July 25, 2010: After several months of conflict and no signs of triumph in favor of Qaddafi or the rebels, some NATO countries suggested that a powerless Qaddafi could be allowed to stay in Libya, a scenario both Tripoli and Benghazi rejected.

July 28, 2010: Rebel army chief and Qadaffi defector Abdul Fatah Younis was put under arrest by the NTC (the National Transitional Council). The NTC later organized a press conference and announced the death of Younis
July 30. 2011: NATO aircraft attacked and disabled 3 Libyan state television transmission dishes in Tripoli, on grounds that Qaddafi was using the media to incite attacks against civilians. The Libyan government claimed that 3 journalists were killed and 15 injured in the attacks.

July, 2011: Genevieve Garrigos, head of Amnesty International in France, admitted that the allegations which she, herself, had helped to spread in February 2011 about mercenaries being in Libya for the Jamahiriya Government "was just a rumor spread by the media." Sliman Bouchuiguir admitted in an interview with Julien Teil that the allegations of deaths by the Jamahiriya Government were without evidence. In addition, he admitted that his information had come from the Libyan National Transitional Council (NTC), adding that at least three of the LLHR members were also members of the NTC.

August 3, 2011: NATO bombed Zliten and Tajura, near Tripoli, and the rebels captured a Qaddafi ship laden with 250,000 barrels of oil.

August 8, 2011: During Ramadan NATO aircraft dropped bombs on four houses in Majer, a rural village near Zliten. The bombs harmed only civilians with 14 killed and 17 wounded. A May 14, 2012 report, "Unacknowledged Deaths" by Human Rights Watch concluded as to this incident: "the concerns about civilian loss of life are heightened by the second strike on the al-Jarud compound when relatives and neighbors were providing assistance after the first strike."

August 9, 2011: NATO bombed a warship in Tripoli's harbor after reportedly observing weapons were being removed from it.

August 16, 2011: Rebel forces supported by NATO air strikes started a 48 hour operation securing key towns such as Gharyan around the capital. They then began cutting off fuel and supply lines, effectively leaving Tripoli under a state of siege.

August 18, 2011: US officials reported that Qaddafi was making preparations to flee to exile in Tunisia with his family.

August 20, 2011: Battle for Tripoli as rebel elements in Tripoli supported by NATO launched a general uprising code named Operation Mermaid Dawn in the city. Many of the weapons used by rebels had been assembled and sent to Tripoli by tugboat. Opposition forces in the city launched a general uprising, surrounding almost every neighborhood, with especially heavy fighting occurring in Fashloom, Tajura, and Souk al Jomaa. Rebels suffered high casualties, while Qaddafi forces also took losses. NATO warplanes supported the operation by conducting bombing runs over government targets in the city.

August 20, 2011: Diplomats of the United States, the United Kingdom and France began working on a UN resolution to release some of the frozen Libyan assets to the NTC. Resistance was met from China and Russia, who felt that the move would formally recognize the NTC as the de facto government of Libya.

August 22, 2011: Tripoli had largely fallen as rebel forces from outside poured into the city, with little resistance from Qaddafi troops. Green Square was taken and renamed to Martyr's Square, and there were reports that three of Qaddafi's sons were captured alive. However later that day, reports came in that Mohammad Qaddafi had escaped. Heavy fighting took place near Qaddafi's compound Bab al Azizia. At night between 22 and 23 August, CNN reporter Matthew Chance spoke to Saif al Islam Qaddafi outside the Rixos Hotel, took pictures of him and a video putting earlier reports about his capture in serious discredit.

August 23, 2011: Rebels seized Qaddafi's compound in Bab al Azizia.

August 25, 2011: UN sanctions committee released $500 million of frozen Libyan assets following a direct request by the US. South Africa only agreed on the condition the money would be used for humanitarian purposes, but blocked the release of a further $1 billion for the NTC itself.

August 27, 2011: Western news websites were reporting and showing pictures of the rebels entering the houses of Qaddafi's sons and daughter in Tripoli. The international media reported the excessive and luxurious lifestyle that their children led though DIGNITY visits to the bombed home of his son showed little by way of extravagance. As the Battle for Tripoli reached a climax in mid August, the Qaddafi family were forced to abandon their fortified compound.

August 28, 2011: Battle of Bani Walid begins. Along with Sirte was one of two final strongholds, outside of Triploi, held by Qaddafi forces. With loyalist forces expelled from Tripoli itself, fighting continued to the south of the city, with attacks on the airport from Tarhuna.

August 29, 30, 2011: NATO aircraft struck two adjacent homes killing 5 family members and wounding another in Bani Walid. A May 14, 2012 Human Rights Report: "Unacknowledged Deaths" reported that NATO claimed the site "was a major command and control node, which was reliant on non-traditional/informal methods to carry out that function." HRW could find no evidence to support this was anything but a civilian site and the surviving family claimed "no relations to the Qadaffi government or military." Qaddafi and the whereabouts of other members of his family remained unknown. A million sum bounty was placed by a group of businessmen, supported by the NTC, on anyone who brings Col. Qaddafi to the NTC, dead or alive. After the fall of Tripoli, son Saadi stated in various media interviews that he had been authorized to negotiate a transfer of power to the NTC.

August 31, 2011: British Royal Air Force flew the first LD 280 million of a shipment of LD 2 billion, that were blocked from entering the country at the start of the conflict. The money was to be handed over direct to the Central Bank of Libya, authorised by the UN on humanitarian grounds, and particularly to pay Libyan Government workers during Eid ul Fitr, some of whom had not been paid for over three months.

September 15, 2011: Libyan Government spokesman Mousa Ibrahmin claimed there had been over 2000 civilian deaths. Nato flew **26,500** sorties since it took charge of Libya mission on 31 March 2011.

September 23, 2011: NATO airstrikes hit a family farm in Gurdabiya killing 3, an elderly man and two young girls, aged 8 and 10. The Human Rights Watch Report: "Unacknowledged Deaths" documented that: "NATO did not provide any information about this strike to the UN Commission of Inquiry or Human Rights Watch."

September 25, 2011: NATO airstrikes hit a home in Sirte, killing 7, three women and four children. According to the May 14, 2012 Human Rights Watch Report: "Unacknowledged Deaths" the civilian home was a target because the owner's brother was a Qadaffi general. The Report concluded: NATO should clarify why the anticipated loss of civilian life from the attack was not excessive compared to the attack's suspected military gain."

October 20, 2011: Sirte fell and Muammar Qaddafi and several other leading regime figures including his son Mutassim were found and killed as they attempted to flee the city. The engagement marked the end of the war.

October 20, 2011: Observations that Libya, that was the economic envy of Africa, "had been bombed back to the Stone Age" by NATO.

October 23, 2011: 3 days after capturing and then killing Qadaffi, NTC declares Libya liberated.

October 25, 2011: NTC allows final services for Qadaffi and then secretly buries him in the Sahara.

October 2011: Sliman Bouchuiguir is selected to represent Libya as Ambassador to Switzerland.

November 2, 2011: International Criminal Court prosecutor Luis Moreno-Ocampo said "there are allegations of crimes committed by NATO forces [and] these allegations will be examined impartially and independently."

November 19, 2011: Saif al Islam was captured in the southern Libyan desert near the Niger border by the fighters from the Zintan Brigades. After his capture he was flown to Zintan where he was held.

November 21, 2011: UN General Assembly votes to end Libya's suspension from the United Nations Human Rights Council.

November 22, 2011: International Criminal Court prosecutor Luis Moreno Ocampo arrived in Libya for talks with the Libyan government. Both Saif al Islam and Abdullah Senussi are currently under indictment by the ICC in The Hague on charges of crimes against humanity, but were supposed to be tried in Libya first.

March 14, 2012: Libya's long-ignored UPR praising its human rights record under the Jamahiryia was finally adopted over the objection of Hillel Neuer and UN Watch.

March, 2012: Documents released in revealed that in 2007 Qadaffi agreed to finance Sarkozy's French election with a $50 million contribution.

April 10, 2012: US-Libya Business Association (USLBA) meets in Tripoli for a five day conference on trade and investment featuring, Boeing, Conoco-Phillips, Dow Chemical, ExxonMobil, Hess, General Electric, Marathon Oil.

May 14, 2012: Human Rights Watch issues report stating that NATO dropped 7,700 bombs on Libya during its 7 month campaign against Qadaffi regime.

May 28, 2012: Military rebel leaders are still in control of Libya and issue new laws designed to stifle pro-democracy organizations. Other laws targeted control of the media in Libya for ensuring the "protection of national unity and social peace."

May 28, 2012: It was revealed that Amnesty International was investigating torture allegations against the new transitional government and dozens of militias that still exist. The human rights organization documented 20 deaths in custody and urged the NTC to secure control of all detention centers in order to control abuse of prisoners.

CONTRIBUTORS

Abayomi Azikiwe is the editor of the Pan-African News Wire, an international electronic press service designed to foster intelligent discussion on the affairs of African people throughout the continent and the world. The press agency was founded in January of 1998 and has published thousands of articles and dispatches in newspapers, magazines, journals, research reports, blogs and websites throughout the world. The PANW represents the only daily international news source on pan-African and global affairs.

Don DeBar is a New York journalist and and host of The Morning Show, airing daily on CPRmetro.org.

Bob Fitrakis is a Professor of Political Science at Columbus State Community College and Executive Director of the Columbus Institute for Contemporary Journalism (CICJ)/CICJ Books as well as the Editor of The Free Press since 1993. As an investigative journalist, he has won 11 major awards. He is the author of six Fitrakis Files books, inter alia Full Spectrum Dominance, and Cops, Cover-ups and Corruption. Fitrakis and Wasserman won a 2005 Project Censored Award, for an article that was listed as number three of the Top 25 Censored Stories, "How a Republican Election Supervisor Manipulated the 2004 Central Ohio Vote: In Black and White". His articles have appeared on other national and local websites and publications including Huffington Post, Common Dreams, motherjones.com, thenation.com, Z magazine, RagBlog, Scoop.co, Bradblog, Salon.com, OpEdNews, Counterpunch, Truthout, tompaine.com, Hustler, larryflynt.com, Alternet, Buzzflash, progressive.org, and smirkingchimp. In 2012, Fitrakis is running for Congress in the 3rd district, central Ohio, in the Green Party primary Match 6, 2012. He serves on the Central Committee of the Franklin County Green Party and is Co-Chair of the Ohio Green Party. He also serves as legal counsel for Occupy Columbus. Fitrakis has a Ph.D in political science from Wayne State University and a J.D. from the Ohio State University Moritz College of Law.

Sara Flounders, a leader of the International Action Center, has edited and co-authored ten books on U.S. wars. In 1992, Sara Flounders coordinated the International War Crimes Tribunal on U.S. War Crimes in Iraq, which held mass hearings in 30 US cities and 20 countries. She helped coordinate the major anti-war demonstrations that drew hundreds of thousands of people into the streets in 2003 before the U.S. invasion of Iraq. Currently she is working with the United National Antiwar Coalition – UNAC. Flounders organized delegations to Iraq during the years of starvation sanctions, visited Sudan after a U.S. missile barrage destroyed a pharmaceutical complex there and Yugoslavia during 78 days of NATO bombing. She has visited Syria, Iran Egypt, Lebanon, the West Bank and Gaza during times of crisis. Focused on growing racism, incarceration, political repression and austerity, Ms. Flounders has spoken at numerous campus and community forums in the US and internationally and been interviewed by many national and international media. Through the creative use of video, internet, mass meetings, major antiwar rallies and international campaigns, she has worked with other committed activists to build confidence in the potential of powerful grassroots movements to make historic change.

Wayne Madsen is a Washington, DC-based investigative journalist, author and syndicated columnist. He has written for *The Village Voice*, *The Progressive*, *Counterpunch*, I*n These Times*, and *The American Conservative*. His columns have appeared in *The Miami Herald*, *Houston Chronicle*, *Philadelphia Inquirer*, *Columbus Dispatch*, *Sacramento Bee*, and *Atlanta Journal-Constitution*, among others. Madsen is the author of *The Handbook of Personal Data Protection* (London: Macmillan, 1992), an acclaimed reference book on international data protection law; *Genocide and Covert Operations in Africa 1993-1999* (Edwin Mellen Press, 1999); co-author of *America's Nightmare: The Presidency of George Bush II* (Dandelion, 2003); author of *Jaded Tasks: Big Oil, Black Ops & Brass Plates* and *Overthrow a Fascist Regime on $15 a Day*. (Trine Day); and author of the forthcoming book, *The Manufacturing of a President:The CIA's Insertion of Barack H. Obama, Jr. into the White House*. Madsen has been a regular contributor on RT. He has also been a frequent political and national security commentator on Fox News and has also appeared on ABC, NBC, CBS, PBS, CNN, BBC, Al Jazeera, and MS-NBC. Madsen has taken on Bill O'Reilly and Sean Hannity on their television shows. He has been invited to testify as a witness before the US House of Representatives, the UN Criminal Tribunal for Rwanda, and a terrorism investigation panel of the French government.

Dr. Christof Lehman is a clinical psychologist, psycho-traumatologist and political consultant. His work with victims of conflict has inspired him to also pursue political work. He has been working as political advisor and consultant for 29 years. Among his former clients were several progressive heads of state and he continues his independent work for peace and justice. He is a life time peace activist, human rights advocate, active at establishing international institutions for the prosecution of war crimes, including the war crimes of privileged nations, and he is a life long advocate for Palestinians right to life, dignity, the right to return, sovereignty and peace within it´s own borders. He is editing the blogg nsnbc-no spin news, where he is regularly publishing his own and others articles that are denied sufficient exposure on corporate and state controlled media.

Stephen Lendman was awarded the Mexican Press Club Award for Interational Investigative Journalism in 2011.A writer and broadcaster. His work is exceedingly widely distributed online, with his articles carried on numerous listservs and websites such as Information Clearing House, Countercurrents, Rense, AltNews, Uruknet, Global Research, Counterpunch, and more. In early 2007, he began regular radio hosting, now The Progressive Radio News Hour on The Progressive Radio Network. He is author of *How Wall Street Fleeces America* (Chinese edition forthcoming), and co-author with J.J. Asongu of *The Iraq Quagmire: The Price of Imperial Arrogance*. He holds a BA from Harvard and an MBA from Wharton.

Mahdi Darius Nazemroaya was awarded the Mexican Press Club Award for Interational Investigative Journalism in 2011. He is a sociologist and noted geopolitical analyst and researcher at the Centre for Research on Globalization in Montreal, Quebec. He is also an geopolitical expert at the Strategic Culture Foundation (SCF) in Moscow, Russia. His texts have been translated into more than twenty languages including German, Russian, Turkish, Spanish, Arabic, and Chinese. His work on Libya was archived by NATO's Multimedia Library under the "NATO and Libya—Special Focus" annals, a collection of articles by leading experts with their analysis on the war in Libya. He reported from Tripoli on the NATO bombings as the special correspondent of Flashpoints. While in Libya, he was with the international press corps when they were trapped in the Rixos Al Nasr Hotel during the fall of Tripoli to NATO and the rebels. Nazemroaya is the author of *The Globalization of NATO* (2012) and *The War on Libya and the Re-Colonization of Africa* (2012). He works at Carleton University, where his teaching duties have included Latin American studies at the Institute of Interdisciplinary Studies (IIS) and African history at the Department of History.

Lizzie Phelan is a 25 year old independent journalist who was in Libya during the NATO bombing campaign and later blitzkrieg of Tripoli. She was one of the few people that reported on the daily crimes being committed by NATO and the widespread resistance by the Libyan people to the NATO aggression. She also visited Syria in January where she similarly sought to expose the media fabrications about events in Syria. Ms Phelan through her reporting seeks to represent the stories of victims of those who violate international law with western powers such as the US and Britain being the worst offenders historically. As well as having worked for Press TV and Russia Today, Ms Phelan has written in a number of publications and produces independent written work via her blog www.lizzie-phelan.blogspot.co.uk and videos on her youtube channels theliberatedzone and theliberatedzonetv.

Keith Harmon Snow is a war correspondent, photographer and independent investigator, and a four time (2003, 2006, 2007, 2010) Project Censored award winner. He is the 2009 Regent's Lecturer in Law & Society at the University of California Santa Barbara, recognized for over a decade of work, outside of academia, contesting official narratives on war crimes, crimes against humanity and genocide while also working as a genocide investigator for the United Nations and other bodies. He has worked at the International Criminal Tribunal on Rwanda and testified on war crimes and crimes against humanity in Central Africa before the high court in Spain.

Julien Teil is Senior Associate at the Centre for the Study of Interventionism, a Paris-based think-tank devoted to studying the legal and factual aspects of interventionism, both political and military. Previously he worked as an independent French journalist and videographer. He also formerly worked for a company specializing in fundraising for NGOs . He was in Libya during the conflict and revealed the lies of the so-called human rights NGOS to expel Libya from the United Nations Human Rights Council which launched the war-process.

T West is a professional in the Information Technology field but also works as a reporter, videographer and musician. He founded and facilitated the CART (Collective Action Round Table) Forums to bring together the various Black ethnic groups to leverage that into investment and business partnerships with upstream industry control. In 2007, he started AfriSynergy Production with an internet presence on YouTube and a blog viewed and engaged by tens of thousands each month with an average viewership between 5 and 6 thousand daily. He works extensively with Pan African and African immigrant groups. He has also spoken at various colleges and universities.

INDEX

ABOUT CYNTHIA MCKINNEY

Cynthia McKinney is an internationally renowned peace advocate and human rights activist. She began this important work on Day One of her political life and hasn't looked back. With her opinions, actions, and even her sense of style, McKinney has inspired both admiration and controversy. In 1988, McKinney won a House seat in the Georgia Legislature against all odds. She was the first African-American woman to represent Atlanta and Fulton County in an at-large district in Georgia's history. She became a household name when she challenged the state's leadership to abide by the Voting Rights Act and grant fair representation to all of Georgia's residents, including the more than 30% who are of African descent. She appealed directly to the United States Justice Department and won. In 1991, speaking from the "well" of the Georgia House of Representatives, she made national headlines when she challenged President George Herbert Walker Bush's decision to make war against Iraq. Despite the vilification by the state's pro-war establishment, her voice for justice and peace was heard by the people.

In 1992, McKinney won a seat in the U.S. House of Representatives in a newly created district, drawn from Atlanta to Savannah. Again, Cynthia made history by becoming the first African-American woman to represent Georgia in the U.S. Congress. Cynthia voted against every war-funding bill put before her. During her tenure, her district was re-drawn several times and re-numbered. McKinney protested the new boundaries, but was still reelected to the seat until the pro-Israel Lobby targeted her because of her support for peace in Palestine. After 11 September 2001, McKinney stated that based on her readings, the President had received warnings and that the matter deserved independent investigation. The criticism she received as a result, combined with being targeted by the pro-Israel lobby, contributed to her defeat in the 2002 election; however, she ran for the seat again and was re-elected in 2004. Once again in Congress, McKinney was a vocal critic of the government's response to Hurricane Katrina. Cynthia introduced legislation to release the documents related to the murders of Dr. Martin Luther King, Jr. and Tupac Shakur. She was the first Member of Congress to file Articles of Impeachment against President George W. Bush and Cynthia was forced out of Congress once more in 2007 when she was targeted for defeat, again, by donations from pro-Israel contributors that flooded into her opponent's campaign coffers. Late in 2007, Cynthia became a Green Party Presidential Candidate. Cynthia won the Green Party nomination for U.S. President and in 2008 ran for President.

In December 2008, Cynthia made international headlines when the Free Gaza boat she was aboard was rammed by the Israeli military as she was attempting to deliver medical supplies to the people of Gaza during Israel's Operation Cast Lead. Cynthia and her fellow humanitarian activists, rescued by Lebanon, never made it to Gaza. In 2009, Cynthia attempted to reach Gaza again, this time armed with crayons, coloring books, and school supplies for the children. She and her fellow human rights workers became the Free Gaza 21 after their boat was overtaken in international waters by the Israeli military and they were kidnapped to Israel. Cynthia spent 7 days in an Israeli prison. Finally, Cynthia entered Gaza by land in July 2009 with George Galloway's 250-volunteer-strong Viva Palestina, USA.

In 2011, Cynthia led a DIGNITY Delegation of alternative and independent journalists to Libya while US and NATO bombs, laced with poisons including depleted uranium, targeted civilian populations. Afterward, she completed a successful 29-city peace tour in the United States and Canada to promote a more peaceful U.S. foreign policy. Cynthia now travels the world speaking out on human rights, nature's rights, and peace while she completes her studies toward obtaining a Ph.D.